MznLnx

Missing Links Exam Preps

Exam Prep for

Geology of National Parks

Harris & Tuttle & Tuttle, 6th Edition

The MznLnx Exam Prep is your link from the texbook and lecture to your exams.
The MznLnx Exam Preps are unauthorized and comprehensive reviews of your textbooks.

All material provided by MznLnx and Rico Publications (c) 2010
Textbook publishers and textbook authors do not particpate in or contribute to these reviews.

MznLnx

Rico Publications

Exam Prep for Geology of National Parks
6th Edition
Harris & Tuttle & Tuttle

Publisher: Raymond Houge
Assistant Editor: Michael Rouger
Text and Cover Designer: Lisa Buckner
Marketing Manager: Sara Swagger
Project Manager, Editorial Production: Jerry Emerson
Art Director: Vernon Lowerui

Product Manager: Dave Mason
Editorial Assitant: Rachel Guzmanji
Pedagogy: Debra Long
Cover Image: Jim Reed/Getty Images
Text and Cover Printer: City Printing, Inc.
Compositor: Media Mix, Inc.

(c) 2010 Rico Publications

ALL RIGHTS RESERVED. No part of this work covered by the copyright may be reproduced or used in any form or by an means--graphic, electronic, or mechanical, including photocopying, recording, taping, Web distribution, information storage, and retrieval systems, or in any other manner--without the written permission of the publisher.

Printed in the United States
ISBN:

For more information about our products, contact us at:
Dave.Mason@RicoPublications.com

For permission to use material from this text or product, submit a request online to:
Dave.Mason@RicoPublications.com

Contents

CHAPTER 1
Grand Canyon National Park — 1

CHAPTER 2
Zion National Park — 12

CHAPTER 3
Bryce Canyon National Park — 18

CHAPTER 4
Capitol Reef National Park — 23

CHAPTER 5
Canyonlands National Park — 29

CHAPTER 6
Arches National Park — 32

CHAPTER 7
Mesa Verde National Park — 35

CHAPTER 8
Petrified Forest National Park — 37

CHAPTER 9
Badlands National Park — 42

CHAPTER 10
Theodore Roosevelt National Park by Rodney M. Feldmann — 46

CHAPTER 11
Kobuk Valley National Park — 48

CHAPTER 12
Great Sand Dunes National Park and Preserve — 52

CHAPTER 13
Cuyahoga Valley National Park by David B. Hacker — 56

CHAPTER 14
Mammoth Cave National Park by Arthur N. Palmer — 66

CHAPTER 15
Wind Cave National Park by Rodney M. Feldmann — 71

CHAPTER 16
Carlsbad Caverns National Park by Arthur N. Palmer — 73

CHAPTER 17
Guadalupe Mountains National Park by Ann F. Budd and Katherine A. Giles — 76

CHAPTER 18
Virgin Islands National Park by Ann F. Budd — 79

CHAPTER 19
Everglades National Park — 82

CHAPTER 20
Biscayne National Park — 84

Contents (Cont.)

CHAPTER 21
Dry Tortugas National Park by Richard Arnold Davis — 85
CHAPTER 22
Voyageurs National Park — 87
CHAPTER 23
Isle Royale National Park — 92
CHAPTER 24
Acadia National Park — 96
CHAPTER 25
Rocky Mountain National Park — 100
CHAPTER 26
Waterton-Glacier International Peace Park — 108
CHAPTER 27
Gates of the Arctic National Park and Preserve — 114
CHAPTER 28
Yosemite National Park by Donald F. Palmer — 116
CHAPTER 29
North Cascades National Park — 122
CHAPTER 30
Olympic National Park — 127
CHAPTER 31
Glacier Bay National Park and Preserve — 131
CHAPTER 32
Wrangell-St. Elias National Park and Preserve by Monte D. Wilson — 135
CHAPTER 33
Kenai Fjords National Park by Donald S. Follows — 138
CHAPTER 34
Denali National Park and Preserve by Phillip Brease — 140
CHAPTER 35
Mount Rainier National Park — 149
CHAPTER 36
Crater Lake National Park — 154
CHAPTER 37
Lassen Volcanic National Park — 157
CHAPTER 38
Katmai National Park and Preserve — 160
CHAPTER 39
Lake Clark National Park and Preserve — 163
CHAPTER 40
Hawaii Volcanoes National Park — 166

Contents (Cont.)

CHAPTER 41
Haleakala National Park — 170
CHAPTER 42
The National Park of American Samoa — 171
CHAPTER 43
Yellowstone National Park — 174
CHAPTER 44
Grand Teton National Park — 182
CHAPTER 45
Great Basin National Park — 185
CHAPTER 46
Saguaro National Park — 189
CHAPTER 47
Joshua Tree National Park by D.D. Trent — 195
CHAPTER 48
Death Valley National Park by Lauren A. Wright and Martin G. Miller — 201
CHAPTER 49
Sequoia and Kings Canyon National Parks by Donald F. Palmer — 205
CHAPTER 50
0, Channel Islands National Park by Donald F Palmer — 209
CHAPTER 51
Redwood National Park by Lisa A. Rossbacher — 211
CHAPTER 52
Hot Springs National Park — 212
CHAPTER 53
Big Bend National Park — 214
CHAPTER 54
Shenandoah National Park — 216
CHAPTER 55
Great Smokey Mountains National Park — 221
CHAPTER 56
Black Canyon of the Gunnison National Park — 224
ANSWER KEY — 230

TO THE STUDENT

COMPREHENSIVE

The *MznLnx* Exam Prep series is designed to help you pass your exams. Editors at MznLnx review your textbooks and then prepare these practice exams to help you master the textbook material. Unlike study guides, workbooks, and practice tests provided by the texbook publisher and textbook authors, *MznLnx* gives you **all** of the material in each chapter in exam form, not just samples, so you can be sure to nail your exam.

MECHANICAL

The MznLnx Exam Prep series creates exams that will help you learn the subject matter as well as test you on your understanding. Each question is designed to help you master the concept. Just working through the exams, you gain an understanding of the subject--its a simple mechanical process that produces success.

INTEGRATED STUDY GUIDE AND REVIEW

MznLnx is not just a set of exams designed to test you, its also a comprehensive review of the subject content. Each exam question is also a review of the concept, making sure that you will get the answer correct without having to go to other sources of material. You learn as you go! Its the easiest way to pass an exam.

HUMOR

Studying can be tedious and dry. MznLnx's instructional design includes moderate humor within the exam questions on occassion, to break the tedium and revitalize the brain

Chapter 1. Grand Canyon National Park

1. The _____ Era, is the most recent of the three classic geological eras and covers the period from 65.5 million years ago to the present. It is marked by the Cretaceous-Tertiary extinction event at the end of the Cretaceous that saw the demise of the last non-avian dinosaurs and the end of the Mesozoic Era. The _____ era is ongoing.
   - a. Cenozoic
   - b. 1509 Istanbul earthquake
   - c. 1700 Cascadia earthquake
   - d. 1703 Genroku earthquake

2. The _____ of any physical feature such as a hill, stream, roof, railroad, or road refers to the amount of inclination of that surface where zero indicates level (with respect to gravity) and larger numbers indicate higher degrees of 'tilt'. Often slope is calculated as a ratio of 'rise over run' in which run is the horizontal distance and rise is the vertical distance.

   There are several systems for expressing slope:

   1. as an angle of inclination from the horizontal of a right triangle. (This is the angle >α opposite the 'rise' side of the triangle.)
   2. as a percentage (also known as the _____), the formula for which is > which could also be expressed as the tangent of the angle of inclination times 100. In the U.S., the _____ is the most commonly used unit for communicating slopes in transportation, surveying, construction, and civil engineering.
   3. as a per mille figure, the formula for which is > which could also be expressed as the tangent of the angle of inclination times 1000. This is commonly used in Europe to denote the incline of a railway.
   4. as a ratio of one part rise per so many parts run. For example, a slope that has a rise of 5 feet for every 100 feet of run would have a slope ratio of 1 in 20.

   Any one of these expressions may be used interchangeably to express the characteristics of a slope. _____ is usually expressed as a percentage, but this may easily be converted to the angle >α from horizontal since that carries the same information.
   - a. Heavy metal
   - b. Grade
   - c. Diamond Head
   - d. Compaction

3. An _____ is a fan-shaped deposit formed where a fast flowing stream flattens, slows, and spreads typically at the exit of a canyon onto a flatter plain. A convergence of neighboring fans into a single apron of deposits against a slope is called a bajada, or compound _____.
   - a. AASHTO Soil Classification System
   - b. AL 129-1
   - c. AL 333
   - d. Alluvial fan

4. _____ is a fluvial process of erosion that lengthens a stream, a valley or a gully at its head and also enlarges its drainage basin. The stream erodes away at the rock and soil at its headwaters in the opposite direction that it flows. Once a stream has begun to cut back, the erosion is sped up by the steep gradient the water is flowing down. As water erodes a path from its headwaters to its mouth at a standing body of water, it tries to cut an ever-shallower path. This leads to increased erosion at the steepest parts, which is _____.
   - a. Headward erosion
   - b. Hydrothermal circulation
   - c. Diagenesis
   - d. Downcutting

Chapter 1. Grand Canyon National Park

5. _____, is a geomorphological phenomenon occurring when a stream or river drainage system or watershed is diverted from its own bed, and flows instead down the bed of a neighbouring stream. This can happen for several reasons, including:

- Tectonic earth movements, where the slope of the land changes, and the stream is tipped out of its former course.
- Natural damming, such as by a landslide or ice sheet.
- Erosion

a. 1509 Istanbul earthquake
b. Stream capture
c. Distributary
d. Meander

6. _____ is the removal of solids (sediment, soil, rock and other particles) in the natural environment. It usually occurs due to transport by wind, water, or ice; by down-slope creep of soil and other material under the force of gravity; or by living organisms, such as burrowing animals, in the case of bioerosion.

_____ is distinguished from weathering, which is the process of chemical or physical breakdown of the minerals in the rocks, although the two processes may occur concurrently.

a. AL 129-1
b. AL 333
c. AASHTO Soil Classification System
d. Erosion

7. _____ is one of the three main rock types (the others being sedimentary and metamorphic rock.) _____ is formed by magma (molten rock) being cooled and becoming solid . They may form with or without crystallization, either below the surface as intrusive (plutonic) rocks or on the surface as extrusive (volcanic) rocks. They make up approximately 95% of the upper part of the Earth's crust, but their great abundance is hidden on the Earth's surface by a relatively thin but widespread layer of sedimentary and metamorphic rocks.

a. Igneous differentiation
b. Igneous rock
c. Ignimbrite
d. Extrusive

8. _____ is the result of the transformation of an existing rock type, the protolith, in a process called metamorphism, which means 'change in form'. The protolith is subjected to heat and pressure (temperatures greater than 150 to 200 >°C and pressures of 1500 bars) causing profound physical and/or chemical change. The protolith may be sedimentary rock, igneous rock or another older _____.

a. Serpentinite
b. Laccolith
c. Pluton
d. Metamorphic rock

9. An _____ is a buried erosion surface separating two rock masses or strata of different ages, indicating that sediment deposition was not continuous. In general, the older layer was exposed to erosion for an interval of time before deposition of the younger, but the term is used to describe any break in the sedimentary geologic record. The phenomenon of angular unconformities was discovered by James Hutton, who found examples at Jedburgh in 1787 and at Siccar Point in 1788.

a. AL 129-1
b. AASHTO Soil Classification System
c. AL 333
d. Unconformity

10. A _____ or dyke in geology is a type of sheet intrusion referring to any geologic body that cuts discordantly across

- planar wall rock structures, such as bedding or foliation
- massive rock formations, like igneous/magmatic intrusions and salt diapirs.

They can therefore be either intrusive or sedimentary in origin.

An intrusive _____ is an igneous body with a very high aspect ratio, which means that its thickness is usually much smaller than the other two dimensions. Thickness can vary from sub-centimeter scale to many meters and the lateral dimensions can extend over many kilometers. A _____ is an intrusion into an opening cross-cutting fissure, shouldering aside other pre-existing layers or bodies of rock; this implies that a _____ is always younger than the rocks that contain it.

  a. Dike
  b. Detritus
  c. Gradualism
  d. Type locality

11. A _____ in geology is an intrusive igneous rock body that crystallized from a magma slowly cooling below the surface of the Earth. _____s include batholiths, dikes, sills, laccoliths, lopoliths, and other igneous bodies. In practice, '_____' usually refers to a distinctive mass of igneous rock, typically kilometers in dimension, without a tabular shape like those of dikes and sills.
  a. Petrology
  b. Matrix
  c. Tephra
  d. Pluton

12. _____ forms a group of medium-grade metamorphic rocks, chiefly notable for the preponderance of lamellar minerals such as micas, chlorite, talc, hornblende, graphite, and others. Quartz often occurs in drawn-out grains to such an extent that a particular form called quartz _____ is produced. By definition, _____ contains more than 50% platy and elongated minerals, often finely interleaved with quartz and feldspar.
  a. Hornfels
  b. Schist
  c. Talc carbonate
  d. Porphyroblast

13. The chemical compound silicon dioxide, also known as _____ , is an oxide of silicon with a chemical formula of SiO_2 and has been known for its hardness since antiquity. _____ is most commonly found in nature as sand or quartz, as well as in the cell walls of diatoms. It is a principal component of most types of glass and substances such as concrete.
  a. 1703 Genroku earthquake
  b. 1509 Istanbul earthquake
  c. 1700 Cascadia earthquake
  d. Silica

14. A marine _____ is a geologic event during which sea level rises relative to the land and the shoreline moves toward higher ground, resulting in flooding. They can be caused either by the land sinking or the ocean basins filling with water (or decreasing in capacity.) Transgresssions and regressions may be caused by tectonic events such as orogenies, severe climate change such as ice ages or isostatic adjustments following removal of ice or sediment load.
  a. Mid-ocean ridge
  b. Headward erosion
  c. Seafloor spreading
  d. Transgression

15. _____ rocks are composed of fragments of pre-existing rock. The term is most commonly, but not uniquely, applied to sedimentary rocks.

_____ metamorphic rocks include breccias formed in faults, as well as some protomylonite and pseudotachylite.

   a. 1703 Genroku earthquake
   b. 1700 Cascadia earthquake
   c. 1509 Istanbul earthquake
   d. Clastic

16. A _____ is a rock consisting of individual stones that have become cemented together. They are sedimentary rocks consisting of rounded fragments and are thus differentiated from breccias, which consist of angular clasts. Both _____s and breccias are characterized by clasts larger than sand (>2 mm).
   a. Pelagic sediments
   b. Keystone
   c. Concretion
   d. Conglomerate

17. _____ refers to the mode of igneous volcanic rock formation in which hot magma from inside the Earth flows out (extrudes) onto the surface as lava or explodes violently into the atmosphere to fall back as pyroclastics or tuff. This is opposed to intrusive rock formation, in which magma does not reach the surface.
   a. Augen
   b. Igneous rock
   c. Ignimbrite
   d. Extrusive

18. _____ is molten rock expelled by a volcano during eruption. When first expelled from a volcanic vent, it is a liquid at temperatures from 700 >°C to 1,200 >°C (1,300 >°F to 2,200 >°F.) Although _____ is quite viscous, with about 100,000 times the viscosity of water, it can flow great distances before cooling and solidifying, because of both its thixotropic and shear thinning properties.
   a. Cinder
   b. Volcanic ash
   c. Pyroclastic flow
   d. Lava

19. _____ is molten rock that is found beneath the surface of the Earth, and may also exist on other terrestrial planets. Besides molten rock, _____ may also contain suspended crystals and gas bubbles. _____ often collects in a _____ chamber inside a volcano. _____ is capable of intrusion into adjacent rocks, extrusion onto the surface as lava, and explosive ejection as tephra to form pyroclastic rock.
   a. Magma
   b. Sedimentary rock
   c. Large igneous provinces
   d. Groundmass

20. _____ is a naturally occurring glass formed as an extrusive igneous rock. It is produced when felsic lava extruded from a volcano cools without crystal growth. _____ is commonly found within the margins of rhyolitic lava flows known as _____ flows, where the chemical composition (high silica content) induces a high viscosity and polymerization degree of the lava.
   a. Obsidian
   b. AL 333
   c. AASHTO Soil Classification System
   d. AL 129-1

21. An _____ is a section of the Earth's oceanic crust and the underlying upper mantle that has been uplifted or emplaced to be exposed within continental crustal rocks. Ophio is Greek for 'snake', lite means 'stone' from the Greek lithos.

The term _____ was originally used by Alexandre Brongniart for an assemblage of green rocks (serpentine, diabase) in the Alps; Steinmann (1927) later modified its use to include serpentine, pillow lava, and chert ('Steinmann's trinity'), again based on occurrences in the Alps.

a. AL 333 b. AL 129-1
c. AASHTO Soil Classification System d. Ophiolite

22. _____ is any particulate matter that can be transported by fluid flow, and which eventually is deposited.

They are most often transported by water (fluvial processes) transported by wind (aeolian processes) and glaciers. Beach sands and river channel deposits are examples of fluvial transport and deposition, though _____ also often settles out of slow-moving or standing water in lakes and oceans.

a. Salt glacier b. Brickearth
c. Fech fech d. Sediment

23. _____ is one of the three main rock types (the others being igneous and metamorphic rock.) _____ is formed by deposition and consolidation of mineral and organic material and from precipitation of minerals from solution. The processes that form _____ occur at the surface of the Earth and within bodies of water.
a. Felsic b. Serpentinite
c. Large igneous provinces d. Sedimentary rock

24. _____ is a fine-grained sedimentary rock whose original constituents were clay minerals or muds. It is characterized by thin laminae breaking with an irregular curving fracture, often splintery and usually parallel to the often-indistinguishable bedding plane. This property is called fissility.
a. Concretion b. Jasperoid
c. Claystone d. Shale

25. In geology, an _____ is a body of igneous rock that has crystallized from molten magma below the surface of the Earth. Bodies of magma that solidify underground before they reach the surface of the earth are called plutons the Roman god of the underworld. Correspondingly, rocks of this kind are also referred to as igneous plutonic rocks or igneous intrusive rocks.
a. AL 333 b. Intrusion
c. AL 129-1 d. AASHTO Soil Classification System

26. In materials science, _____ is the distribution of crystallographic orientations of a polycrystalline sample. A sample in which these orientations are fully random is said to have no _____. If the crystallographic orientations are not random, but have some preferred orientation, then the sample has a weak, strong, or moderate _____.
a. Diamond Head b. Geothermal
c. Texture d. Platform

27. _____ is a type of foliated metamorphic rock primarily composed of quartz, sericite mica, and chlorite; the rock represents a gradation in the degree of metamorphism between slate and mica schist. Minute crystals of graphite, sericite, or chlorite impart a silky, sometimes golden sheen to the surfaces of cleavage (or schistosity.) _____ is formed from the continued metamorphism of slate.
a. Phyllite b. 1700 Cascadia earthquake
c. 1703 Genroku earthquake d. 1509 Istanbul earthquake

28. _____ is a hard metamorphic rock which was originally sandstone. Sandstone is converted into _____ through heating and pressure usually related to tectonic compression within orogenic belts. Pure _____ is usually white to grey, though _____s often occur in various shades of pink and red due to varying amounts of iron oxide .
   a. Talc carbonate
   b. Slate
   c. Hornfels
   d. Quartzite

29. _____ is a fine-grained, foliated, homogeneous metamorphic rock derived from an original shale-type sedimentary rock composed of clay or volcanic ash through low grade regional metamorphism. The result is a foliated rock in which the foliation may not correspond to the original sedimentary layering. _____ is frequently grey in colour especially when seen en masse covering roofs.
   a. Shock metamorphism
   b. Talc carbonate
   c. Cataclasite
   d. Slate

30. In structural geology, an _____ is a fold that is convex up and has its oldest beds at its core. The term is not to be confused with antiform, which is a purely descriptive term for any fold that is convex up. Therefore if age relationships (i.e. younging direction) between various strata are unknown, the term antiform must be used.
   a. AASHTO Soil Classification System
   b. AL 333
   c. AL 129-1
   d. Anticline

31. The term _____ is used in geology when one or a stack of originally flat and planar surfaces, such as sedimentary strata, are bent or curved as a result of plastic (i.e. permanent) deformation. Synsedimentary _____s are those due to slumping of sedimentary material before it is lithified. _____s in rocks vary in size from microscopic crinkles to mountain-sized _____s.
   a. 1509 Istanbul earthquake
   b. 1700 Cascadia earthquake
   c. 1703 Genroku earthquake
   d. Fold

32. A _____ is a step-like fold consisting of a zone of steeper dip within an otherwise horizontal or gently-dipping sequence.

_____s may be formed in several different ways

- By differential compaction over an underlying structure, particularly a large fault at the edge of a basin due to the greater compactibility of the basin fill, the amplitude of the fold will die out gradually upwards e.g.

- By mild reactivation of an earlier extensional fault during a phase of inversion causing folding in the overlying sequence e.g.

- As a form of fault propagation fold during upward propagation of an extensional fault in basement into an overlying cover sequence e.g.

- As a form of fault propagation fold during upward propagation of a reverse fault in basement into an overlying cover sequence e.g.

   a. Syncline
   b. Structural geology
   c. Monocline
   d. Crenulation

33. In structural geology, a _____ is a downward-curving fold, with layers that dip toward the center of the structure. A synclinorium is a large _____ with superimposed smaller folds.

On a geologic map, they are recognized by a sequence of rock layers that grow progressively younger, followed by the youngest layer at the fold's center or hinge, and by a reverse sequence of the same rock layers on the opposite side of the hinge.

  a. Syncline
  b. Structural geology
  c. Shear
  d. Sag pond

34. In geology, a _____ or _____ line is a planar fracture in rock in which the rock on one side of the fracture has moved with respect to the rock on the other side. Large _____s within the Earth's crust are the result of differential or shear motion and active _____ zones are the causal locations of most earthquakes. Earthquakes are caused by energy release during rapid slippage along a _____.
  a. Cleavage
  b. Fault
  c. Drainage system
  d. Compaction

35. Since faults do not usually consist of a single, clean fracture, the term fault zone is used when referring to the zone of complex deformation that is associated with the fault plane. The two sides of a non-vertical fault are called the _____ and footwall. By definition, the _____ occurs above the fault and the footwall occurs below the fault.
  a. Reverse fault
  b. Fault plane
  c. 1509 Istanbul earthquake
  d. Hanging wall

36. A _____ is the opposite of a normal fault -- the hanging wall moves up relative to the footwall. They are indicative of shortening of the crust. The dip of a _____ is relatively steep, greater than 45>°.
  a. Hanging wall
  b. 1509 Istanbul earthquake
  c. Fault plane
  d. Reverse fault

37. The fault surface of _____ is usually near vertical and the footwall moves either left or right or laterally with very little vertical motion. _____ with left-lateral motion are also known as sinistral faults. Those with right-lateral motion are also known as dextral faults.
  a. Suspended load
  b. Star dunes
  c. Strike-slip faults
  d. Pahoehoe lava

38. A _____ is a type of fault in which rocks of lower stratigraphic position are pushed up and over higher strata. They are often recognized because they place older rocks above younger. _____s are the result of compressional forces.
  a. Convergent boundary
  b. Mantle convection
  c. Thrust fault
  d. Continental drift

39. The _____ is the first geological period of the Phanerozoic eon, lasting from 542 ± 0.3 million years ago to 488.3 ± 1.7 million years ago (ICS, 2004); it is succeeded by the Ordovician. Its subdivisions, and indeed its base, are somewhat in flux. The period was established by Adam Sedgwick, who named it after Cambria, the classical name for Wales, where Britain's _____ rocks are best exposed.
  a. 1700 Cascadia earthquake
  b. 1509 Istanbul earthquake
  c. Cambrian
  d. 1703 Genroku earthquake

40. The _____ is a physiographic region of the Intermontane Plateaus, roughly centered on the Four Corners region of the southwestern United States. The province covers an area of 337,000 km² within western Colorado, northwestern New Mexico, southern and eastern Utah, and northern Arizona. About 90% of the area is drained by the Colorado River and its main tributaries; the Green, San Juan and Little Colorado.

Development of the province has in large part been influenced by structural features in its oldest rocks. Part of the Wasatch Line and its various faults form the western edge of the province. Faults that run parallel to the Wasatch Fault that lies along the Wasatch Range form the boundaries between the plateaus in the High Plateaus Section. The Uinta Basin, Uncompahgre Uplift, and the Paradox Basin were also created by movement along structural weaknesses in the region's oldest rock.

a. 1700 Cascadia earthquake
b. Colorado Plateau
c. 1509 Istanbul earthquake
d. 1703 Genroku earthquake

41. The _____ , usually abbreviated K for its German translation Kreide, is a geologic period and system from circa >145.5 >± 4 to >65.5 >± 0.3 million years ago . In the geologic timescale, the _____ follows on the Jurassic period and is followed by the Paleogene period. It is the youngest period of the Mesozoic era, and at 80 million years long, the longest period of the Phanerozoic eon. The end of the _____ defines the boundary between the Mesozoic and Cenozoic eras.
a. Campanian
b. Hauterivian
c. Cretaceous
d. Valanginian

42. The _____ is a geologic period and system of the Paleozoic era spanning from >416 to 359.2 million years ago (ICS, 2004.).

During the _____ Period, which occurred in the Paleozoic era, the first fish evolved legsand started to walk on land as tetrapods around 365 Ma.

a. 1509 Istanbul earthquake
b. Xitun Formation
c. Devonian
d. Gogo Formation

43. The _____ Era is one of three geologic eras of the Phanerozoic eon. The division of time into eras dates back to Giovanni Arduino, in the 18th century, although his original name for the era now called the '_____' was 'Secondary' (making the modern era the 'Tertiary'.)

The _____ was a time of tectonic, climatic and evolutionary activity. The continents gradually shifted from a state of connectedness into their present configuration; the drifting provided for speciation and other important evolutionary developments.

a. 1509 Istanbul earthquake
b. Mesozoic
c. 1700 Cascadia earthquake
d. 1703 Genroku earthquake

44. The _____ is a geologic subperiod and stratigraphic subsystem of the Carboniferous Period. It is the earliest/lowermost of two divisions of the Carboniferous, lasting from roughly 359 to 318 Ma (million years ago.) As with most other geochronologic units, the rock beds that define the _____ are well identified, but the exact start and end dates are uncertain by a few million years.

a. Calciferous sandstone
b. Mississippian
c. Pennsylvanian
d. Dinantian

45. The _____ is the earliest of three geologic eras of the Phanerozoic eon. The _____ spanned from roughly 542 to 251 million years ago (ICS, 2004), and is subdivided into six geologic periods; from oldest to youngest they are: the Cambrian, Ordovician, Silurian, Devonian, Carboniferous, and Permian.

The _____ covers the time from the first appearance of abundant, soft-shelled fossils to the time when the continents were beginning to be dominated by large, relatively sophisticated reptiles and modern plants. The lower (oldest) boundary was classically set at the first appearance of creatures known as trilobites and archeocyathids.

a. 1703 Genroku earthquake
b. Paleozoic
c. 1509 Istanbul earthquake
d. 1700 Cascadia earthquake

46. In geology and earth science, a _____ is an area of highland, usually consisting of relatively flat terrain. A highly eroded _____ is called a dissected _____. A volcanic _____ is a _____ produced by volcanic activity.
a. 1703 Genroku earthquake
b. 1509 Istanbul earthquake
c. 1700 Cascadia earthquake
d. Plateau

47. A _____ is the shadow a rain drop has before it lands on the ground, with respect to prevailing wind direction. In a more geographical sense, a _____ is an area of land that has suffered desertification from proximity to mountain ranges. The mountains block the passage of rain-producing weather systems, casting a 'shadow' of dryness behind them.
a. 1700 Cascadia earthquake
b. 1703 Genroku earthquake
c. 1509 Istanbul earthquake
d. Rain shadow

48. In geology, a _____ is a place where the Earth's crust and lithosphere are being pulled apart and is an example of extensional tectonics.

Typical _____ features are a central linear downdropped fault segment, called a graben, with parallel normal faulting and _____-flank uplifts on either side forming a _____ valley, where the _____ remains above sea level. The axis of the _____ area commonly contains volcanic rocks and active volcanism is a part of many, but not all active _____ systems.

a. 1700 Cascadia earthquake
b. 1509 Istanbul earthquake
c. 1703 Genroku earthquake
d. Rift

49. _____ is a sedimentary rock composed mainly of sand-size mineral or rock grains. Most _____ is composed of quartz and/or feldspar because these are the most common minerals in the Earth's crust. Like sand, _____ may be any color, but the most common colors are tan, brown, yellow, red, gray and white.
a. Superficial deposits
b. Claystone
c. Shale
d. Sandstone

50. _____ is the geological process by which material is added to a landform or land mass. Fluids such as wind and water, as well as sediment gravity flows, transport previously eroded sediment, which, at the loss of enough kinetic energy in the fluid, is deposited, building up layers of sediment.

_____ occurs when the forces responsible for sediment transportation are no longer sufficient to overcome the forces of particle weight and friction, which resist motion.

- a. Deposition
- b. Mid-ocean ridge
- c. Headward erosion
- d. Saltation

51. In geography and geology, a _____ is a significant vertical, or near vertical, rock exposure. _____s are formed as erosion landforms due to the processes of erosion and weathering that produce them. _____s are common on coasts, in mountainous areas, escarpments and along rivers. _____s are usually formed by rock that is resistant to erosion and weathering. Sedimentary rocks are most likely to form sandstone, limestone, chalk, and dolomite. Igneous rocks, such as granite and basalt also often form _____s.

- a. Cliff
- b. 1703 Genroku earthquake
- c. 1700 Cascadia earthquake
- d. 1509 Istanbul earthquake

52. In geology, a _____ is a continental area covered by relatively flat or gently tilted, mainly sedimentary strata, which overlie a basement of consolidated igneous or metamorphic rocks of an earlier deformation. They as well as, shields and the basement rocks together constitute cratons.

It is also common practice to use the term _____ as a very general term for a sequence of shallow water carbonate _____.

- a. Texture
- b. Platform
- c. Combe
- d. Compaction

53. In geology a _____ is the smallest division of a geologic formation or stratigraphic rock series marked by well-defined divisional planes (bedding planes) separating it from layers above and below. A _____ is the smallest lithostratigraphic unit, usually ranging in thickness from a centimeter to several meters and distinguishable from _____s above and below it. _____s can be differentiated in various ways, including rock or mineral type and particle size.

- a. Biozones
- b. Cyclostratigraphy
- c. Bed
- d. Sequence stratigraphy

54. _____ is the difference in degree of discoloration, disintegration, etc., of rocks of different kinds exposed to the same environment. Quartz deposits in basaltic flows will weather slower than the surrounding rock, while being exposed to the same forces of weathering.

_____ occurs when some parts of a rock weathers at different rates than others.

- a. Gravitational erosion
- b. Toreva block
- c. Coastal erosion
- d. Differential weathering

55. The _____ is the epoch from 1.8 million to 11550 years BP covering the world's recent period of repeated glaciations. The _____ epoch follows the Pliocene epoch and is followed by the Holocene epoch. The _____ is the third epoch of the Neogene period or 6th epoch of the Cenozoic Era. The end of the _____ corresponds with the retreat of the last continental glacier. It also corresponds with the end of the Paleolithic age used in archaeology.

a. Late Pleistocene
b. Sicilian Stage
c. Pleistocene
d. Tyrrhenian

56. _____ is a term given to an accumulation of broken rock fragments at the base of crags, mountain cliffs, or valley shoulders. Landforms associated with these materials are sometimes called _____ slopes or talus piles. These deposits typically have a concave upwards form, while the maximum inclination of such deposits corresponds to the angle of repose of the mean debris size.
   a. 1509 Istanbul earthquake
   b. Scree
   c. 1703 Genroku earthquake
   d. 1700 Cascadia earthquake

57. The _____ is a a term for a geologic period 65 million to 1.8 million years ago. The _____ covered the time span between the superseded Secondary period and an out-of-date definition of the Quaternary period. The period began with the demise of the non-avian dinosaurs in the Cretaceous-_____ extinction event, at start of the Cenozoic era, spanning to beginning of the most recent Ice Age, at the end of the Pliocene epoch.
   a. Tertiary
   b. Logarithmic Spiral Beach
   c. Loihi Seamount
   d. Historical geology

Chapter 2. Zion National Park

1. A _____ is a tributary valley with the floor at a higher relief than the main channel into which it flows. They are most commonly associated with U-shaped valleys when a tributary glacier flows into a glacier of larger volume. The main glacier erodes a deep U-shaped valley with nearly vertical sides while the tributary glacier, with a smaller volume of ice, makes a shallower U-shaped valley.
   a. 1509 Istanbul earthquake
   b. Hanging valley
   c. 1700 Cascadia earthquake
   d. 1703 Genroku earthquake

2. _____ is a form of mass wasting event that occurs when loosely consolidated materials or rock layers move a short distance down a slope. The landmass and the surface it _____s upon is called a failure surface. When the movement occurs in soil, there is often a distinctive rotational movement to the mass, that cuts vertically through bedding planes (landslides take place along a bedding plane or fault). This rotational movement moves along a curved slip surface of regolith (the failure surface) which overlies bedrock. This results in internal deformation of the moving mass consisting chiefly of overturned folds called 'sheath folds.'
   a. Soil
   b. Topsoil
   c. 1509 Istanbul earthquake
   d. Slump

3. An _____ is the result of a sudden release of energy in the Earth's crust that creates seismic waves. They are recorded with a seismometer or the related and mostly obsolete Richter magnitude, with a magnitude 3 or lower _____ being mostly imperceptible and magnitude 7 causing serious damage over large areas.
   a. AL 333
   b. Earthquake
   c. AASHTO Soil Classification System
   d. AL 129-1

4. In geology the term _____ refers to a fracture in rock where there has been no lateral movement in the plane of the fracture (up, down or sideways) of one side relative to the other. This makes it different from a fault which is defined as a fracture in rock where one side slides laterally past to the other. _____s normally have a regular spacing related to either the mechanical properties of the individual rock or the thickness of the layer involved.
   a. 1703 Genroku earthquake
   b. 1700 Cascadia earthquake
   c. 1509 Istanbul earthquake
   d. Joint

5. _____ is an igneous rock of volcanic origin.

They are usually fine-grained or aphanitic to glassy in texture. They often contain clasts of other rocks and phenocrysts.

   a. Vesicular texture
   b. Volcanic rock
   c. Large igneous provinces
   d. Petrology

6. The _____ is a geologic formation that is spread across the U.S. states of northern Arizona, Nevada, Utah, western New Mexico, and western Colorado. The _____ is controversially considered to be synonymous to Dockum Group in eastern Colorado, eastern New Mexico, southwestern Kansas, the Oklahoma panhandle, and western Texas. The _____ is sometimes colloquially used as a geologic formation within the Dockum in New Mexico and occasionally in Texas.
   a. Dali
   b. Melange
   c. Nodule
   d. Chinle

Chapter 2. Zion National Park

7. A _____ is a rock consisting of individual stones that have become cemented together. They are sedimentary rocks consisting of rounded fragments and are thus differentiated from breccias, which consist of angular clasts. Both _____s and breccias are characterized by clasts larger than sand (>2 mm).
   a. Conglomerate
   b. Keystone
   c. Concretion
   d. Pelagic sediments

8. A _____ is a large emplacement of igneous intrusive rock that forms from cooled magma deep in the Earth's crust. they are almost always made mostly of felsic or intermediate rock-types, such as granite, quartz monzonite, or diorite

   Although they may appear uniform, _____s are in fact structures with complex histories and compositions.

   a. Country rock
   b. Welded tuff
   c. Litchfieldite
   d. Batholith

9. _____ is molten rock that is found beneath the surface of the Earth, and may also exist on other terrestrial planets. Besides molten rock, _____ may also contain suspended crystals and gas bubbles. _____ often collects in a _____ chamber inside a volcano. _____ is capable of intrusion into adjacent rocks, extrusion onto the surface as lava, and explosive ejection as tephra to form pyroclastic rock.
   a. Magma
   b. Groundmass
   c. Sedimentary rock
   d. Large igneous provinces

10. A _____ is an underwater mountain range, typically having a valley known as a rift running along its spine, formed by plate tectonics. This type of oceanic ridge is characteristic of what is known as an oceanic spreading center, which is responsible for seafloor spreading. The uplifted sea floor results from convection currents which rise in the mantle as magma at a linear weakness in the oceanic crust, and emerge as lava, creating new crust upon cooling.
    a. Hydrothermal
    b. Mid-ocean ridge
    c. Hydrothermal circulation
    d. Hydraulic action

11. The _____ are hemispheric-scale long but narrow topographic depressions of the sea floor. They are also the deepest parts of the ocean floor.

    _____ define one of the most important natural boundaries on the Earth's solid surface, thatlie between two lithospheric plates. There are three types of lithospheric plate boundaries: divergent (where lithosphere and oceanic crust is created at mid-ocean ridges), convergent (where one lithospheric plate sinks beneath another and returns to the mantle), and transform (where two lithospheric plates slide past each other).

    a. AL 333
    b. AASHTO Soil Classification System
    c. AL 129-1
    d. Oceanic trenches

12. _____ describes the large scale motions of Earth's lithosphere. The theory encompasses the older concepts of continental drift, developed during the first decades of the 20th century by Alfred Wegener, and seafloor spreading, understood during the 1960s.

The outermost part of the Earth's interior is made up of two layers: the lithosphere and the asthenosphere.

a. Mantle convection
b. Plate tectonics
c. Continental crust
d. Nappe

13. In geology, a _____ is a place where the Earth's crust and lithosphere are being pulled apart and is an example of extensional tectonics.

Typical _____ features are a central linear downdropped fault segment, called a graben, with parallel normal faulting and _____-flank uplifts on either side forming a _____ valley, where the _____ remains above sea level. The axis of the _____ area commonly contains volcanic rocks and active volcanism is a part of many, but not all active _____ systems.

a. 1509 Istanbul earthquake
b. Rift
c. 1703 Genroku earthquake
d. 1700 Cascadia earthquake

14. The _____ is a continental transform fault that runs a length of roughly 800 miles (1,300 km) through California in the United States. The fault's motion is right-lateral strike-slip (horizontal motion.) It forms the tectonic boundary between the Pacific Plate and the North American Plate.

a. 1509 Istanbul earthquake
b. San Andreas fault
c. 1703 Genroku earthquake
d. 1700 Cascadia earthquake

15. In geology, _____ is the process that takes place at convergent boundaries by which one tectonic plate moves under another tectonic plate, sinking into the Earth's mantle, as the plates converge. A _____ zone is an area on Earth where two tectonic plates move towards one another and _____ occurs. Rates of _____ are typically measured in centimeters per year, with the average rate of convergence being approximately 2 to 8 centimeters per year (about the rate a fingernail grows.)

a. Mirovia
b. Continental collision
c. Motagua Fault
d. Subduction

16. In geology, a _____ or _____ line is a planar fracture in rock in which the rock on one side of the fracture has moved with respect to the rock on the other side. Large _____s within the Earth's crust are the result of differential or shear motion and active _____ zones are the causal locations of most earthquakes. Earthquakes are caused by energy release during rapid slippage along a _____.

a. Cleavage
b. Compaction
c. Drainage system
d. Fault

17. A _____ is a mountain rising from the ocean seafloor that does not reach to the water's surface (sea level), and thus is not an island. These are typically formed from extinct volcanoes, that rise abruptly and are usually found rising from a seafloor of 1,000-4,000 meters depth. They are defined by oceanographers as independent features that rise to at least 1,000 meters above the seafloor.

a. 1703 Genroku earthquake
b. 1509 Istanbul earthquake
c. Seamount
d. 1700 Cascadia earthquake

18. The lithosphere is broken up into what are called _____. In the case of Earth, there are eight major and many minor plates The lithospheric plates ride on the asthenosphere. These plates move in relation to one another at one of three types of plate boundaries: convergent, or collisional boundaries; divergent boundaries, also called spreading centers; and transform boundaries.

Chapter 2. Zion National Park

a. Supercontinent cycle
c. Nappe
b. Tectonic plates
d. Continental drift

19. _____s is a field of study within geology concerned generally with the structures within the lithosphere of the Earth and particularly with the forces and movements that have operated in a region to create these structures.

_____s is concerned with the orogenies and _____ development of cratons and _____ terranes as well as the earthquake and volcanic belts which directly affect much of the global population. _____ studies are also important for understanding erosion patterns in geomorphology and as guides for the economic geologist searching for petroleum and metallic ores.

a. Cocos Plate
c. Fault trace
b. Rivera Plate
d. Tectonic

20. _____ is a field of study within geology concerned generally with the structures within the lithosphere of the Earth and particularly with the forces and movements that have operated in a region to create these structures.

_____ is concerned with the orogenies and tectonic development of cratons and tectonic terranes as well as the earthquake and volcanic belts which directly affect much of the global population. Tectonic studies are also important for understanding erosion patterns in geomorphology and as guides for the economic geologist searching for petroleum and metallic ores.

a. Fault trace
c. Rivera Plate
b. Cocos Plate
d. Tectonics

21. The _____ is a physiographic region of the Intermontane Plateaus, roughly centered on the Four Corners region of the southwestern United States. The province covers an area of 337,000 km^2 within western Colorado, northwestern New Mexico, southern and eastern Utah, and northern Arizona. About 90% of the area is drained by the Colorado River and its main tributaries; the Green, San Juan and Little Colorado.

Development of the province has in large part been influenced by structural features in its oldest rocks. Part of the Wasatch Line and its various faults form the western edge of the province. Faults that run parallel to the Wasatch Fault that lies along the Wasatch Range form the boundaries between the plateaus in the High Plateaus Section. The Uinta Basin, Uncompahgre Uplift, and the Paradox Basin were also created by movement along structural weaknesses in the region's oldest rock.

a. Colorado Plateau
c. 1703 Genroku earthquake
b. 1700 Cascadia earthquake
d. 1509 Istanbul earthquake

22. The _____ , usually abbreviated K for its German translation Kreide, is a geologic period and system from circa >145.5 >± 4 to >65.5 >± 0.3 million years ago . In the geologic timescale, the _____ follows on the Jurassic period and is followed by the Paleogene period. It is the youngest period of the Mesozoic era, and at 80 million years long, the longest period of the Phanerozoic eon. The end of the _____ defines the boundary between the Mesozoic and Cenozoic eras.

a. Campanian
c. Hauterivian
b. Valanginian
d. Cretaceous

23. The _____ is a geologic subperiod and stratigraphic subsystem of the Carboniferous Period. It is the earliest/lowermost of two divisions of the Carboniferous, lasting from roughly 359 to 318 Ma (million years ago.) As with most other geochronologic units, the rock beds that define the _____ are well identified, but the exact start and end dates are uncertain by a few million years.
    a. Mississippian
    b. Pennsylvanian
    c. Dinantian
    d. Calciferous sandstone

24. The _____ is a tectonic plate covering most of North America, Greenland and part of Siberia. It extends eastward to the Mid-Atlantic Ridge and westward to the Chersky Range in eastern Siberia. The plate includes both continental and oceanic crust. The interior of the main continental landmass includes an extensive granitic core called a craton. Along most of the edges of this craton are fragments of crustal material called terranes, accreted to the craton by tectonic actions over the long span of geologic time. It is believed that much of North America west of the Rockies is composed of such terranes.
    a. Scotia Plate
    b. Kula Plate
    c. North American plate
    d. New Hebrides Plate

25. _____ was the supercontinent that is theorized to have existed during the Paleozoic and Mesozoic eras about 250 million years ago, before the component continents were separated into their current configuration.

The name was first used by the German originator of the continental drift theory, Alfred Wegener, in the 1920 edition of his book The Origin of Continents and Oceans , in which a postulated supercontinent _____ played a key role.

The single enormous ocean which surrounded Pangaea is known as Panthalassa.

    a. 1509 Istanbul earthquake
    b. Pangea
    c. 1703 Genroku earthquake
    d. 1700 Cascadia earthquake

26. In geology and earth science, a _____ is an area of highland, usually consisting of relatively flat terrain. A highly eroded _____ is called a dissected _____. A volcanic _____ is a _____ produced by volcanic activity.
    a. Plateau
    b. 1703 Genroku earthquake
    c. 1509 Istanbul earthquake
    d. 1700 Cascadia earthquake

27. _____ is the principle that the same scientific laws and processes are constant throughout space and time. It applies specifically to sciences that require a long timescale such as geology, astronomy, and paleontology. It was first defined by Charles Lyell (1797 - 1875), who incorporated James Hutton's gradualism into the idea of _____.
    a. AL 129-1
    b. Uniformitarianism
    c. AASHTO Soil Classification System
    d. AL 333

28. _____ is the removal of solids (sediment, soil, rock and other particles) in the natural environment. It usually occurs due to transport by wind, water, or ice; by down-slope creep of soil and other material under the force of gravity; or by living organisms, such as burrowing animals, in the case of bioerosion.

_____ is distinguished from weathering, which is the process of chemical or physical breakdown of the minerals in the rocks, although the two processes may occur concurrently.

a. AL 333
c. AL 129-1
b. AASHTO Soil Classification System
d. Erosion

29. _____ is molten rock expelled by a volcano during eruption. When first expelled from a volcanic vent, it is a liquid at temperatures from 700 >°C to 1,200 >°C (1,300 >°F to 2,200 >°F.) Although _____ is quite viscous, with about 100,000 times the viscosity of water, it can flow great distances before cooling and solidifying, because of both its thixotropic and shear thinning properties.

a. Lava
c. Cinder
b. Volcanic ash
d. Pyroclastic flow

Chapter 3. Bryce Canyon National Park

1. In geography and geology, a _____ is a significant vertical, or near vertical, rock exposure. _____s are formed as erosion landforms due to the processes of erosion and weathering that produce them. _____s are common on coasts, in mountainous areas, escarpments and along rivers. _____s are usually formed by rock that is resistant to erosion and weathering. Sedimentary rocks are most likely to form sandstone, limestone, chalk, and dolomite. Igneous rocks, such as granite and basalt also often form _____s.
   a. Cliff
   b. 1509 Istanbul earthquake
   c. 1703 Genroku earthquake
   d. 1700 Cascadia earthquake

2. _____, is a geomorphological phenomenon occurring when a stream or river drainage system or watershed is diverted from its own bed, and flows instead down the bed of a neighbouring stream. This can happen for several reasons, including:

   - Tectonic earth movements, where the slope of the land changes, and the stream is tipped out of its former course.
   - Natural damming, such as by a landslide or ice sheet.
   - Erosion

   a. Stream capture
   b. 1509 Istanbul earthquake
   c. Meander
   d. Distributary

3. The _____ of any physical feature such as a hill, stream, roof, railroad, or road refers to the amount of inclination of that surface where zero indicates level (with respect to gravity) and larger numbers indicate higher degrees of 'tilt'. Often slope is calculated as a ratio of 'rise over run' in which run is the horizontal distance and rise is the vertical distance.

   There are several systems for expressing slope:

   1. as an angle of inclination from the horizontal of a right triangle. (This is the angle >α opposite the 'rise' side of the triangle.)
   2. as a percentage (also known as the _____), the formula for which is ⬚> which could also be expressed as the tangent of the angle of inclination times 100. In the U.S., the _____ is the most commonly used unit for communicating slopes in transportation, surveying, construction, and civil engineering.
   3. as a per mille figure, the formula for which is ⬚> which could also be expressed as the tangent of the angle of inclination times 1000. This is commonly used in Europe to denote the incline of a railway.
   4. as a ratio of one part rise per so many parts run. For example, a slope that has a rise of 5 feet for every 100 feet of run would have a slope ratio of 1 in 20.

   Any one of these expressions may be used interchangeably to express the characteristics of a slope. _____ is usually expressed as a percentage, but this may easily be converted to the angle >α from horizontal since that carries the same information.

   a. Diamond Head
   b. Compaction
   c. Heavy metal
   d. Grade

Chapter 3. Bryce Canyon National Park

4. _____, also called erosional _____ or downward erosion or vertical erosion is a geological process that deepens the channel of a stream or valley by removing material from the stream's bed or the valley's floor. How fast _____ occurs depends on the stream's base level, which is the lowest point to which the stream can erode. Sea level is the ultimate base level, but many streams have a higher 'temporary' base level because they empty into another body of water that is above sea level or encounter bedrock that resists erosion.
- a. Downcutting
- b. Stoping
- c. Hydrothermal
- d. Deposition

5. The _____ epoch (55.8 >± 0.2 - 33.9 >± 0.1 Ma) is a major division of the geologic timescale and the second epoch of the Palaeogene period in the Cenozoic era. The _____ spans the time from the end of the Paleocene epoch to the beginning of the Oligocene epoch. The start of the _____ is marked by the emergence of the first modern mammals.
- a. AL 129-1
- b. AASHTO Soil Classification System
- c. Eocene
- d. AL 333

6. A _____ is a natural formation (or landform) where a rock arch forms, with a natural passageway through underneath. Most _____es form as a narrow ridge, walled by cliffs, become narrower from erosion, with a softer rock stratum under the cliff-forming stratum gradually eroding out until the rock shelters thus formed meet underneath the ridge, thus forming the arch. They commonly form where cliffs are subject to erosion from the sea, rivers or weathering (sub-aerial processes); the processes 'find' weaknesses in rocks and work on them, making them bigger until they break through.
- a. 1700 Cascadia earthquake
- b. 1703 Genroku earthquake
- c. Natural arch
- d. 1509 Istanbul earthquake

7. _____ is the process by which the freezing of water-saturated soil causes the deformation and upward thrust of the ground surface. This process can damage plant roots through breaking or desiccation, cause cracks in pavement, and damage the foundations of buildings, even below the frost line. Moist, fine-grained soil at certain temperatures is most susceptible to _____.
- a. 1700 Cascadia earthquake
- b. 1509 Istanbul earthquake
- c. 1703 Genroku earthquake
- d. Frost heaving

8. _____ can also be called frost shattering or frost-wedging. This type of weathering is common in mountain areas where the temperature is around freezing point. Frost induced weathering, although often attributed to the expansion of freezing water captured in cracks, is generally independent of the water-to-ice expansion. It has long been known that moist soils expand or frost heave upon freezing as a result of water migrating along from unfrozen areas via thin films to collect at growing ice lenses. This same phenomena occurs within pore spaces of rocks.
- a. 1509 Istanbul earthquake
- b. Physical weathering
- c. Weathering
- d. Frost disintegration

9. _____ is the decomposition of Earth rocks, soils and their minerals through direct contact with the planet's atmosphere. _____ occurs in situ, or 'with no movement', and thus should not be confused with erosion, which involves the movement of rocks and minerals by agents such as water, ice, wind and gravity.

Two important classifications of _____ processes exist -- physical and chemical _____.

a. 1700 Cascadia earthquake
b. Weathering
c. Physical weathering
d. 1509 Istanbul earthquake

10. _____ is a type of chemical weathering that creates rounded boulders and helps to create domed monoliths. This should not be confused with stream abrasion, a physical process which also creates rounded rocks on a much smaller scale. A good example of _____ can be found in the Alabama Hills area of eastern California.
a. Headward erosion
b. Diagenesis
c. Hydrothermal
d. Spheroidal weathering

11. In geology the term _____ refers to a fracture in rock where there has been no lateral movement in the plane of the fracture (up, down or sideways) of one side relative to the other. This makes it different from a fault which is defined as a fracture in rock where one side slides laterally past to the other. _____s normally have a regular spacing related to either the mechanical properties of the individual rock or the thickness of the layer involved.
a. 1703 Genroku earthquake
b. Joint
c. 1700 Cascadia earthquake
d. 1509 Istanbul earthquake

12. The _____ , usually abbreviated K for its German translation Kreide, is a geologic period and system from circa >145.5 >± 4 to >65.5 >± 0.3 million years ago . In the geologic timescale, the _____ follows on the Jurassic period and is followed by the Paleogene period. It is the youngest period of the Mesozoic era, and at 80 million years long, the longest period of the Phanerozoic eon. The end of the _____ defines the boundary between the Mesozoic and Cenozoic eras.
a. Hauterivian
b. Valanginian
c. Campanian
d. Cretaceous

13. A _____ is a tall thin spire of rock that protrudes from the bottom of an arid drainage basin or badland. _____s are composed of soft sedimentary rock and are topped by a piece of harder, less easily-eroded stone that protects the column from the elements.

They are mainly located in the desert in dry, hot areas.

a. 1700 Cascadia earthquake
b. 1703 Genroku earthquake
c. 1509 Istanbul earthquake
d. Hoodoo

14. _____ is a fine-grained sedimentary rock whose original constituents were clay minerals or muds. It is characterized by thin laminae breaking with an irregular curving fracture, often splintery and usually parallel to the often-indistinguishable bedding plane. This property is called fissility.
a. Jasperoid
b. Concretion
c. Claystone
d. Shale

15. _____ is a term given to an accumulation of broken rock fragments at the base of crags, mountain cliffs, or valley shoulders. Landforms associated with these materials are sometimes called _____ slopes or talus piles. These deposits typically have a concave upwards form, while the maximum inclination of such deposits corresponds to the angle of repose of the mean debris size.
a. 1703 Genroku earthquake
b. 1700 Cascadia earthquake
c. 1509 Istanbul earthquake
d. Scree

16. _____ is the geological process by which material is added to a landform or land mass. Fluids such as wind and water, as well as sediment gravity flows, transport previously eroded sediment, which, at the loss of enough kinetic energy in the fluid, is deposited, building up layers of sediment.

_____ occurs when the forces responsible for sediment transportation are no longer sufficient to overcome the forces of particle weight and friction, which resist motion.

a. Headward erosion
c. Mid-ocean ridge
b. Saltation
d. Deposition

17. _____ is the removal of solids (sediment, soil, rock and other particles) in the natural environment. It usually occurs due to transport by wind, water, or ice; by down-slope creep of soil and other material under the force of gravity; or by living organisms, such as burrowing animals, in the case of bioerosion.

_____ is distinguished from weathering, which is the process of chemical or physical breakdown of the minerals in the rocks, although the two processes may occur concurrently.

a. AL 129-1
c. AL 333
b. AASHTO Soil Classification System
d. Erosion

18. _____ is a naturally occurring granular material composed of finely divided rock and mineral particles.

As the term is used by geologists, _____ particles range in diameter from 0.0625 (or $>^1\!\!/_{16}$ mm, or 62.5 micrometers) to 2 millimeters. An individual particle in this range size is termed a _____ grain.

a. 1703 Genroku earthquake
c. 1509 Istanbul earthquake
b. Sand
d. 1700 Cascadia earthquake

19. The _____ or Palaeocene, 'early dawn of the recent' is a geologic epoch that lasted from 65.5 >± 0.3 Ma to 55.8 >± 0.2 Ma (million years ago.) It is the first epoch of the Palaeogene Period in the modern Cenozoic era. As with most other older geologic periods, the strata that define the epoch's beginning and end are well identified but the exact date of the end is uncertain.

a. Paleocene
c. 1700 Cascadia earthquake
b. 1509 Istanbul earthquake
d. 1703 Genroku earthquake

20. The _____ is a a term for a geologic period 65 million to 1.8 million years ago. The _____ covered the time span between the superseded Secondary period and an out-of-date definition of the Quaternary period. The period began with the demise of the non-avian dinosaurs in the Cretaceous-_____ extinction event, at start of the Cenozoic era, spanning to beginning of the most recent Ice Age, at the end of the Pliocene epoch.

a. Loihi Seamount
c. Historical geology
b. Tertiary
d. Logarithmic Spiral Beach

21. The _____ is a physiographic region of the Intermontane Plateaus, roughly centered on the Four Corners region of the southwestern United States. The province covers an area of 337,000 km² within western Colorado, northwestern New Mexico, southern and eastern Utah, and northern Arizona. About 90% of the area is drained by the Colorado River and its main tributaries; the Green, San Juan and Little Colorado.

Development of the province has in large part been influenced by structural features in its oldest rocks. Part of the Wasatch Line and its various faults form the western edge of the province. Faults that run parallel to the Wasatch Fault that lies along the Wasatch Range form the boundaries between the plateaus in the High Plateaus Section. The Uinta Basin, Uncompahgre Uplift, and the Paradox Basin were also created by movement along structural weaknesses in the region's oldest rock.

   a. 1700 Cascadia earthquake   b. Colorado Plateau
   c. 1509 Istanbul earthquake   d. 1703 Genroku earthquake

22. A _____ is a rock consisting of individual stones that have become cemented together. They are sedimentary rocks consisting of rounded fragments and are thus differentiated from breccias, which consist of angular clasts. Both _____ s and breccias are characterized by clasts larger than sand (>2 mm).
   a. Pelagic sediments   b. Concretion
   c. Keystone   d. Conglomerate

23. A _____ is an elevated area of land with a flat top and sides that are usually steep cliffs. It takes its name from its characteristic table-top shape. It is a characteristic landform of arid environments, particularly the southwestern United States.

_____s form usually in areas where horizontally layered rocks are uplifted by tectonic activity, but may form also in its absence.

_____s are formed by weathering and erosion. Variations in the ability of different types of rock to resist weathering and erosion cause the weaker types of rocks to be eroded away, leaving the more resistant types of rocks topographically higher relative to their surroundings. This process is called differential erosion.

   a. Mesa   b. 1509 Istanbul earthquake
   c. Palustrine   d. Truncated spur

24. In geology and earth science, a _____ is an area of highland, usually consisting of relatively flat terrain. A highly eroded _____ is called a dissected _____. A volcanic _____ is a _____ produced by volcanic activity.
   a. 1509 Istanbul earthquake   b. 1700 Cascadia earthquake
   c. Plateau   d. 1703 Genroku earthquake

Chapter 4. Capitol Reef National Park

1. The term _____ is used in geology when one or a stack of originally flat and planar surfaces, such as sedimentary strata, are bent or curved as a result of plastic (i.e. permanent) deformation. Synsedimentary _____s are those due to slumping of sedimentary material before it is lithified. _____s in rocks vary in size from microscopic crinkles to mountain-sized _____s.
   a. 1700 Cascadia earthquake
   b. Fold
   c. 1509 Istanbul earthquake
   d. 1703 Genroku earthquake

2. In geology and earth science, a _____ is an area of highland, usually consisting of relatively flat terrain. A highly eroded _____ is called a dissected _____. A volcanic _____ is a _____ produced by volcanic activity.
   a. 1703 Genroku earthquake
   b. 1509 Istanbul earthquake
   c. Plateau
   d. 1700 Cascadia earthquake

3. A _____ is a step-like fold consisting of a zone of steeper dip within an otherwise horizontal or gently-dipping sequence.

   _____s may be formed in several different ways

   - By differential compaction over an underlying structure, particularly a large fault at the edge of a basin due to the greater compactibility of the basin fill, the amplitude of the fold will die out gradually upwards e.g.

   - By mild reactivation of an earlier extensional fault during a phase of inversion causing folding in the overlying sequence e.g.

   - As a form of fault propagation fold during upward propagation of an extensional fault in basement into an overlying cover sequence e.g.

   - As a form of fault propagation fold during upward propagation of a reverse fault in basement into an overlying cover sequence e.g.

   a. Structural geology
   b. Crenulation
   c. Syncline
   d. Monocline

4. The _____ Era, is the most recent of the three classic geological eras and covers the period from 65.5 million years ago to the present. It is marked by the Cretaceous-Tertiary extinction event at the end of the Cretaceous that saw the demise of the last non-avian dinosaurs and the end of the Mesozoic Era. The _____ era is ongoing.
   a. Cenozoic
   b. 1509 Istanbul earthquake
   c. 1703 Genroku earthquake
   d. 1700 Cascadia earthquake

5. The _____ is a physiographic region of the Intermontane Plateaus, roughly centered on the Four Corners region of the southwestern United States. The province covers an area of 337,000 km^2 within western Colorado, northwestern New Mexico, southern and eastern Utah, and northern Arizona. About 90% of the area is drained by the Colorado River and its main tributaries; the Green, San Juan and Little Colorado.

Development of the province has in large part been influenced by structural features in its oldest rocks. Part of the Wasatch Line and its various faults form the western edge of the province. Faults that run parallel to the Wasatch Fault that lies along the Wasatch Range form the boundaries between the plateaus in the High Plateaus Section. The Uinta Basin, Uncompahgre Uplift, and the Paradox Basin were also created by movement along structural weaknesses in the region's oldest rock.

   a. 1509 Istanbul earthquake
   b. Colorado Plateau
   c. 1700 Cascadia earthquake
   d. 1703 Genroku earthquake

6. _____ is the geomorphic process by which soil, regolith, and rock move downslope under the force of gravity. Types of _____ include creep, slides, flows, topples, and falls, each with its own characteristic features, and taking place over timescales from seconds to years. _____ occurs on both terrestrial and submarine slopes, and has been observed on Earth, Mars, and Venus.
   a. 1700 Cascadia earthquake
   b. 1509 Istanbul earthquake
   c. Soil liquefaction
   d. Mass wasting

7. A _____ or mudslide is the most rapid (up to 80 km/h, or 50 mph) and fluid type of downhill mass wasting. It is a rapid movement of a large mass of mud formed from loose earth and water. Similar terms are mudslide (not very liquid), mud stream, debris flow (e.g. in high mountains), j>ökulhlaup, and lahar
   a. 1703 Genroku earthquake
   b. 1700 Cascadia earthquake
   c. 1509 Istanbul earthquake
   d. Mudflow

8. The _____ of any physical feature such as a hill, stream, roof, railroad, or road refers to the amount of inclination of that surface where zero indicates level (with respect to gravity) and larger numbers indicate higher degrees of 'tilt'. Often slope is calculated as a ratio of 'rise over run' in which run is the horizontal distance and rise is the vertical distance.

There are several systems for expressing slope:

1. as an angle of inclination from the horizontal of a right triangle. (This is the angle >α opposite the 'rise' side of the triangle.)

2. as a percentage (also known as the _____), the formula for which is $\boxed{\times}$> which could also be expressed as the tangent of the angle of inclination times 100. In the U.S., the _____ is the most commonly used unit for communicating slopes in transportation, surveying, construction, and civil engineering.

3. as a per mille figure, the formula for which is $\boxed{\times}$> which could also be expressed as the tangent of the angle of inclination times 1000. This is commonly used in Europe to denote the incline of a railway.

4. as a ratio of one part rise per so many parts run. For example, a slope that has a rise of 5 feet for every 100 feet of run would have a slope ratio of 1 in 20.

Any one of these expressions may be used interchangeably to express the characteristics of a slope. _____ is usually expressed as a percentage, but this may easily be converted to the angle >α from horizontal since that carries the same information.

a. Grade
b. Heavy metal
c. Diamond Head
d. Compaction

9. _____ is a term given to an accumulation of broken rock fragments at the base of crags, mountain cliffs, or valley shoulders. Landforms associated with these materials are sometimes called _____ slopes or talus piles. These deposits typically have a concave upwards form, while the maximum inclination of such deposits corresponds to the angle of repose of the mean debris size.

a. Scree
b. 1703 Genroku earthquake
c. 1509 Istanbul earthquake
d. 1700 Cascadia earthquake

10. _____ is one of the three main rock types (the others being sedimentary and metamorphic rock.) _____ is formed by magma (molten rock) being cooled and becoming solid . They may form with or without crystallization, either below the surface as intrusive (plutonic) rocks or on the surface as extrusive (volcanic) rocks. They make up approximately 95% of the upper part of the Earth's crust, but their great abundance is hidden on the Earth's surface by a relatively thin but widespread layer of sedimentary and metamorphic rocks.

a. Igneous differentiation
b. Ignimbrite
c. Extrusive
d. Igneous rock

11. A _____ is an elevated area of land with a flat top and sides that are usually steep cliffs. It takes its name from its characteristic table-top shape. It is a characteristic landform of arid environments, particularly the southwestern United States.

_____s form usually in areas where horizontally layered rocks are uplifted by tectonic activity, but may form also in its absence.

_____s are formed by weathering and erosion. Variations in the ability of different types of rock to resist weathering and erosion cause the weaker types of rocks to be eroded away, leaving the more resistant types of rocks topographically higher relative to their surroundings. This process is called differential erosion.

a. 1509 Istanbul earthquake
b. Truncated spur
c. Palustrine
d. Mesa

12. A _____ is a natural formation (or landform) where a rock arch forms, with a natural passageway through underneath. Most _____es form as a narrow ridge, walled by cliffs, become narrower from erosion, with a softer rock stratum under the cliff-forming stratum gradually eroding out until the rock shelters thus formed meet underneath the ridge, thus forming the arch. They commonly form where cliffs are subject to erosion from the sea, rivers or weathering (sub-aerial processes); the processes 'find' weaknesses in rocks and work on them, making them bigger until they break through.

a. 1700 Cascadia earthquake
b. Natural arch
c. 1509 Istanbul earthquake
d. 1703 Genroku earthquake

13. An _____ is a section of the Earth's oceanic crust and the underlying upper mantle that has been uplifted or emplaced to be exposed within continental crustal rocks. Ophio is Greek for 'snake', lite means 'stone' from the Greek lithos.

The term _____ was originally used by Alexandre Brongniart for an assemblage of green rocks (serpentine, diabase) in the Alps; Steinmann (1927) later modified its use to include serpentine, pillow lava, and chert ('Steinmann's trinity'), again based on occurrences in the Alps.

a. AL 333
b. Ophiolite
c. AASHTO Soil Classification System
d. AL 129-1

14. _____ is a term for a formation in rivers caused by a whirlpool eroding a hole into rock. The abrasion is mainly caused by the circular motion of small sediments such as small stones in the river. The interiors of _____s tend to be smooth and regular, unlike a plunge pool.
   a. 1700 Cascadia earthquake
   b. 1509 Istanbul earthquake
   c. Subsidence
   d. Pothole

15. _____, is a geomorphological phenomenon occurring when a stream or river drainage system or watershed is diverted from its own bed, and flows instead down the bed of a neighbouring stream. This can happen for several reasons, including:

   - Tectonic earth movements, where the slope of the land changes, and the stream is tipped out of its former course.
   - Natural damming, such as by a landslide or ice sheet.
   - Erosion

   a. Distributary
   b. Stream capture
   c. 1509 Istanbul earthquake
   d. Meander

16. A _____ or dyke in geology is a type of sheet intrusion referring to any geologic body that cuts discordantly across

   - planar wall rock structures, such as bedding or foliation
   - massive rock formations, like igneous/magmatic intrusions and salt diapirs.

They can therefore be either intrusive or sedimentary in origin.

An intrusive _____ is an igneous body with a very high aspect ratio, which means that its thickness is usually much smaller than the other two dimensions. Thickness can vary from sub-centimeter scale to many meters and the lateral dimensions can extend over many kilometers. A _____ is an intrusion into an opening cross-cutting fissure, shouldering aside other pre-existing layers or bodies of rock; this implies that a _____ is always younger than the rocks that contain it.

   a. Type locality
   b. Detritus
   c. Gradualism
   d. Dike

17. The chemical compound silicon dioxide, also known as _____ , is an oxide of silicon with a chemical formula of SiO_2 and has been known for its hardness since antiquity. _____ is most commonly found in nature as sand or quartz, as well as in the cell walls of diatoms. It is a principal component of most types of glass and substances such as concrete.
   a. 1509 Istanbul earthquake
   b. 1700 Cascadia earthquake
   c. 1703 Genroku earthquake
   d. Silica

18. _____ is the decomposition of Earth rocks, soils and their minerals through direct contact with the planet's atmosphere. _____ occurs in situ, or 'with no movement', and thus should not be confused with erosion, which involves the movement of rocks and minerals by agents such as water, ice, wind and gravity.

Two important classifications of _____ processes exist -- physical and chemical _____.

a. 1509 Istanbul earthquake
b. 1700 Cascadia earthquake
c. Weathering
d. Physical weathering

19. _____ is the removal of solids (sediment, soil, rock and other particles) in the natural environment. It usually occurs due to transport by wind, water, or ice; by down-slope creep of soil and other material under the force of gravity; or by living organisms, such as burrowing animals, in the case of bioerosion.

_____ is distinguished from weathering, which is the process of chemical or physical breakdown of the minerals in the rocks, although the two processes may occur concurrently.

a. AL 333
b. AL 129-1
c. AASHTO Soil Classification System
d. Erosion

20. An _____ is a fan-shaped deposit formed where a fast flowing stream flattens, slows, and spreads typically at the exit of a canyon onto a flatter plain. A convergence of neighboring fans into a single apron of deposits against a slope is called a bajada, or compound _____.

a. AASHTO Soil Classification System
b. AL 129-1
c. AL 333
d. Alluvial fan

21. The _____ is a geologic formation that is spread across the U.S. states of northern Arizona, Nevada, Utah, western New Mexico, and western Colorado. The _____ is controversially considered to be synonymous to Dockum Group in eastern Colorado, eastern New Mexico, southwestern Kansas, the Oklahoma panhandle, and western Texas. The _____ is sometimes colloquially used as a geologic formation within the Dockum in New Mexico and occasionally in Texas.

a. Nodule
b. Chinle
c. Dali
d. Melange

22. A _____ is a rapid flooding of geomorphic low-lying areas - washes, rivers and streams. It is caused by heavy rain associated with a thunderstorm, hurricane, or tropical storm. _____s can also occur after the collapse of an ice dam, or a human structure, such as a dam, for example, the Johnstown Flood of 1889.

a. 1509 Istanbul earthquake
b. Lake breakout
c. 1700 Cascadia earthquake
d. Flash flood

23. The _____ is a geologic period and system that extends from about 251 to 199 Mya (million years ago.) As the first period of the Mesozoic Era, the _____ follows the Permian and is followed by the Jurassic. Both the start and end of the _____ are marked by major extinction events.

a. Rhaetian
b. 1700 Cascadia earthquake
c. 1509 Istanbul earthquake
d. Triassic

24. The _____ is a distinctive sequence of Late Jurassic sedimentary rock that is found in the western United States, which has been the most fertile source of dinosaur fossils in North America. It is composed of mudstone, sandstone, siltstone and limestone and is light grey, greenish gray, or red. Most of the fossils occur in the green siltstone beds and lower sandstones, relics of the rivers and floodplains of the Jurassic period.

a. 1700 Cascadia earthquake
b. 1703 Genroku earthquake
c. 1509 Istanbul earthquake
d. Morrison Formation

25. _____ is a fine-grained sedimentary rock whose original constituents were clay minerals or muds. It is characterized by thin laminae breaking with an irregular curving fracture, often splintery and usually parallel to the often-indistinguishable bedding plane. This property is called fissility.
   a. Shale
   b. Claystone
   c. Concretion
   d. Jasperoid

26. The _____ is a a term for a geologic period 65 million to 1.8 million years ago. The _____ covered the time span between the superseded Secondary period and an out-of-date definition of the Quaternary period. The period began with the demise of the non-avian dinosaurs in the Cretaceous-_____ extinction event, at start of the Cenozoic era, spanning to beginning of the most recent Ice Age, at the end of the Pliocene epoch.
   a. Loihi Seamount
   b. Logarithmic Spiral Beach
   c. Historical geology
   d. Tertiary

27. The _____ is the epoch from 1.8 million to 11550 years BP covering the world's recent period of repeated glaciations. The _____ epoch follows the Pliocene epoch and is followed by the Holocene epoch. The _____ is the third epoch of the Neogene period or 6th epoch of the Cenozoic Era. The end of the _____ corresponds with the retreat of the last continental glacier. It also corresponds with the end of the Paleolithic age used in archaeology.
   a. Sicilian Stage
   b. Tyrrhenian
   c. Late Pleistocene
   d. Pleistocene

28. _____, also known as the Pleistocene glaciation, the current ice age or simply the ice age, refers to the period of the last few million years in which permanent ice sheets were established in Antarctica and perhaps Greenland, and fluctuating ice sheets have occurred elsewhere The major effects of the ice age were erosion and deposition of material over large parts of the continents, modification of river systems, creation of millions of lakes, changes in sea level, development of pluvial lakes far from the ice margins, isostatic adjustment of the crust, and abnormal winds. It affected oceans, flooding, and biological communities.
   a. Snowball Earth
   b. Wolstonian Stage
   c. Rock glaciers
   d. Quaternary glaciation

Chapter 5. Canyonlands National Park

1. _____ is a dark coating found on exposed rock surfaces in arid environments.

_____ forms only on physically stable rock surfaces that are no longer subject to frequent precipitation, fracturing or wind abrasion. The varnish is primarily composed of particles of clay along with iron and manganese oxides. There is also a host of trace elements and almost always some organic matter. The color of the varnish varies from shades of brown to black.

 a. 1509 Istanbul earthquake
 b. 1700 Cascadia earthquake
 c. Desert varnish
 d. 1703 Genroku earthquake

2. A _____ is a mountain rising from the ocean seafloor that does not reach to the water's surface (sea level), and thus is not an island. These are typically formed from extinct volcanoes, that rise abruptly and are usually found rising from a seafloor of 1,000-4,000 meters depth. They are defined by oceanographers as independent features that rise to at least 1,000 meters above the seafloor.
 a. Seamount
 b. 1700 Cascadia earthquake
 c. 1703 Genroku earthquake
 d. 1509 Istanbul earthquake

3. A _____ is a type of structural dome formed when a thick bed of evaporite minerals found at depth intrudes vertically into surrounding rock strata, forming a diapir.

The salt that forms these domes was deposited within restricted marine basins. Due to restricted flow of water into a basin, evaporation occurs resulting in the precipitation of salts from solution, depositing evaporites.

 a. Salt dome
 b. 1703 Genroku earthquake
 c. 1509 Istanbul earthquake
 d. 1700 Cascadia earthquake

4. In geology the term _____ refers to a fracture in rock where there has been no lateral movement in the plane of the fracture (up, down or sideways) of one side relative to the other. This makes it different from a fault which is defined as a fracture in rock where one side slides laterally past to the other. _____s normally have a regular spacing related to either the mechanical properties of the individual rock or the thickness of the layer involved.
 a. 1509 Istanbul earthquake
 b. 1700 Cascadia earthquake
 c. 1703 Genroku earthquake
 d. Joint

5. A _____ is an elevated area of land with a flat top and sides that are usually steep cliffs. It takes its name from its characteristic table-top shape. It is a characteristic landform of arid environments, particularly the southwestern United States.

_____s form usually in areas where horizontally layered rocks are uplifted by tectonic activity, but may form also in its absence.

_____s are formed by weathering and erosion. Variations in the ability of different types of rock to resist weathering and erosion cause the weaker types of rocks to be eroded away, leaving the more resistant types of rocks topographically higher relative to their surroundings. This process is called differential erosion.

 a. Palustrine
 b. Mesa
 c. 1509 Istanbul earthquake
 d. Truncated spur

6. _____ is a fine-grained sedimentary rock whose original constituents were clay minerals or muds. It is characterized by thin laminae breaking with an irregular curving fracture, often splintery and usually parallel to the often-indistinguishable bedding plane. This property is called fissility.
   a. Jasperoid
   b. Shale
   c. Concretion
   d. Claystone

7. A _____ is a depressed block of land bordered by parallel faults.

   A _____ is the result of a block of land being downthrown producing a valley with a distinct scarp on each side.

   _____ are produced from parallel normal faults, where the hanging wall is downthrown and the footwall is upthrown. The faults typically dip toward the center of the _____ from both sides.

   a. Graben
   b. Sag pond
   c. Michoud fault
   d. Shear

8. _____ is a term for a formation in rivers caused by a whirlpool eroding a hole into rock. The abrasion is mainly caused by the circular motion of small sediments such as small stones in the river. The interiors of _____s tend to be smooth and regular, unlike a plunge pool.
   a. 1509 Istanbul earthquake
   b. 1700 Cascadia earthquake
   c. Pothole
   d. Subsidence

9. The _____ is a geologic subperiod and stratigraphic subsystem of the Carboniferous Period. It is the later subperiod of the Carboniferous, lasting from roughly 318.1>± 1.3 to 299>± 0.8 Ma (million years ago.) As with most other geochronologic units, the rock beds that define the _____ are well identified, but the exact date of the start and end are uncertain by a few million years.
   a. Mississippian
   b. Pennsylvanian
   c. Dinantian
   d. Calciferous sandstone

10. The _____ is a geologic formation that is spread across the U.S. states of northern Arizona, Nevada, Utah, western New Mexico, and western Colorado. The _____ is controversially considered to be synonymous to Dockum Group in eastern Colorado, eastern New Mexico, southwestern Kansas, the Oklahoma panhandle, and western Texas. The _____ is sometimes colloquially used as a geologic formation within the Dockum in New Mexico and occasionally in Texas.
    a. Dali
    b. Nodule
    c. Chinle
    d. Melange

11. The _____ Era is one of three geologic eras of the Phanerozoic eon. The division of time into eras dates back to Giovanni Arduino, in the 18th century, although his original name for the era now called the '_____' was 'Secondary' (making the modern era the 'Tertiary'.)

The _____ was a time of tectonic, climatic and evolutionary activity. The continents gradually shifted from a state of connectedness into their present configuration; the drifting provided for speciation and other important evolutionary developments.

a. Mesozoic
b. 1509 Istanbul earthquake
c. 1703 Genroku earthquake
d. 1700 Cascadia earthquake

12. A _____ is a forest in which tree trunks have fossilized. That is, the wood in the trunks have turned into petrified wood, where organic cells have decomposed and are replaced by minerals, while preserving the structure of the wood.
   a. 1509 Istanbul earthquake
   b. Petrified Forest
   c. Phaneritic
   d. 1700 Cascadia earthquake

13. The _____ is the epoch from 1.8 million to 11550 years BP covering the world's recent period of repeated glaciations. The _____ epoch follows the Pliocene epoch and is followed by the Holocene epoch. The _____ is the third epoch of the Neogene period or 6th epoch of the Cenozoic Era. The end of the _____ corresponds with the retreat of the last continental glacier. It also corresponds with the end of the Paleolithic age used in archaeology.
   a. Sicilian Stage
   b. Pleistocene
   c. Late Pleistocene
   d. Tyrrhenian

Chapter 6. Arches National Park

1. A _____ is a natural formation (or landform) where a rock arch forms, with a natural passageway through underneath. Most _____es form as a narrow ridge, walled by cliffs, become narrower from erosion, with a softer rock stratum under the cliff-forming stratum gradually eroding out until the rock shelters thus formed meet underneath the ridge, thus forming the arch. They commonly form where cliffs are subject to erosion from the sea, rivers or weathering (sub-aerial processes); the processes 'find' weaknesses in rocks and work on them, making them bigger until they break through.
   a. Natural arch
   b. 1700 Cascadia earthquake
   c. 1509 Istanbul earthquake
   d. 1703 Genroku earthquake

2. The _____ is the earliest of three geologic eras of the Phanerozoic eon. The _____ spanned from roughly 542 to 251 million years ago (ICS, 2004), and is subdivided into six geologic periods; from oldest to youngest they are: the Cambrian, Ordovician, Silurian, Devonian, Carboniferous, and Permian.

   The _____ covers the time from the first appearance of abundant, soft-shelled fossils to the time when the continents were beginning to be dominated by large, relatively sophisticated reptiles and modern plants. The lower (oldest) boundary was classically set at the first appearance of creatures known as trilobites and archeocyathids.

   a. 1700 Cascadia earthquake
   b. 1509 Istanbul earthquake
   c. 1703 Genroku earthquake
   d. Paleozoic

3. The _____ , usually abbreviated K for its German translation Kreide, is a geologic period and system from circa >145.5 >± 4 to >65.5 >± 0.3 million years ago . In the geologic timescale, the _____ follows on the Jurassic period and is followed by the Paleogene period. It is the youngest period of the Mesozoic era, and at 80 million years long, the longest period of the Phanerozoic eon. The end of the _____ defines the boundary between the Mesozoic and Cenozoic eras.
   a. Valanginian
   b. Hauterivian
   c. Campanian
   d. Cretaceous

4. The _____ Period is the geologic time period after the Neogene Period, spanning 1.805 +/- 0.005 million years ago to the present. The _____ includes two geologic epochs: the Pleistocene and the Holocene Epoch.

   There is an ongoing debate of the status of _____ -- a recent proposal from International Commission on Stratigraphy (ICS) was to make _____ a subperiod under Neogene, but that was retracted after criticism from International Union for _____ Research (INQUA), so instead ICS and INQUA agreed to erect _____ as an Era, above Neogene, and to place the base for _____ at 2.588 >± 3.005, the base for Gelasian Stage.

   a. Tributary
   b. Yilgarn Craton
   c. Quaternary
   d. Geomorphology

5. In structural geology, an _____ is a fold that is convex up and has its oldest beds at its core. The term is not to be confused with antiform, which is a purely descriptive term for any fold that is convex up. Therefore if age relationships (i.e. younging direction) between various strata are unknown, the term antiform must be used.
   a. AL 129-1
   b. AASHTO Soil Classification System
   c. Anticline
   d. AL 333

6. _____ is a cryptocrystalline form of silica, composed of very fine intergrowths of the minerals quartz and moganite. These are both silica minerals, but they differ in that quartz has a trigonal crystal structure, whilst moganite is monoclinic.

Chapter 6. Arches National Park

_____ has a waxy luster, and may be semitransparent or translucent.

a. Silicate minerals
b. 1509 Istanbul earthquake
c. Chalcedony
d. Mineraloid

7. The _____ is a geologic formation that is spread across the U.S. states of northern Arizona, Nevada, Utah, western New Mexico, and western Colorado. The _____ is controversially considered to be synonymous to Dockum Group in eastern Colorado, eastern New Mexico, southwestern Kansas, the Oklahoma panhandle, and western Texas. The _____ is sometimes colloquially used as a geologic formation within the Dockum in New Mexico and occasionally in Texas.

a. Nodule
b. Chinle
c. Melange
d. Dali

8. _____ is a colloid hydrogel consisting of fine granular matter (such as sand or silt), clay, and salt water. In the name, as in that of quicksilver (mercury), 'quick' does not mean 'fast,' but 'living' (cf. the expression the quick and the dead.)

a. Sediment
b. Brickearth
c. Fech fech
d. Quicksand

9. The _____ is a distinctive sequence of Late Jurassic sedimentary rock that is found in the western United States, which has been the most fertile source of dinosaur fossils in North America. It is composed of mudstone, sandstone, siltstone and limestone and is light grey, greenish gray, or red. Most of the fossils occur in the green siltstone beds and lower sandstones, relics of the rivers and floodplains of the Jurassic period.

a. 1509 Istanbul earthquake
b. 1703 Genroku earthquake
c. Morrison Formation
d. 1700 Cascadia earthquake

10. The _____ was a period of mountain building in western North America, which started in the Late Cretaceous, 70 to 80 million years ago, and ended 35 to 55 million years ago. The exact duration and ages of beginning and end of the orogeny are in dispute, as is the cause. The _____ occurred in a series of pulses, with quiescent phases intervening. The major feature that was created by this orogeny was the Rocky Mountains, but evidence of this orogeny can be found from Alaska to northern Mexico, with the easternmost extent of the mountain-building represented by the Black Hills of South Dakota.

a. Nevadan orogeny
b. Pan-African orogeny
c. Kaikoura Orogeny
d. Laramide orogeny

11. _____ refers to natural mountain building, and may be studied as a tectonic structural event, (b) as a geographical event, and (c) a chronological event. Orogenic events (a) cause distinctive structural phenomena and related tectonic activity, (b) affect certain regions of rocks and crust, and (c) happen within a specific period of time.

a. Alice Springs Orogeny
b. Orogeny
c. Antler orogeny
d. Orogenesis

12. The _____ is a a term for a geologic period 65 million to 1.8 million years ago. The _____ covered the time span between the superseded Secondary period and an out-of-date definition of the Quaternary period. The period began with the demise of the non-avian dinosaurs in the Cretaceous-_____ extinction event, at start of the Cenozoic era, spanning to beginning of the most recent Ice Age, at the end of the Pliocene epoch.

a. Logarithmic Spiral Beach
b. Loihi Seamount
c. Tertiary
d. Historical geology

13. In geology, a _____ or _____ line is a planar fracture in rock in which the rock on one side of the fracture has moved with respect to the rock on the other side. Large _____s within the Earth's crust are the result of differential or shear motion and active _____ zones are the causal locations of most earthquakes. Earthquakes are caused by energy release during rapid slippage along a _____.
a. Compaction
b. Drainage system
c. Cleavage
d. Fault

Chapter 7. Mesa Verde National Park

1. A _____ is an elevated area of land with a flat top and sides that are usually steep cliffs. It takes its name from its characteristic table-top shape. It is a characteristic landform of arid environments, particularly the southwestern United States.

   _____s form usually in areas where horizontally layered rocks are uplifted by tectonic activity, but may form also in its absence.

   _____s are formed by weathering and erosion. Variations in the ability of different types of rock to resist weathering and erosion cause the weaker types of rocks to be eroded away, leaving the more resistant types of rocks topographically higher relative to their surroundings. This process is called differential erosion.

   a. Truncated spur
   b. 1509 Istanbul earthquake
   c. Mesa
   d. Palustrine

2. The _____ , usually abbreviated K for its German translation Kreide, is a geologic period and system from circa >145.5 >± 4 to >65.5 >± 0.3 million years ago . In the geologic timescale, the _____ follows on the Jurassic period and is followed by the Paleogene period. It is the youngest period of the Mesozoic era, and at 80 million years long, the longest period of the Phanerozoic eon. The end of the _____ defines the boundary between the Mesozoic and Cenozoic eras.
   a. Campanian
   b. Cretaceous
   c. Valanginian
   d. Hauterivian

3. In geography and geology, a _____ is a significant vertical, or near vertical, rock exposure. _____s are formed as erosion landforms due to the processes of erosion and weathering that produce them. _____s are common on coasts, in mountainous areas, escarpments and along rivers. _____s are usually formed by rock that is resistant to erosion and weathering. Sedimentary rocks are most likely to form sandstone, limestone, chalk, and dolomite. Igneous rocks, such as granite and basalt also often form _____s.
   a. 1703 Genroku earthquake
   b. 1700 Cascadia earthquake
   c. 1509 Istanbul earthquake
   d. Cliff

4. A _____ is a mountain rising from the ocean seafloor that does not reach to the water's surface (sea level), and thus is not an island. These are typically formed from extinct volcanoes, that rise abruptly and are usually found rising from a seafloor of 1,000-4,000 meters depth. They are defined by oceanographers as independent features that rise to at least 1,000 meters above the seafloor.
   a. 1703 Genroku earthquake
   b. 1509 Istanbul earthquake
   c. Seamount
   d. 1700 Cascadia earthquake

5. _____ is a homogeneous, typically nonstratified, porous, friable, slightly coherent, often calcareous, fine-grained, silty, pale yellow or buff, windblown (aeolian) sediment. It generally occurs as a widespread blanket deposit that covers areas of hundreds of square kilometers and tens of meters thick. _____ often stands in either steep or vertical faces.
   a. 1703 Genroku earthquake
   b. 1509 Istanbul earthquake
   c. 1700 Cascadia earthquake
   d. Loess

6. A _____ is a gently inclined erosional surface carved into bedrock. It is thinly covered with Fluvial gravel that has developed at the foot of mountains. It develops when running water erodes most of the mass of the mountain. It is typically a concave surface gently sloping away from mountainous desert areas.

a. Gradualism
b. Pediment
c. Stream Load
d. Patterned ground

7. _____ is the naturally occurring, unconsolidated or loose covering on the Earth's surface. _____ is composed of particles of broken rock that have been altered by chemical, biological and environmental processes including weathering and erosion. _____ is different from its parent rock(s) source(s), altered by interactions between the lithosphere, hydrosphere, atmosphere, and the biosphere.
 a. Topsoil
 b. 1509 Istanbul earthquake
 c. Soil
 d. Slump

8. _____ is a measure of the void spaces in a material, and is measured as a fraction, between 0-1, or as a percentage between 0-100%. The term is used in multiple fields including ceramics, metallurgy, materials, manufacturing, earth sciences and construction.

Used in geology, hydrogeology, soil science, and building science, the _____ of a porous medium (such as rock or sediment) describes the fraction of void space in the material, where the void may contain, for example, air or water.

 a. Saltwater intrusion
 b. Phreatic zone
 c. Permeability
 d. Porosity

9. _____, is a geomorphological phenomenon occurring when a stream or river drainage system or watershed is diverted from its own bed, and flows instead down the bed of a neighbouring stream. This can happen for several reasons, including:

- Tectonic earth movements, where the slope of the land changes, and the stream is tipped out of its former course.
- Natural damming, such as by a landslide or ice sheet.
- Erosion

 a. Meander
 b. Distributary
 c. 1509 Istanbul earthquake
 d. Stream capture

10. _____ is a fine-grained sedimentary rock whose original constituents were clay minerals or muds. It is characterized by thin laminae breaking with an irregular curving fracture, often splintery and usually parallel to the often-indistinguishable bedding plane. This property is called fissility.
 a. Claystone
 b. Concretion
 c. Shale
 d. Jasperoid

11. The _____ is a a term for a geologic period 65 million to 1.8 million years ago. The _____ covered the time span between the superseded Secondary period and an out-of-date definition of the Quaternary period. The period began with the demise of the non-avian dinosaurs in the Cretaceous-_____ extinction event, at start of the Cenozoic era, spanning to beginning of the most recent Ice Age, at the end of the Pliocene epoch.
 a. Logarithmic Spiral Beach
 b. Historical geology
 c. Loihi Seamount
 d. Tertiary

Chapter 8. Petrified Forest National Park

1. _____ is a microcrystalline variety of quartz, chiefly chalcedony, characterised by its fineness of grain and brightness of color. Although _____s may be found in various kinds of rock, they are classically associated with volcanic rocks but can be common in certain metamorphic rocks.

Colorful _____s and other chalcedonies were obtained over 3,000 years ago from the Achates River, now called Dirillo, in Sicily.

   a. Agate
   c. AL 333
   b. AASHTO Soil Classification System
   d. AL 129-1

2. A _____ is a forest in which tree trunks have fossilized. That is, the wood in the trunks have turned into petrified wood, where organic cells have decomposed and are replaced by minerals, while preserving the structure of the wood.
   a. 1700 Cascadia earthquake
   c. Petrified Forest
   b. 1509 Istanbul earthquake
   d. Phaneritic

3. The _____, usually abbreviated K for its German translation Kreide, is a geologic period and system from circa >145.5 >± 4 to >65.5 >± 0.3 million years ago. In the geologic timescale, the _____ follows on the Jurassic period and is followed by the Paleogene period. It is the youngest period of the Mesozoic era, and at 80 million years long, the longest period of the Phanerozoic eon. The end of the _____ defines the boundary between the Mesozoic and Cenozoic eras.
   a. Cretaceous
   c. Campanian
   b. Hauterivian
   d. Valanginian

4. The _____ Period is the geologic time period after the Neogene Period, spanning 1.805 +/- 0.005 million years ago to the present. The _____ includes two geologic epochs: the Pleistocene and the Holocene Epoch.

There is an ongoing debate of the status of _____ -- a recent proposal from International Commission on Stratigraphy (ICS) was to make _____ a subperiod under Neogene, but that was retracted after criticism from International Union for _____ Research (INQUA), so instead ICS and INQUA agreed to erect _____ as an Era, above Neogene, and to place the base for _____ at 2.588 >± 3.005, the base for Gelasian Stage.

   a. Tributary
   c. Geomorphology
   b. Yilgarn Craton
   d. Quaternary

5. _____ refers to natural mountain building, and may be studied as a tectonic structural event, (b) as a geographical event, and (c) a chronological event. Orogenic events (a) cause distinctive structural phenomena and related tectonic activity, (b) affect certain regions of rocks and crust, and (c) happen within a specific period of time.
   a. Orogenesis
   c. Antler orogeny
   b. Alice Springs Orogeny
   d. Orogeny

6. _____ is a cryptocrystalline form of silica, composed of very fine intergrowths of the minerals quartz and moganite. These are both silica minerals, but they differ in that quartz has a trigonal crystal structure, whilst moganite is monoclinic.

_____ has a waxy luster, and may be semitransparent or translucent.

a. Chalcedony
b. Mineraloid
c. 1509 Istanbul earthquake
d. Silicate minerals

7. The chemical compound silicon dioxide, also known as _____ , is an oxide of silicon with a chemical formula of SiO_2 and has been known for its hardness since antiquity. _____ is most commonly found in nature as sand or quartz, as well as in the cell walls of diatoms. It is a principal component of most types of glass and substances such as concrete.
   a. Silica
   b. 1509 Istanbul earthquake
   c. 1703 Genroku earthquake
   d. 1700 Cascadia earthquake

8. _____ is the most common metalloid. It is a chemical element, which has the symbol Si and atomic number 14. The atomic mass is 28.0855. As the eighth most common element in the universe by mass, _____ very rarely occurs as the pure free element in nature, but is more widely distributed in dusts, planetoids and planets as various forms of _____ dioxide or silicates. On Earth, _____ is the second most abundant element (after oxygen) in the crust, making up 25.7% of the crust by mass.
   a. 1703 Genroku earthquake
   b. 1700 Cascadia earthquake
   c. 1509 Istanbul earthquake
   d. Silicon

9. The chemical compound _____, also known as silica, is an oxide of silicon with a chemical formula of SiO_2 and has been known for its hardness since antiquity. Silica is most commonly found in nature as sand or quartz, as well as in the cell walls of diatoms. It is a principal component of most types of glass and substances such as concrete.
   a. 1509 Istanbul earthquake
   b. 1700 Cascadia earthquake
   c. 1703 Genroku earthquake
   d. Silicon dioxide

10. _____ is a type of fossil: it consists of fossil wood where all the organic materials have been replaced with minerals , while retaining the original structure of the wood. The petrifaction process occurs underground, when wood becomes buried under sediment and is initially preserved due to a lack of oxygen. Mineral-rich water flowing through the sediment deposits minerals in the plant's cells and as the plant's lignin and cellulose decay away, a stone mould forms in its place.
    a. Pteridospermatophyta
    b. Glossopteris
    c. 1509 Istanbul earthquake
    d. Petrified wood

11. The _____ is a geologic formation that is spread across the U.S. states of northern Arizona, Nevada, Utah, western New Mexico, and western Colorado. The _____ is controversially considered to be synonymous to Dockum Group in eastern Colorado, eastern New Mexico, southwestern Kansas, the Oklahoma panhandle, and western Texas. The _____ is sometimes colloquially used as a geologic formation within the Dockum in New Mexico and occasionally in Texas.
    a. Nodule
    b. Melange
    c. Dali
    d. Chinle

12. _____ is a process of fossilization in which mineral deposits form internal casts of organism. Carried by water, these minerals fill the spaces within organic tissue. Because of the nature of the casts, _____ is particularly useful in studies of the internal structures of organisms, usually of plants.
    a. Saltation
    b. Permineralization
    c. Deposition
    d. Hydrothermal circulation

Chapter 8. Petrified Forest National Park

13. A _____ is a type of arid terrain where softer sedimentary rocks and clay-rich soils have been extensively eroded by wind and water. It can resemble malpaís, a terrain of volcanic rocks. Canyons, ravines, gullies, hoodoos and other such geological forms are common in _____.
   a. 1700 Cascadia earthquake
   b. Badlands
   c. 1703 Genroku earthquake
   d. 1509 Istanbul earthquake

14. _____ is a sedimentary rock, a hardened deposit of calcium carbonate. This calcium carbonate cements together other materials, including gravel, sand, clay, and silt. It is found in aridisol and mollisol soil orders.
   a. 1700 Cascadia earthquake
   b. 1509 Istanbul earthquake
   c. Caliche
   d. 1703 Genroku earthquake

15. A _____ is a desert surface that is covered with closely packed, interlocking angular or rounded rock fragments of pebble and cobble size.

Several theories have been proposed for their formation. The more common theory is that they form by the gradual removal of the sand, dust and other fine grained material by the wind and intermittent rain leaving only the larger fragments behind.

   a. 1703 Genroku earthquake
   b. 1700 Cascadia earthquake
   c. 1509 Istanbul earthquake
   d. Desert pavement

16. _____ is a dark coating found on exposed rock surfaces in arid environments.

_____ forms only on physically stable rock surfaces that are no longer subject to frequent precipitation, fracturing or wind abrasion. The varnish is primarily composed of particles of clay along with iron and manganese oxides. There is also a host of trace elements and almost always some organic matter. The color of the varnish varies from shades of brown to black.

   a. 1509 Istanbul earthquake
   b. 1700 Cascadia earthquake
   c. 1703 Genroku earthquake
   d. Desert varnish

17. _____ are the preserved remains or traces of animals, plants, and other organisms from the remote past. The totality of _____, both discovered and undiscovered, and their placement in fossiliferous rock formations and sedimentary layers (strata) is known as the fossil record. The study of _____ across geological time, how they were formed, and the evolutionary relationships between taxa (phylogeny) are some of the most important functions of the science of paleontology.
   a. 1703 Genroku earthquake
   b. Fossils
   c. 1509 Istanbul earthquake
   d. 1700 Cascadia earthquake

18. _____ are images created by removing part of a rock surface by incising, pecking, carving, and abrading. Outside North America, scholars often use terms such as 'carving', 'engraving', or other descriptions of the technique to refer to such images. _____ are found world-wide, and are often associated with prehistoric peoples.
   a. 1509 Istanbul earthquake
   b. 1700 Cascadia earthquake
   c. 1703 Genroku earthquake
   d. Petroglyphs

19. The _____ is a geologic period and system that extends from about 251 to 199 Mya (million years ago.) As the first period of the Mesozoic Era, the _____ follows the Permian and is followed by the Jurassic. Both the start and end of the _____ are marked by major extinction events.
   a. Triassic
   b. 1700 Cascadia earthquake
   c. Rhaetian
   d. 1509 Istanbul earthquake

20. _____ are rocks that have been abraded, pitted, etched, grooved, or polished by wind-driven sand or ice crystals. These geomorphic features are most typically found in arid environments where there is little vegetation to interfere with aeolian particle transport, where there are frequently strong winds, and where there is a steady but not overwhelming supply of sand.

_____ can be abraded to eye-catching natural sculptures.

   a. Fault breccia
   b. Coprolite
   c. 1509 Istanbul earthquake
   d. Ventifacts

21. _____ is an absorbent aluminium phyllosilicate, generally impure clay consisting mostly of montmorillonite. There are a few types of _____s and their names depend on the dominant elements, such as K, Na, Ca, and Al. As noted in several places in the geologic literature, there are some nomenclatorial problems with the classification of _____ clays.
   a. 1509 Istanbul earthquake
   b. Bentonite
   c. 1703 Genroku earthquake
   d. 1700 Cascadia earthquake

22. The _____ is the earliest of three geologic eras of the Phanerozoic eon. The _____ spanned from roughly 542 to 251 million years ago (ICS, 2004), and is subdivided into six geologic periods; from oldest to youngest they are: the Cambrian, Ordovician, Silurian, Devonian, Carboniferous, and Permian.

The _____ covers the time from the first appearance of abundant, soft-shelled fossils to the time when the continents were beginning to be dominated by large, relatively sophisticated reptiles and modern plants. The lower (oldest) boundary was classically set at the first appearance of creatures known as trilobites and archeocyathids.

   a. 1703 Genroku earthquake
   b. 1700 Cascadia earthquake
   c. Paleozoic
   d. 1509 Istanbul earthquake

23. The _____ is a geological epoch which began approximately 11 700 years ago (10 000 ^{14}C years ago). According to traditional geological thinking, the _____ continues to the present. The _____ is part of the Neogene and Quaternary periods.
   a. Neoglaciation
   b. 1509 Istanbul earthquake
   c. Holocene
   d. 1700 Cascadia earthquake

24. The _____ is the epoch from 1.8 million to 11550 years BP covering the world's recent period of repeated glaciations. The _____ epoch follows the Pliocene epoch and is followed by the Holocene epoch. The _____ is the third epoch of the Neogene period or 6th epoch of the Cenozoic Era. The end of the _____ corresponds with the retreat of the last continental glacier. It also corresponds with the end of the Paleolithic age used in archaeology.

a. Sicilian Stage
b. Tyrrhenian
c. Late Pleistocene
d. Pleistocene

25. In geology and climatology, a _____ was an extended period of abundant rainfall lasting many thousands of years. The term is especially applied to such periods during the Pleistocene Epoch. A minor, short _____ may be termed a 'subpluvial'.

　a. Polar front
　b. Pluvial
　c. 1509 Istanbul earthquake
　d. Mesosphere

26. A _____ is a mass of molten rock (tephra) larger than 65 mm (2.5 inches) in diameter, formed when a volcano ejects viscous fragments of lava during an eruption. They cool into solid fragments before they reach the ground. Lava bombs can be thrown many kilometres from an erupting vent, and often acquire aerodynamic shapes during their flight.

　a. 1509 Istanbul earthquake
　b. 1700 Cascadia earthquake
　c. 1703 Genroku earthquake
　d. Volcanic bomb

27. _____ is the removal of solids (sediment, soil, rock and other particles) in the natural environment. It usually occurs due to transport by wind, water, or ice; by down-slope creep of soil and other material under the force of gravity; or by living organisms, such as burrowing animals, in the case of bioerosion.

_____ is distinguished from weathering, which is the process of chemical or physical breakdown of the minerals in the rocks, although the two processes may occur concurrently.

　a. AL 129-1
　b. AASHTO Soil Classification System
　c. AL 333
　d. Erosion

Chapter 9. Badlands National Park

1. The _____ Era, is the most recent of the three classic geological eras and covers the period from 65.5 million years ago to the present. It is marked by the Cretaceous-Tertiary extinction event at the end of the Cretaceous that saw the demise of the last non-avian dinosaurs and the end of the Mesozoic Era. The _____ era is ongoing.
    a. 1509 Istanbul earthquake
    b. 1703 Genroku earthquake
    c. 1700 Cascadia earthquake
    d. Cenozoic

2. _____ are the preserved remains or traces of animals, plants, and other organisms from the remote past. The totality of _____, both discovered and undiscovered, and their placement in fossiliferous rock formations and sedimentary layers (strata) is known as the fossil record. The study of _____ across geological time, how they were formed, and the evolutionary relationships between taxa (phylogeny) are some of the most important functions of the science of paleontology.
    a. 1509 Istanbul earthquake
    b. 1700 Cascadia earthquake
    c. 1703 Genroku earthquake
    d. Fossils

3. The _____ is the epoch from 1.8 million to 11550 years BP covering the world's recent period of repeated glaciations. The _____ epoch follows the Pliocene epoch and is followed by the Holocene epoch. The _____ is the third epoch of the Neogene period or 6th epoch of the Cenozoic Era. The end of the _____ corresponds with the retreat of the last continental glacier. It also corresponds with the end of the Paleolithic age used in archaeology.
    a. Late Pleistocene
    b. Sicilian Stage
    c. Pleistocene
    d. Tyrrhenian

4. The _____ , usually abbreviated K for its German translation Kreide, is a geologic period and system from circa >145.5 >± 4 to >65.5 >± 0.3 million years ago . In the geologic timescale, the _____ follows on the Jurassic period and is followed by the Paleogene period. It is the youngest period of the Mesozoic era, and at 80 million years long, the longest period of the Phanerozoic eon. The end of the _____ defines the boundary between the Mesozoic and Cenozoic eras.
    a. Campanian
    b. Valanginian
    c. Hauterivian
    d. Cretaceous

5. A _____ is a type of arid terrain where softer sedimentary rocks and clay-rich soils have been extensively eroded by wind and water. It can resemble malpa>ís, a terrain of volcanic rocks. Canyons, ravines, gullies, hoodoos and other such geological forms are common in _____.
    a. Badlands
    b. 1509 Istanbul earthquake
    c. 1703 Genroku earthquake
    d. 1700 Cascadia earthquake

6. A _____ is an old and stable part of the continental crust that has survived the merging and splitting of continents and supercontinents for at least 500 million years. Some are over two billion years old. They are generally found in the interiors of continents and are characteristically composed of ancient crystalline basement crust of lightweight felsic igneous rock such as granite.
    a. Craton
    b. Wyoming craton
    c. Superior craton
    d. Sebakwe proto-craton

7. _____ is an extinct genus of Hyaenodonts, a group of Creodonts. Some species of this genus were amongst the largest terrestrial carnivorous mammals of their time, others were only of the size of a marten. _____ was one of the latest genera of the Hyaenodonts and is known from the Late Eocene to Early Miocene.
    a. 1509 Istanbul earthquake
    b. 1703 Genroku earthquake
    c. Hyaenodon
    d. 1700 Cascadia earthquake

8. The _____ are a small, isolated mountain range rising from the Great Plains of North America in western South Dakota and extending into Wyoming, USA. Set off from the main body of the Rocky Mountains, the region is something of a geological anomaly--accurately described as an 'island of trees in a sea of grass'. The _____ encompass the _____ National Forest and are home to the tallest peaks of continental North America east of the Rockies.
  a. Thirtynine Mile volcanic field
  b. Monument Valley
  c. Paleorrota
  d. Black Hills

9. In the geosciences, _____ can have two meanings. The first meaning, common in geology and paleontology, refers to a former soil preserved by burial underneath either sediments (alluvium or loess) or volcanic deposits (Volcanic ash), which in case of older deposits have lithified into rock. In Quaternary geology, sedimentology, paleoclimatology, and geology in general, it is the typical and accepted practice to use the term '_____' to designate such 'fossil' soils found buried within either sedimentary or volcanic deposits exposed in all continents as illustrated by Rettallack (2001), Kraus (1999), and innumerable other published papers and books.
  a. Soil structure
  b. Slickenside
  c. Soil horizon
  d. Paleosol

10. The _____ is a a term for a geologic period 65 million to 1.8 million years ago. The _____ covered the time span between the superseded Secondary period and an out-of-date definition of the Quaternary period. The period began with the demise of the non-avian dinosaurs in the Cretaceous-_____ extinction event, at start of the Cenozoic era, spanning to beginning of the most recent Ice Age, at the end of the Pliocene epoch.
  a. Logarithmic Spiral Beach
  b. Tertiary
  c. Loihi Seamount
  d. Historical geology

11. _____ is an absorbent aluminium phyllosilicate, generally impure clay consisting mostly of montmorillonite. There are a few types of _____s and their names depend on the dominant elements, such as K, Na, Ca, and Al. As noted in several places in the geologic literature, there are some nomenclatorial problems with the classification of _____ clays.
  a. Bentonite
  b. 1703 Genroku earthquake
  c. 1509 Istanbul earthquake
  d. 1700 Cascadia earthquake

12. _____ is the decomposition of Earth rocks, soils and their minerals through direct contact with the planet's atmosphere. _____ occurs in situ, or 'with no movement', and thus should not be confused with erosion, which involves the movement of rocks and minerals by agents such as water, ice, wind and gravity.

Two important classifications of _____ processes exist -- physical and chemical _____.

  a. Weathering
  b. 1700 Cascadia earthquake
  c. Physical weathering
  d. 1509 Istanbul earthquake

13. _____ is the removal of solids (sediment, soil, rock and other particles) in the natural environment. It usually occurs due to transport by wind, water, or ice; by down-slope creep of soil and other material under the force of gravity; or by living organisms, such as burrowing animals, in the case of bioerosion.

_____ is distinguished from weathering, which is the process of chemical or physical breakdown of the minerals in the rocks, although the two processes may occur concurrently.

| a. AASHTO Soil Classification System | b. AL 333 |
| c. Erosion | d. AL 129-1 |

14. In geology, a _____ or _____ line is a planar fracture in rock in which the rock on one side of the fracture has moved with respect to the rock on the other side. Large _____s within the Earth's crust are the result of differential or shear motion and active _____ zones are the causal locations of most earthquakes. Earthquakes are caused by energy release during rapid slippage along a _____.
   a. Compaction
   b. Cleavage
   c. Drainage system
   d. Fault

15. _____ rocks are composed of fragments of pre-existing rock. The term is most commonly, but not uniquely, applied to sedimentary rocks.

_____ metamorphic rocks include breccias formed in faults, as well as some protomylonite and pseudotachylite.

   a. 1703 Genroku earthquake
   b. 1509 Istanbul earthquake
   c. Clastic
   d. 1700 Cascadia earthquake

16. _____ is the geomorphic process by which soil, regolith, and rock move downslope under the force of gravity. Types of _____ include creep, slides, flows, topples, and falls, each with its own characteristic features, and taking place over timescales from seconds to years. _____ occurs on both terrestrial and submarine slopes, and has been observed on Earth, Mars, and Venus.
   a. Soil liquefaction
   b. 1509 Istanbul earthquake
   c. Mass wasting
   d. 1700 Cascadia earthquake

17. An _____ is a fan-shaped deposit formed where a fast flowing stream flattens, slows, and spreads typically at the exit of a canyon onto a flatter plain. A convergence of neighboring fans into a single apron of deposits against a slope is called a bajada, or compound _____.
   a. AL 333
   b. AASHTO Soil Classification System
   c. AL 129-1
   d. Alluvial fan

18. A _____ or dyke in geology is a type of sheet intrusion referring to any geologic body that cuts discordantly across

- planar wall rock structures, such as bedding or foliation
- massive rock formations, like igneous/magmatic intrusions and salt diapirs.

They can therefore be either intrusive or sedimentary in origin.

An intrusive _____ is an igneous body with a very high aspect ratio, which means that its thickness is usually much smaller than the other two dimensions. Thickness can vary from sub-centimeter scale to many meters and the lateral dimensions can extend over many kilometers. A _____ is an intrusion into an opening cross-cutting fissure, shouldering aside other pre-existing layers or bodies of rock; this implies that a _____ is always younger than the rocks that contain it.

a. Gradualism
b. Detritus
c. Dike
d. Type locality

19. _____ occurs when a soil is sodic. When a sodic soil is wetted the clay particles are forced apart. This is generally a major cause of erosion.
   a. Seismic inversion
   b. Schreyerite
   c. Geomicrobiology
   d. Dispersion

20. A _____ is a volume of sedimentary rock in which a mineral cement fills the porosity (i.e. the spaces between the sediment grains.) _____s are often ovoid or spherical in shape, although irregular shapes also occur.
   a. Sedimentary deposits
   b. Mudstone
   c. Sandstone
   d. Concretion

21. _____ is a fine-grained sedimentary rock whose original constituents were clay minerals or muds. It is characterized by thin laminae breaking with an irregular curving fracture, often splintery and usually parallel to the often-indistinguishable bedding plane. This property is called fissility.
   a. Jasperoid
   b. Concretion
   c. Claystone
   d. Shale

1. _____ is one of the three main rock types (the others being igneous and metamorphic rock.) _____ is formed by deposition and consolidation of mineral and organic material and from precipitation of minerals from solution. The processes that form _____ occur at the surface of the Earth and within bodies of water.
   a. Felsic
   b. Serpentinite
   c. Large igneous provinces
   d. Sedimentary rock

2. A _____ is a volume of sedimentary rock in which a mineral cement fills the porosity (i.e. the spaces between the sediment grains.) _____s are often ovoid or spherical in shape, although irregular shapes also occur.
   a. Sandstone
   b. Sedimentary deposits
   c. Mudstone
   d. Concretion

3. The _____ or Palaeocene, 'early dawn of the recent' is a geologic epoch that lasted from 65.5 >± 0.3 Ma to 55.8 >± 0.2 Ma (million years ago.) It is the first epoch of the Palaeogene Period in the modern Cenozoic era. As with most other older geologic periods, the strata that define the epoch's beginning and end are well identified but the exact date of the end is uncertain.
   a. Paleocene
   b. 1703 Genroku earthquake
   c. 1700 Cascadia earthquake
   d. 1509 Istanbul earthquake

4. The _____ is the earliest of three geologic eras of the Phanerozoic eon. The _____ spanned from roughly 542 to 251 million years ago (ICS, 2004), and is subdivided into six geologic periods; from oldest to youngest they are: the Cambrian, Ordovician, Silurian, Devonian, Carboniferous, and Permian.

   The _____ covers the time from the first appearance of abundant, soft-shelled fossils to the time when the continents were beginning to be dominated by large, relatively sophisticated reptiles and modern plants. The lower (oldest) boundary was classically set at the first appearance of creatures known as trilobites and archeocyathids.

   a. 1509 Istanbul earthquake
   b. 1700 Cascadia earthquake
   c. 1703 Genroku earthquake
   d. Paleozoic

5. _____ is a type of fossil: it consists of fossil wood where all the organic materials have been replaced with minerals, while retaining the original structure of the wood. The petrifaction process occurs underground, when wood becomes buried under sediment and is initially preserved due to a lack of oxygen. Mineral-rich water flowing through the sediment deposits minerals in the plant's cells and as the plant's lignin and cellulose decay away, a stone mould forms in its place.
   a. Pteridospermatophyta
   b. Glossopteris
   c. Petrified wood
   d. 1509 Istanbul earthquake

6. The _____ is the epoch from 1.8 million to 11550 years BP covering the world's recent period of repeated glaciations. The _____ epoch follows the Pliocene epoch and is followed by the Holocene epoch. The _____ is the third epoch of the Neogene period or 6th epoch of the Cenozoic Era. The end of the _____ corresponds with the retreat of the last continental glacier. It also corresponds with the end of the Paleolithic age used in archaeology.
   a. Pleistocene
   b. Late Pleistocene
   c. Tyrrhenian
   d. Sicilian Stage

7. _____ is a textural term for macrovesicular volcanic rock. It is commonly, but not exclusively, basaltic or andesitic in composition. _____ is light as a result of numerous macroscopic ellipsoidal vesicles, but most _____ has a specific gravity greater than 1, and sinks in water.

   a. Lopolith
   c. Charnockite
   b. Scoria
   d. Coldwell Complex

8. The _____ Era is one of three geologic eras of the Phanerozoic eon. The division of time into eras dates back to Giovanni Arduino, in the 18th century, although his original name for the era now called the '_____' was 'Secondary' (making the modern era the 'Tertiary'.)

The _____ was a time of tectonic, climatic and evolutionary activity. The continents gradually shifted from a state of connectedness into their present configuration; the drifting provided for speciation and other important evolutionary developments.

   a. 1703 Genroku earthquake
   c. 1509 Istanbul earthquake
   b. Mesozoic
   d. 1700 Cascadia earthquake

Chapter 11. Kobuk Valley National Park

1. A _____ is flat or nearly flat land adjacent to a stream or river that experiences occasional or periodic flooding. It includes the floodway, which consists of the stream channel and adjacent areas that carry flood flows, and the flood fringe, which are areas covered by the flood, but which do not experience a strong current.

They generally contain unconsolidated sediments, often extending below the bed of the stream.

   a. 1509 Istanbul earthquake
   b. 1700 Cascadia earthquake
   c. 1703 Genroku earthquake
   d. Floodplain

2. The _____ is the earliest of three geologic eras of the Phanerozoic eon. The _____ spanned from roughly 542 to 251 million years ago (ICS, 2004), and is subdivided into six geologic periods; from oldest to youngest they are: the Cambrian, Ordovician, Silurian, Devonian, Carboniferous, and Permian.

The _____ covers the time from the first appearance of abundant, soft-shelled fossils to the time when the continents were beginning to be dominated by large, relatively sophisticated reptiles and modern plants. The lower (oldest) boundary was classically set at the first appearance of creatures known as trilobites and archeocyathids.

   a. 1700 Cascadia earthquake
   b. 1509 Istanbul earthquake
   c. 1703 Genroku earthquake
   d. Paleozoic

3. A _____, in biogeography, is an isthmus or wider land connection between otherwise separate areas, which allows terrestrial animals and plants to cross over and colonise new lands. They can be created by marine regression, in which sea levels fall, exposing shallow, previously submerged sections of continental shelf; or when new land is created by plate tectonics; or occasionally when the sea floor rises due to post-glacial rebound after an ice age.
   a. 1509 Istanbul earthquake
   b. Polar deserts
   c. Land Bridge
   d. 1700 Cascadia earthquake

4. In geology, _____ or _____ soil is soil at or below the freezing point of water (0 >°C or 32 >°F) for two or more years. Ice is not always present, as may be in the case of nonporous bedrock, but it frequently occurs and it may be in amounts exceeding the potential hydraulic saturation of the ground material. Most _____ is located in high latitudes (i.e. land in close proximity to the North and South poles), but alpine _____ may exist at high altitudes in much lower latitudes.
   a. 1703 Genroku earthquake
   b. 1700 Cascadia earthquake
   c. 1509 Istanbul earthquake
   d. Permafrost

5. In geology, the term '_____' refers to structures or minerals from a parent rock that did not undergo metamorphosis when the surrounding rock did, or to rock that survived a destructive geologic process.
   a. 1703 Genroku earthquake
   b. 1509 Istanbul earthquake
   c. 1700 Cascadia earthquake
   d. Relict

6. _____ is a naturally occurring granular material composed of finely divided rock and mineral particles.

As the term is used by geologists, _____ particles range in diameter from 0.0625 (or $>^1\!/_{16}$ mm, or 62.5 micrometers) to 2 millimeters. An individual particle in this range size is termed a _____ grain.

a. 1509 Istanbul earthquake
b. 1700 Cascadia earthquake
c. 1703 Genroku earthquake
d. Sand

7. An _____ is a fan-shaped deposit formed where a fast flowing stream flattens, slows, and spreads typically at the exit of a canyon onto a flatter plain. A convergence of neighboring fans into a single apron of deposits against a slope is called a bajada, or compound _____.
a. AL 129-1
b. AASHTO Soil Classification System
c. Alluvial fan
d. AL 333

8. A _____ in general is a bend in a sinuous watercourse. A _____ is formed when the moving water in a river erodes the outer banks and widens its valley. A stream of any volume may assume a meandering course, alternatively eroding sediments from the outside of a bend and depositing them on the inside.
a. Stream capture
b. Distributary
c. 1509 Istanbul earthquake
d. Meander

9. An _____ is a U-shaped body of water formed when a wide meander from the mainstem of a river is cut off to create a lake. This landform is called an _____ for the distinctive curved shape that results from this process. In Australia, an _____ is called a billabong.
a. AL 129-1
b. AL 333
c. AASHTO Soil Classification System
d. Oxbow lake

10. In the earth sciences and geology sub-fields, a _____ or physical feature comprises a geomorphological unit, and is largely defined by its surface form and location in the landscape, as part of the terrain, and as such, is typically an element of topography. _____ elements also include seascape and oceanic waterbody interface features such as bays, peninsulas, seas and so forth, including sub-surface terrain features such as submersed mountain ranges, volcanoes, and the great ocean basins under the thin skin of water, for the whole earth is the province and domain of geology. This panorama in Great Smoky Mountains National Park has the readily identifiable physical features of a rolling plain, actually part of a broad valley, distant foothills, and a backdrop of the old much weathered Appalachian mountain range.

_____s are categorised by characteristic physical attributes such as elevation, slope, orientation, stratification, rock exposure, and soil type.

a. 1700 Cascadia earthquake
b. Polar deserts
c. 1509 Istanbul earthquake
d. Landform

11. A _____, dike (or dyke), embankment, floodbank or stopbank is a natural or artificial slope or wall to regulate water levels. It is usually earthen and often parallel to the course of a river or the coast.
a. 1700 Cascadia earthquake
b. 1703 Genroku earthquake
c. 1509 Istanbul earthquake
d. Levee

12. A _____ is a depositional feature of streams. _____s are found in abundance in mature or meandering streams. They are crescent-shaped and located on the inside of a stream bend, being very similar to, though often smaller than towheads, or river islands. They are composed of sediment that is well sorted and typically reflects the overall capacity of the stream.

a. 1700 Cascadia earthquake
b. Point bar
c. 1509 Istanbul earthquake
d. 1703 Genroku earthquake

13. A _____ dune is an arc-shaped sand ridge, comprising well-sorted sand. This type of dune possesses two 'horns' that face downwind, with the slip face (the downwind slope) at the angle of repose, or approximately 32 degrees. The upwind side is packed by the wind, and stands at about 15 degrees. Simple _____ dunes may stretch from meters to a hundred meters or so between the tips of the horns.
    a. 1509 Istanbul earthquake
    b. 1700 Cascadia earthquake
    c. 1703 Genroku earthquake
    d. Barchan

14. In stratigraphy, _____ is the native consolidated rock underlying the surface of a terrestrial planet, usually the Earth. Above the _____ is usually an area of broken and weathered unconsolidated rock in the basal subsoil. The top of the _____ is known as rockhead and identifying this, via excavations, drilling or geophysical methods, is an important task in most civil engineering projects.
    a. Biozones
    b. Bedrock
    c. Polystrate
    d. Sequence stratigraphy

15. _____ are sandy depressions in a sand dune ecosystem (psammosere) caused by the removal of sediments by wind.

_____ occur in partially vegetated dunefields or sandhills. _____ form when a patch of protective vegetation is lost, allowing strong winds to 'blow out' sand and form a depression.

    a. Pothole
    b. 1700 Cascadia earthquake
    c. 1509 Istanbul earthquake
    d. Blowouts

16. In geology, _____ is a specific type of particle transport by fluids such as wind, or the denser fluid water. It occurs when loose material is removed from a bed and carried by the fluid, before being transported back to the surface. Examples include pebble transport by rivers, sand drift over desert surfaces, soil blowing over fields, or even snow drift over smooth surfaces such as those in the Arctic or Canadian Prairies.
    a. Downcutting
    b. Saltation
    c. Stoping
    d. Wave pounding

17. The _____ Era is one of three geologic eras of the Phanerozoic eon. The division of time into eras dates back to Giovanni Arduino, in the 18th century, although his original name for the era now called the '_____' was 'Secondary' (making the modern era the 'Tertiary'.)

The _____ was a time of tectonic, climatic and evolutionary activity. The continents gradually shifted from a state of connectedness into their present configuration; the drifting provided for speciation and other important evolutionary developments.

    a. 1703 Genroku earthquake
    b. 1509 Istanbul earthquake
    c. 1700 Cascadia earthquake
    d. Mesozoic

18. The _____ Period is the geologic time period after the Neogene Period, spanning 1.805 +/- 0.005 million years ago to the present. The _____ includes two geologic epochs: the Pleistocene and the Holocene Epoch.

There is an ongoing debate of the status of _____ -- a recent proposal from International Commission on Stratigraphy (ICS) was to make _____ a subperiod under Neogene, but that was retracted after criticism from International Union for _____ Research (INQUA), so instead ICS and INQUA agreed to erect _____ as an Era, above Neogene, and to place the base for _____ at 2.588 >± 3.005, the base for Gelasian Stage.

- a. Geomorphology
- b. Yilgarn Craton
- c. Tributary
- d. Quaternary

19. The _____ is a a term for a geologic period 65 million to 1.8 million years ago. The _____ covered the time span between the superseded Secondary period and an out-of-date definition of the Quaternary period. The period began with the demise of the non-avian dinosaurs in the Cretaceous-_____ extinction event, at start of the Cenozoic era, spanning to beginning of the most recent Ice Age, at the end of the Pliocene epoch.
- a. Logarithmic Spiral Beach
- b. Loihi Seamount
- c. Tertiary
- d. Historical geology

20. The _____ is the epoch from 1.8 million to 11550 years BP covering the world's recent period of repeated glaciations. The _____ epoch follows the Pliocene epoch and is followed by the Holocene epoch. The _____ is the third epoch of the Neogene period or 6th epoch of the Cenozoic Era. The end of the _____ corresponds with the retreat of the last continental glacier. It also corresponds with the end of the Paleolithic age used in archaeology.
- a. Pleistocene
- b. Tyrrhenian
- c. Late Pleistocene
- d. Sicilian Stage

Chapter 12. Great Sand Dunes National Park and Preserve

1. The _____ Era, is the most recent of the three classic geological eras and covers the period from 65.5 million years ago to the present. It is marked by the Cretaceous-Tertiary extinction event at the end of the Cretaceous that saw the demise of the last non-avian dinosaurs and the end of the Mesozoic Era. The _____ era is ongoing.

   a. 1509 Istanbul earthquake
   b. Cenozoic
   c. 1703 Genroku earthquake
   d. 1700 Cascadia earthquake

2. The _____ is a geological eon representing a period before the first abundant complex life on Earth. The _____ extended from 2500 Ma to 542.0 >± 1.0 Ma (million years ago), and is the most recent part of the old, informally named 'e;Precambrian'e; time.

The Proterozoic consists of 3 geologic eras, from oldest to youngest:

- Paleoproterozoic
- Mesoproterozoic
- Neoproterozoic

The well-identified events were:

- The transition to an oxygenated atmosphere during the Mesoproterozoic.
- Several glaciations, including the hypothesized Snowball Earth during the Cryogenian period in the late Neoproterozoic.
- The Ediacaran Period (635 to 542 Ma) which is characterized by the evolution of abundant soft-bodied multicellular organisms.

The geoloic record of the Proterozoic is much better than that for the preceding Archean. In contrast to the deep-water deposits of the Archean, the Proterozoic features many strata that were laid down in extensive shallow epicontinental seas; furthermore, many of these rocks are less metamorphosed than Archean-age ones, and plenty are unaltered.

   a. 1700 Cascadia earthquake
   b. 1703 Genroku earthquake
   c. 1509 Istanbul earthquake
   d. Proterozoic Eon

3. _____ is a naturally occurring granular material composed of finely divided rock and mineral particles.

As the term is used by geologists, _____ particles range in diameter from 0.0625 (or $>^1\!/_{16}$ mm, or 62.5 micrometers) to 2 millimeters. An individual particle in this range size is termed a _____ grain.

   a. 1700 Cascadia earthquake
   b. 1509 Istanbul earthquake
   c. 1703 Genroku earthquake
   d. Sand

4. In geology, _____ is a specific type of particle transport by fluids such as wind, or the denser fluid water. It occurs when loose material is removed from a bed and carried by the fluid, before being transported back to the surface. Examples include pebble transport by rivers, sand drift over desert surfaces, soil blowing over fields, or even snow drift over smooth surfaces such as those in the Arctic or Canadian Prairies.

a. Downcutting
b. Wave pounding
c. Stoping
d. Saltation

5. Radially symmetrical, _____ are pyramidal sand mounds with slipfaces on three or more arms that radiate from the high center of the mound. They tend to accumulate in areas with multidirectional wind regimes. _____ grow upward rather than laterally. They dominate the Grand Erg Oriental of the Sahara. In other deserts, they occur around the margins of the sand seas, particularly near topographic barriers. In the southeast Badain Jaran Desert of China, the _____ are up to 500 meters tall and may be the tallest dunes on Earth.
   a. Star dunes
   b. Historical geology
   c. Loihi Seamount
   d. Pahoehoe lava

6. A _____ dune is an arc-shaped sand ridge, comprising well-sorted sand. This type of dune possesses two 'horns' that face downwind, with the slip face (the downwind slope) at the angle of repose, or approximately 32 degrees. The upwind side is packed by the wind, and stands at about 15 degrees. Simple _____ dunes may stretch from meters to a hundred meters or so between the tips of the horns.
   a. Barchan
   b. 1509 Istanbul earthquake
   c. 1703 Genroku earthquake
   d. 1700 Cascadia earthquake

7. A _____ is one of a number of channel types and has a channel that consists of a network of small channels separated by small and often temporary islands called braid bars or, in British usage, aits or eyots. Braided streams occur in rivers with high slope and/or large sediment load (Schumm and Kahn 1972.) Braided channels are also typical of environments that dramatically decrease channel depth, and consequently channel velocity, such as river deltas, alluvial fans and peneplains.

_____s, as distinct from meandering rivers, occur when a threshold level of sediment load or slope is reached. Geologically speaking an increase in sediment load will over time increase the slope of the river, so these two conditions can be considered synonymous and consequently a variation of slope can model a variation in sediment load.

   a. Meander
   b. Stream capture
   c. 1509 Istanbul earthquake
   d. Braided river

8. An _____ is a fan-shaped deposit formed where a fast flowing stream flattens, slows, and spreads typically at the exit of a canyon onto a flatter plain. A convergence of neighboring fans into a single apron of deposits against a slope is called a bajada, or compound _____.
   a. AASHTO Soil Classification System
   b. AL 129-1
   c. AL 333
   d. Alluvial fan

9. The _____ is the earliest of three geologic eras of the Phanerozoic eon. The _____ spanned from roughly 542 to 251 million years ago (ICS, 2004), and is subdivided into six geologic periods; from oldest to youngest they are: the Cambrian, Ordovician, Silurian, Devonian, Carboniferous, and Permian.

The _____ covers the time from the first appearance of abundant, soft-shelled fossils to the time when the continents were beginning to be dominated by large, relatively sophisticated reptiles and modern plants. The lower (oldest) boundary was classically set at the first appearance of creatures known as trilobites and archeocyathids.

a. 1700 Cascadia earthquake
b. 1509 Istanbul earthquake
c. 1703 Genroku earthquake
d. Paleozoic

10. The _____ is a geologic subperiod and stratigraphic subsystem of the Carboniferous Period. It is the later subperiod of the Carboniferous, lasting from roughly 318.1>± 1.3 to 299>± 0.8 Ma (million years ago.) As with most other geochronologic units, the rock beds that define the _____ are well identified, but the exact date of the start and end are uncertain by a few million years.
   a. Calciferous sandstone
   b. Pennsylvanian
   c. Mississippian
   d. Dinantian

11. The _____ is an informal name for the supereon comprising the eons of the geologic timescale that came before the current Phanerozoic eon. It spans from the formation of Earth around 4500 Mya (million years ago) to the evolution of abundant macroscopic hard-shelled animals, which marked the beginning of the Cambrian, the first period of the first era of the Phanerozoic eon, some 542 Mya. It is named after the Roman name for Wales - Cambria - where rocks from this age were first studied.
   a. Precambrian
   b. 1509 Istanbul earthquake
   c. 1703 Genroku earthquake
   d. 1700 Cascadia earthquake

12. The _____ Era is one of three geologic eras of the Phanerozoic eon. The division of time into eras dates back to Giovanni Arduino, in the 18th century, although his original name for the era now called the '_____' was 'Secondary' (making the modern era the 'Tertiary'.)

The _____ was a time of tectonic, climatic and evolutionary activity. The continents gradually shifted from a state of connectedness into their present configuration; the drifting provided for speciation and other important evolutionary developments.

   a. 1700 Cascadia earthquake
   b. 1703 Genroku earthquake
   c. 1509 Istanbul earthquake
   d. Mesozoic

13. An _____ is a section of the Earth's oceanic crust and the underlying upper mantle that has been uplifted or emplaced to be exposed within continental crustal rocks. Ophio is Greek for 'snake', lite means 'stone' from the Greek lithos.

The term _____ was originally used by Alexandre Brongniart for an assemblage of green rocks (serpentine, diabase) in the Alps; Steinmann (1927) later modified its use to include serpentine, pillow lava, and chert ('Steinmann's trinity'), again based on occurrences in the Alps.

   a. AL 129-1
   b. Ophiolite
   c. AASHTO Soil Classification System
   d. AL 333

14. _____ is the second most abundant mineral in the Earth's continental crust. It is made up of a framework of silicon-oxygen tetrahedra SiO_4, with each silicon shared between two oxygens to give the overall formula SiO_2. _____ has a hardness of 7 on the Mohs scale and a density of 2.65 g/cm³.
   a. 1509 Istanbul earthquake
   b. Shocked quartz
   c. 1700 Cascadia earthquake
   d. Quartz

15. _____ is a common and widely distributed type of rock formed by high-grade regional metamorphic processes from pre-existing formations that were originally either igneous or sedimentary rocks. Gneissic rocks are usually medium to coarse foliated and largely recrystallized but do not carry large quantities of micas, chlorite or other platy minerals. _____es that are metamorphosed igneous rocks or their equivalent are termed granite _____es, diorite _____es, etc.
   a. 1703 Genroku earthquake
   b. 1700 Cascadia earthquake
   c. 1509 Istanbul earthquake
   d. Gneiss

16. The _____ is the epoch from 1.8 million to 11550 years BP covering the world's recent period of repeated glaciations. The _____ epoch follows the Pliocene epoch and is followed by the Holocene epoch. The _____ is the third epoch of the Neogene period or 6th epoch of the Cenozoic Era. The end of the _____ corresponds with the retreat of the last continental glacier. It also corresponds with the end of the Paleolithic age used in archaeology.
   a. Sicilian Stage
   b. Late Pleistocene
   c. Tyrrhenian
   d. Pleistocene

17. In geology, a _____ or _____ line is a planar fracture in rock in which the rock on one side of the fracture has moved with respect to the rock on the other side. Large _____s within the Earth's crust are the result of differential or shear motion and active _____ zones are the causal locations of most earthquakes. Earthquakes are caused by energy release during rapid slippage along a _____.
   a. Drainage system
   b. Fault
   c. Cleavage
   d. Compaction

18. A _____ is a depressed block of land bordered by parallel faults.

A _____ is the result of a block of land being downthrown producing a valley with a distinct scarp on each side.

_____ are produced from parallel normal faults, where the hanging wall is downthrown and the footwall is upthrown. The faults typically dip toward the center of the _____ from both sides.

   a. Michoud fault
   b. Sag pond
   c. Shear
   d. Graben

19. In geology and earth science, a _____ is an area of highland, usually consisting of relatively flat terrain. A highly eroded _____ is called a dissected _____. A volcanic _____ is a _____ produced by volcanic activity.
   a. 1509 Istanbul earthquake
   b. 1700 Cascadia earthquake
   c. 1703 Genroku earthquake
   d. Plateau

Chapter 13. Cuyahoga Valley National Park by David B. Hacker

1. The _____ is a geologic period and system of the Paleozoic era spanning from >416 to 359.2 million years ago (ICS, 2004.).

During the _____ Period, which occurred in the Paleozoic era, the first fish evolved legsand started to walk on land as tetrapods around 365 Ma.

   a. 1509 Istanbul earthquake   b. Devonian
   c. Xitun Formation   d. Gogo Formation

2. The _____ is the epoch from 1.8 million to 11550 years BP covering the world's recent period of repeated glaciations. The _____ epoch follows the Pliocene epoch and is followed by the Holocene epoch. The _____ is the third epoch of the Neogene period or 6th epoch of the Cenozoic Era. The end of the _____ corresponds with the retreat of the last continental glacier. It also corresponds with the end of the Paleolithic age used in archaeology.

   a. Sicilian Stage   b. Late Pleistocene
   c. Tyrrhenian   d. Pleistocene

3. The _____ is an informal name for the supereon comprising the eons of the geologic timescale that came before the current Phanerozoic eon. It spans from the formation of Earth around 4500 Mya (million years ago) to the evolution of abundant macroscopic hard-shelled animals, which marked the beginning of the Cambrian, the first period of the first era of the Phanerozoic eon, some 542 Mya. It is named after the Roman name for Wales - Cambria - where rocks from this age were first studied.

   a. Precambrian   b. 1509 Istanbul earthquake
   c. 1703 Genroku earthquake   d. 1700 Cascadia earthquake

4. The _____ is a a term for a geologic period 65 million to 1.8 million years ago. The _____ covered the time span between the superseded Secondary period and an out-of-date definition of the Quaternary period. The period began with the demise of the non-avian dinosaurs in the Cretaceous-_____ extinction event, at start of the Cenozoic era, spanning to beginning of the most recent Ice Age, at the end of the Pliocene epoch.

   a. Loihi Seamount   b. Historical geology
   c. Logarithmic Spiral Beach   d. Tertiary

5. _____ is a naturally occurring granular material composed of finely divided rock and mineral particles.

As the term is used by geologists, _____ particles range in diameter from 0.0625 (or $>^1\!/_{16}$ mm, or 62.5 micrometers) to 2 millimeters. An individual particle in this range size is termed a _____ grain.

   a. 1509 Istanbul earthquake   b. 1700 Cascadia earthquake
   c. 1703 Genroku earthquake   d. Sand

6. The _____ is the earliest of three geologic eras of the Phanerozoic eon. The _____ spanned from roughly 542 to 251 million years ago (ICS, 2004), and is subdivided into six geologic periods; from oldest to youngest they are: the Cambrian, Ordovician, Silurian, Devonian, Carboniferous, and Permian.

The _____ covers the time from the first appearance of abundant, soft-shelled fossils to the time when the continents were beginning to be dominated by large, relatively sophisticated reptiles and modern plants. The lower (oldest) boundary was classically set at the first appearance of creatures known as trilobites and archeocyathids.

   a. 1509 Istanbul earthquake
   b. Paleozoic
   c. 1703 Genroku earthquake
   d. 1700 Cascadia earthquake

7. The _____ is the primary federal law in the United States governing water pollution. Commonly abbreviated as the _____, the act established the symbolic goals of eliminating releases to water of high amounts of toxic substances, eliminating additional water pollution by 1985, and ensuring that surface waters would meet standards necessary for human sports and recreation by 1983.

The principal body of law currently in effect is based on the Federal Water Pollution Control Amendments of 1972, which significantly expanded and strengthened earlier legislation.

   a. Clean Water Act
   b. General Mining Act of 1872
   c. Rule of Capture
   d. Surface Mining Control and Reclamation Act

8. A _____ is a rock consisting of individual stones that have become cemented together. They are sedimentary rocks consisting of rounded fragments and are thus differentiated from breccias, which consist of angular clasts. Both _____s and breccias are characterized by clasts larger than sand (>2 mm).
   a. Keystone
   b. Concretion
   c. Conglomerate
   d. Pelagic sediments

9. _____ is a fine-grained sedimentary rock whose original constituents were clay minerals or muds. It is characterized by thin laminae breaking with an irregular curving fracture, often splintery and usually parallel to the often-indistinguishable bedding plane. This property is called fissility.
   a. Claystone
   b. Shale
   c. Concretion
   d. Jasperoid

10. In stratigraphy, _____ is the native consolidated rock underlying the surface of a terrestrial planet, usually the Earth. Above the _____ is usually an area of broken and weathered unconsolidated rock in the basal subsoil. The top of the _____ is known as rockhead and identifying this, via excavations, drilling or geophysical methods, is an important task in most civil engineering projects.
   a. Polystrate
   b. Biozones
   c. Bedrock
   d. Sequence stratigraphy

11. In geology, _____ refers to inclined sedimentary structures in a horizontal unit of rock. These tilted structures are deposits from bedforms such as ripples and dunes, and they indicate that the depositional environment contained a flowing fluid (typically, water or wind.) This is a case in geology when original depositional layering is tilted, and that the tilting is not a result of post-depositional deformation.
   a. Geomicrobiology
   b. Gibraltar Arc
   c. Contact metamorphism
   d. Cross-bedding

12. _____ is one of the three main rock types (the others being igneous and metamorphic rock.) _____ is formed by deposition and consolidation of mineral and organic material and from precipitation of minerals from solution. The processes that form _____ occur at the surface of the Earth and within bodies of water.
   a. Felsic
   b. Serpentinite
   c. Large igneous provinces
   d. Sedimentary rock

13. A _____ is one of a number of channel types and has a channel that consists of a network of small channels separated by small and often temporary islands called braid bars or, in British usage, aits or eyots. Braided streams occur in rivers with high slope and/or large sediment load (Schumm and Kahn 1972.) Braided channels are also typical of environments that dramatically decrease channel depth, and consequently channel velocity, such as river deltas, alluvial fans and peneplains.

_____s, as distinct from meandering rivers, occur when a threshold level of sediment load or slope is reached. Geologically speaking an increase in sediment load will over time increase the slope of the river, so these two conditions can be considered synonymous and consequently a variation of slope can model a variation in sediment load.

   a. Meander
   b. Stream capture
   c. 1509 Istanbul earthquake
   d. Braided river

14. An _____ is a fan-shaped deposit formed where a fast flowing stream flattens, slows, and spreads typically at the exit of a canyon onto a flatter plain. A convergence of neighboring fans into a single apron of deposits against a slope is called a bajada, or compound _____.
   a. AL 333
   b. Alluvial fan
   c. AASHTO Soil Classification System
   d. AL 129-1

15. A _____ is a moraine that forms at the end of the glacier called the snout.

They mark the maximum advance of the glacier. An end moraine is at the present boundary of the glacier. They are one of the most prominent types of moraines in the Arctic. One famous _____ is the Giant's Wall in Norway.

   a. Glacial plucking
   b. Bull Lake glaciation
   c. Firn
   d. Terminal moraine

16. A _____ is any glacially formed accumulation of unconsolidated glacial debris (soil and rock) which can occur in currently glaciated and formerly glaciated regions, such as those areas acted upon by a past ice age. This debris may have been plucked off the valley floor as a glacier advanced or it may have fallen off the valley walls as a result of frost wedging. _____s may be composed of silt like glacial flour to large boulders.
   a. Moraine
   b. 1509 Istanbul earthquake
   c. 1703 Genroku earthquake
   d. 1700 Cascadia earthquake

17. _____, is a type of salt weathering common on coastal and semi-arid granites, sandstones and limestones. _____ is not limited to natural settings and can be seen to develop on buildings where a rate of development can be established. This rate can be as fast as several centimeters in 100 years

a. Cross-bedding
b. Metamorphic reaction
c. Patterned ground
d. Honeycomb weathering

18. A _____ or mudslide is the most rapid (up to 80 km/h, or 50 mph) and fluid type of downhill mass wasting. It is a rapid movement of a large mass of mud formed from loose earth and water. Similar terms are mudslide (not very liquid), mud stream, debris flow (e.g. in high mountains), j>ökulhlaup, and lahar
   a. 1509 Istanbul earthquake
   b. 1700 Cascadia earthquake
   c. 1703 Genroku earthquake
   d. Mudflow

19. A _____ is a depositional feature of streams. _____s are found in abundance in mature or meandering streams. They are crescent-shaped and located on the inside of a stream bend, being very similar to, though often smaller than towheads, or river islands. They are composed of sediment that is well sorted and typically reflects the overall capacity of the stream.
   a. 1700 Cascadia earthquake
   b. 1509 Istanbul earthquake
   c. Point bar
   d. 1703 Genroku earthquake

20. _____ is unsorted glacial sediment. Glacial drift is a general term for the coarsely graded and extremely heterogeneous sediments of glacial origin. Glacial _____ is that part of glacial drift which was deposited directly by the glacier. In cases where _____ has been indurated or lithified by subsequent burial into solid rock, it is known as the sedimentary rock tillite.
   a. 1703 Genroku earthquake
   b. 1509 Istanbul earthquake
   c. 1700 Cascadia earthquake
   d. Till

21. _____ is the decomposition of Earth rocks, soils and their minerals through direct contact with the planet's atmosphere. _____ occurs in situ, or 'with no movement', and thus should not be confused with erosion, which involves the movement of rocks and minerals by agents such as water, ice, wind and gravity.

Two important classifications of _____ processes exist -- physical and chemical _____.

   a. 1509 Istanbul earthquake
   b. Physical weathering
   c. Weathering
   d. 1700 Cascadia earthquake

22. The _____ is a middle Paleozoic mountain building event (orogeny), especially in the northern Appalachians, between New York and Newfoundland. The _____ most greatly affected the Northern Appalachian region (New England northeastward into the Gasp>é region of Canada.) The _____ should not be regarded as a single tectonic event, but rather as an orogenic era.
   a. Orogenesis
   b. Acadian orogeny
   c. Alpine orogeny
   d. Alice Springs Orogeny

23. An _____ is a downslope viscous flow of fine grained materials that have been saturated with water, and moves under the pull of gravity. They are an intermediate type of mass wasting that is between downhill creep and mudflow. The types of materials that are susceptible to _____s are clay, fine sand and silt, and fine-grained pyroclastic material.
   a. AL 129-1
   b. AASHTO Soil Classification System
   c. AL 333
   d. Earthflow

24. A _____ is flat or nearly flat land adjacent to a stream or river that experiences occasional or periodic flooding. It includes the floodway, which consists of the stream channel and adjacent areas that carry flood flows, and the flood fringe, which are areas covered by the flood, but which do not experience a strong current.

They generally contain unconsolidated sediments, often extending below the bed of the stream.

   a. Floodplain
   b. 1509 Istanbul earthquake
   c. 1703 Genroku earthquake
   d. 1700 Cascadia earthquake

25. _____ is the geomorphic process by which soil, regolith, and rock move downslope under the force of gravity. Types of _____ include creep, slides, flows, topples, and falls, each with its own characteristic features, and taking place over timescales from seconds to years. _____ occurs on both terrestrial and submarine slopes, and has been observed on Earth, Mars, and Venus.

   a. Soil liquefaction
   b. Mass wasting
   c. 1700 Cascadia earthquake
   d. 1509 Istanbul earthquake

26. A _____ in general is a bend in a sinuous watercourse. A _____ is formed when the moving water in a river erodes the outer banks and widens its valley. A stream of any volume may assume a meandering course, alternatively eroding sediments from the outside of a bend and depositing them on the inside.

   a. Stream capture
   b. Distributary
   c. 1509 Istanbul earthquake
   d. Meander

27. An _____ is a U-shaped body of water formed when a wide meander from the mainstem of a river is cut off to create a lake. This landform is called an _____ for the distinctive curved shape that results from this process. In Australia, an _____ is called a billabong.

   a. AL 129-1
   b. AASHTO Soil Classification System
   c. AL 333
   d. Oxbow lake

28. _____ is a form of mass wasting event that occurs when loosely consolidated materials or rock layers move a short distance down a slope. The landmass and the surface it _____s upon is called a failure surface. When the movement occurs in soil, there is often a distinctive rotational movement to the mass, that cuts vertically through bedding planes (landslides take place along a bedding plane or fault). This rotational movement moves along a curved slip surface of regolith (the failure surface) which overlies bedrock. This results in internal deformation of the moving mass consisting chiefly of overturned folds called 'sheath folds.'

   a. Slump
   b. Soil
   c. 1509 Istanbul earthquake
   d. Topsoil

29. A _____, dike (or dyke), embankment, floodbank or stopbank is a natural or artificial slope or wall to regulate water levels. It is usually earthen and often parallel to the course of a river or the coast.

   a. 1509 Istanbul earthquake
   b. Levee
   c. 1703 Genroku earthquake
   d. 1700 Cascadia earthquake

30. _____ refers to natural mountain building, and may be studied as a tectonic structural event, (b) as a geographical event, and (c) a chronological event. Orogenic events (a) cause distinctive structural phenomena and related tectonic activity, (b) affect certain regions of rocks and crust, and (c) happen within a specific period of time.

a. Orogenesis
b. Alice Springs Orogeny
c. Antler orogeny
d. Orogeny

31. The _____ is the first geological period of the Phanerozoic eon, lasting from 542 ± 0.3 million years ago to 488.3 ± 1.7 million years ago (ICS, 2004); it is succeeded by the Ordovician. Its subdivisions, and indeed its base, are somewhat in flux. The period was established by Adam Sedgwick, who named it after Cambria, the classical name for Wales, where Britain's _____ rocks are best exposed.
   a. 1509 Istanbul earthquake
   b. Cambrian
   c. 1703 Genroku earthquake
   d. 1700 Cascadia earthquake

32. The _____ is a geologic period and system, the second of six of the Paleozoic era, and covers the time between 488.3>±1.7 to 443.7>±1.5 million years ago (ICS, 2004.) It follows the Cambrian period and is followed by the Silurian period. The _____ was defined by Charles Lapworth in 1879, to resolve a dispute between followers of Adam Sedgwick and Roderick Murchison, who were placing the same rock beds in northern Wales into the Cambrian and Silurian periods respectively.
   a. AL 129-1
   b. AASHTO Soil Classification System
   c. AL 333
   d. Ordovician

33. The _____ was a great mountain building period that perhaps had the greatest overall effect on the geologic structure of basement rocks within the New York Bight region. The effects of this orogeny are most apparent throughout New England, but the sediments derived from mountainous areas formed in the northeast can be traced throughout the Appalachians and midcontinental North America.

Beginning in Cambrian time, about 550 million years ago, the Iapetus Ocean began to grow progressively narrower.

   a. Trans-Hudson orogeny
   b. Taconic Orogeny
   c. Sevier orogeny
   d. Nevadan orogeny

34. The _____ Era, is the most recent of the three classic geological eras and covers the period from 65.5 million years ago to the present. It is marked by the Cretaceous-Tertiary extinction event at the end of the Cretaceous that saw the demise of the last non-avian dinosaurs and the end of the Mesozoic Era. The _____ era is ongoing.
   a. 1703 Genroku earthquake
   b. 1509 Istanbul earthquake
   c. 1700 Cascadia earthquake
   d. Cenozoic

35. The _____ Era is one of three geologic eras of the Phanerozoic eon. The division of time into eras dates back to Giovanni Arduino, in the 18th century, although his original name for the era now called the '_____' was 'Secondary' (making the modern era the 'Tertiary'.)

The _____ was a time of tectonic, climatic and evolutionary activity. The continents gradually shifted from a state of connectedness into their present configuration; the drifting provided for speciation and other important evolutionary developments.

   a. Mesozoic
   b. 1509 Istanbul earthquake
   c. 1700 Cascadia earthquake
   d. 1703 Genroku earthquake

36. The _____ is a geologic subperiod and stratigraphic subsystem of the Carboniferous Period. It is the later subperiod of the Carboniferous, lasting from roughly 318.1>± 1.3 to 299>± 0.8 Ma (million years ago.) As with most other geochronologic units, the rock beds that define the _____ are well identified, but the exact date of the start and end are uncertain by a few million years.

a. Mississippian
b. Calciferous sandstone
c. Dinantian
d. Pennsylvanian

37. _____, also known as the Pleistocene glaciation, the current ice age or simply the ice age, refers to the period of the last few million years in which permanent ice sheets were established in Antarctica and perhaps Greenland, and fluctuating ice sheets have occurred elsewhere The major effects of the ice age were erosion and deposition of material over large parts of the continents, modification of river systems, creation of millions of lakes, changes in sea level, development of pluvial lakes far from the ice margins, isostatic adjustment of the crust, and abnormal winds. It affected oceans, flooding, and biological communities.

a. Rock glaciers
b. Quaternary glaciation
c. Wolstonian Stage
d. Snowball Earth

38. A _____ is a large, slow-moving mass of ice, formed from compacted layers of snow, that slowly deforms and flows in response to gravity and high pressure.

_____ ice is the largest reservoir of fresh water on Earth, and second only to oceans as the largest reservoir of total water.

a. Little Ice Age
b. Keeling Curve
c. Deforestation
d. Glacier

39. _____ is a carbonate mineral and the most stable polymorph of calcium carbonate ($CaCO_3$.) The other polymorphs are the minerals aragonite and vaterite. Aragonite will change to _____ at 470>°C, and vaterite is even less stable.

_____ is a common constituent of sedimentary rocks, limestone in particular, much of which is formed from the shells of dead marine organisms. Approximately 10% of sedimentary rock is limestone.

a. 1703 Genroku earthquake
b. Calcite
c. 1700 Cascadia earthquake
d. 1509 Istanbul earthquake

40. In chemistry, a _____ is a salt or ester of carbonic acid.

To test for the presence of the _____ anion in a salt, the addition of dilute mineral acid (e.g. hydrochloric acid) will yield carbon dioxide gas.

_____-containing salts are industrially and mineralogically ubiquitous.

a. 1703 Genroku earthquake
b. 1700 Cascadia earthquake
c. 1509 Istanbul earthquake
d. Carbonate

41. _____ are a class of sedimentary rocks composed primarily of carbonate minerals. The two major types are limestone and dolomite, composed of calcite (CaCO$_3$) and the mineral dolomite (CaMg(CO$_3$)$_2$) respectively. Chalk and tufa are also minor sedimentary carbonates.
   a. Shale
   b. Diatomaceous earth
   c. Carbonate rocks
   d. Dolostone

42. _____ is the name of a sedimentary carbonate rock and a mineral, both composed of calcium magnesium carbonate CaMg$_2$ found in crystals.

   _____ rock (also dolostone) is composed predominantly of the mineral _____. Limestone that is partially replaced by _____ is referred to as dolomitic limestone, or in old U.S. geologic literature as magnesian limestone.

   a. Dolostone
   b. Pelagic sediments
   c. Superficial deposits
   d. Dolomite

43. A _____ is a mountain rising from the ocean seafloor that does not reach to the water's surface (sea level), and thus is not an island. These are typically formed from extinct volcanoes, that rise abruptly and are usually found rising from a seafloor of 1,000-4,000 meters depth. They are defined by oceanographers as independent features that rise to at least 1,000 meters above the seafloor.
   a. 1703 Genroku earthquake
   b. 1700 Cascadia earthquake
   c. 1509 Istanbul earthquake
   d. Seamount

44. _____ is a sedimentary rock composed largely of the mineral calcite (calcium carbonate: CaCO$_3$.) The deposition of _____ strata is often a by-product and indicator of biological activity in the geologic record. Calcium (along with nitrogen, phosphorus, and potassium) is a key mineral to plant nutrition: soils overlying _____ bedrock tend to be pre-fertilized with calcium.
   a. 1509 Istanbul earthquake
   b. 1703 Genroku earthquake
   c. Limestone
   d. 1700 Cascadia earthquake

45. An _____ is a section of the Earth's oceanic crust and the underlying upper mantle that has been uplifted or emplaced to be exposed within continental crustal rocks. Ophio is Greek for 'snake', lite means 'stone' from the Greek lithos.

The term _____ was originally used by Alexandre Brongniart for an assemblage of green rocks (serpentine, diabase) in the Alps; Steinmann (1927) later modified its use to include serpentine, pillow lava, and chert ('Steinmann's trinity'), again based on occurrences in the Alps.

   a. AASHTO Soil Classification System
   b. AL 129-1
   c. AL 333
   d. Ophiolite

46. _____ is a carbonate mineral, one of the two common, naturally occurring polymorphs of calcium carbonate, CaCO$_3$. The other polymorph is the mineral calcite. _____'s crystal lattice differs from that of calcite, resulting in a different crystal shape, an orthorhombic system with acicular crystals.
   a. Apatite
   b. AASHTO Soil Classification System
   c. Aragonite
   d. AL 129-1

47. Traditionally, _____ compounds are considered to be of a mineral, not biological, origin. Complementarily, most organic compounds are traditionally viewed as being of biological origin. Over the past century, the precise classification of _____ vs organic compounds has become less important to scientists, primarily because the majority of known compounds are synthetic and not of natural origin.

Minerals are mainly oxides and sulfides, which are strictly _____. In fact, most of the earth and the universe is _____. Although the components of the Earth's crust are well elucidated, the processes of mineralization and the composition of the deep mantle remain active areas of investigation, which are mainly covered in geology-oriented venues.

a. AL 129-1
b. AASHTO Soil Classification System
c. Inorganic
d. AL 333

48. The _____ is the area in an aquifer, below the water table, in which relatively all pores and fractures are saturated with water. The _____ may fluctuate with changes of season and during wet and dry periods.

a. Phreatic zone
b. Saltwater intrusion
c. Porosity
d. Permeability

49. A _____, commonly known as a cave formation, is a secondary mineral deposit formed in a cave. They are typically formed in limestone or dolostone solutional caves.

Water seeping through cracks in a cave's surrounding bedrock may dissolve certain compounds, usually calcite and aragonite , or gypsum (calcium sulfate.)

a. Speleothem
b. 1509 Istanbul earthquake
c. 1703 Genroku earthquake
d. 1700 Cascadia earthquake

50. _____ is water collecting on the ground or in a stream, river, lake, wetland, or ocean; it is related to water collecting as groundwater or atmospheric water.

_____ is naturally replenished by precipitation and naturally lost through discharge to evaporation, and sub-surface seepage into the groundwater. Although there are other sources of groundwater, such as connate water and magmatic water, precipitation is the major one and groundwater originated in this way is called meteoric water.

a. Surface water
b. Streamflow
c. Stemflow
d. Hydrograph

51. _____ is a sedimentary rock. It is a natural chemical precipitate of carbonate minerals; typically aragonite, but often recrystallized to, or primarily, calcite.

_____ forms as calcium carbonate is deposited from the water of mineral springs or rivulets that are saturated with dissolved calcium bicarbonate. The spring water from which the calcium carbonate precipitates can be hot, warm or cold. The rate of deposition increases with the temperature of the water, or alternatively, when biotic material accelerates the process of precipitation.

a. 1509 Istanbul earthquake
b. 1700 Cascadia earthquake
c. Travertine
d. 1703 Genroku earthquake

52. The _____, also termed the unsaturated zone, is the portion of Earth between the land surface and the phreatic zone or zone of saturation. It extends from the top of the ground surface to the water table. Water in the _____ has a pressure head less than atmospheric pressure, and is retained by a combination of adhesion, and capillary action (capillary groundwater.)
   a. Vadose zone
   b. Hydraulic conductivity
   c. Water cycle
   d. Strahler stream order

53. The _____ is the level at which the ground water pressure is equal to atmospheric pressure. It may be conveniently visualized as the 'surface' of the ground water in a given vicinity. It usually coincides with the phreatic surface, but can be many feet above it. As water infiltrates through pore spaces in the soil, it first passes through the zone of aeration, where the soil is unsaturated. At increasing depths water fills in more spaces, until the zone of saturation is reached. The relatively horizontal plane atop this zone constitutes the _____.
   a. Rock bolt
   b. Shaft construction
   c. Crosshole sonic logging
   d. Water table

Chapter 14. Mammoth Cave National Park by Arthur N. Palmer

1. _____ is a landscape shaped by the dissolution of a layer or layers of soluble bedrock, usually carbonate rock such as limestone or dolomite.

Due to subterranean drainage, there may be very limited surface water, even to the absence of all rivers and lakes. Many karst regions display distinctive surface features, with sinkholes or dolines being the most common.

   a. Andrija Mohorovičić
   b. Amblypoda
   c. Karst topography
   d. Ambulocetus

2. In geology and earth science, a _____ is an area of highland, usually consisting of relatively flat terrain. A highly eroded _____ is called a dissected _____. A volcanic _____ is a _____ produced by volcanic activity.

   a. 1509 Istanbul earthquake
   b. 1703 Genroku earthquake
   c. Plateau
   d. 1700 Cascadia earthquake

3. _____ is a sedimentary rock. It is a natural chemical precipitate of carbonate minerals; typically aragonite, but often recrystallized to, or primarily, calcite.

_____ forms as calcium carbonate is deposited from the water of mineral springs or rivulets that are saturated with dissolved calcium bicarbonate. The spring water from which the calcium carbonate precipitates can be hot, warm or cold. The rate of deposition increases with the temperature of the water, or alternatively, when biotic material accelerates the process of precipitation.

   a. Travertine
   b. 1700 Cascadia earthquake
   c. 1703 Genroku earthquake
   d. 1509 Istanbul earthquake

4. _____ is a carbonate mineral, one of the two common, naturally occurring polymorphs of calcium carbonate, $CaCO_3$. The other polymorph is the mineral calcite. _____'s crystal lattice differs from that of calcite, resulting in a different crystal shape, an orthorhombic system with acicular crystals.

   a. Aragonite
   b. AL 129-1
   c. AASHTO Soil Classification System
   d. Apatite

5. _____, a branch of geology, studies rock layers and layering (stratification.) It is primarily used in the study of sedimentary and layered volcanic rocks. _____ includes two related subfields: lithologic or lithostratigraphy and biologic _____ or biostratigraphy.

   a. 1703 Genroku earthquake
   b. Stratigraphy
   c. 1509 Istanbul earthquake
   d. 1700 Cascadia earthquake

6. The _____ is a a term for a geologic period 65 million to 1.8 million years ago. The _____ covered the time span between the superseded Secondary period and an out-of-date definition of the Quaternary period. The period began with the demise of the non-avian dinosaurs in the Cretaceous-_____ extinction event, at start of the Cenozoic era, spanning to beginning of the most recent Ice Age, at the end of the Pliocene epoch.

   a. Tertiary
   b. Loihi Seamount
   c. Logarithmic Spiral Beach
   d. Historical geology

7. The _____ is the area in an aquifer, below the water table, in which relatively all pores and fractures are saturated with water. The _____ may fluctuate with changes of season and during wet and dry periods.

a. Permeability
b. Porosity
c. Saltwater intrusion
d. Phreatic zone

8. A _____, commonly known as a cave formation, is a secondary mineral deposit formed in a cave. They are typically formed in limestone or dolostone solutional caves.

Water seeping through cracks in a cave's surrounding bedrock may dissolve certain compounds, usually calcite and aragonite , or gypsum (calcium sulfate.)

a. 1703 Genroku earthquake
b. 1700 Cascadia earthquake
c. 1509 Istanbul earthquake
d. Speleothem

9. The _____, also termed the unsaturated zone, is the portion of Earth between the land surface and the phreatic zone or zone of saturation . It extends from the top of the ground surface to the water table. Water in the _____ has a pressure head less than atmospheric pressure, and is retained by a combination of adhesion , and capillary action (capillary groundwater.)

a. Water cycle
b. Hydraulic conductivity
c. Vadose zone
d. Strahler stream order

10. The _____ is the level at which the ground water pressure is equal to atmospheric pressure. It may be conveniently visualized as the 'surface' of the ground water in a given vicinity. It usually coincides with the phreatic surface, but can be many feet above it. As water infiltrates through pore spaces in the soil, it first passes through the zone of aeration, where the soil is unsaturated. At increasing depths water fills in more spaces, until the zone of saturation is reached. The relatively horizontal plane atop this zone constitutes the _____.

a. Shaft construction
b. Crosshole sonic logging
c. Rock bolt
d. Water table

11. _____ is the chemical element with the symbol Ca and atomic number 20. It has an atomic mass of 40.078 amu. _____ is a soft grey alkaline earth metal, and is the fifth most abundant element by mass in the Earth's crust.

a. Calcium
b. Wollastonite
c. 1700 Cascadia earthquake
d. 1509 Istanbul earthquake

12. _____ is a chemical compound with the chemical formula $CaCO_3$. It is a common substance found in rock in all parts of the world, and is the main component of shells of marine organisms, snails, pearls, and eggshells. _____ is the active ingredient in agricultural lime, and is usually the principal cause of hard water.

a. 1703 Genroku earthquake
b. 1509 Istanbul earthquake
c. 1700 Cascadia earthquake
d. Calcium carbonate

13. In chemistry, a _____ is a salt or ester of carbonic acid.

To test for the presence of the _____ anion in a salt, the addition of dilute mineral acid (e.g. hydrochloric acid) will yield carbon dioxide gas.

_____-containing salts are industrially and mineralogically ubiquitous.

a. Carbonate
b. 1509 Istanbul earthquake
c. 1703 Genroku earthquake
d. 1700 Cascadia earthquake

14. _____ is the name of a sedimentary carbonate rock and a mineral, both composed of calcium magnesium carbonate $CaMg_2$ found in crystals.

_____ rock (also dolostone) is composed predominantly of the mineral _____. Limestone that is partially replaced by _____ is referred to as dolomitic limestone, or in old U.S. geologic literature as magnesian limestone.

a. Superficial deposits
b. Pelagic sediments
c. Dolostone
d. Dolomite

15. _____ is a sedimentary rock composed largely of the mineral calcite (calcium carbonate: $CaCO_3$.) The deposition of _____ strata is often a by-product and indicator of biological activity in the geologic record. Calcium (along with nitrogen, phosphorus, and potassium) is a key mineral to plant nutrition: soils overlying _____ bedrock tend to be pre-fertilized with calcium.

a. 1703 Genroku earthquake
b. 1700 Cascadia earthquake
c. 1509 Istanbul earthquake
d. Limestone

16. The _____ is a geologic subperiod and stratigraphic subsystem of the Carboniferous Period. It is the earliest/lowermost of two divisions of the Carboniferous, lasting from roughly 359 to 318 Ma (million years ago.) As with most other geochronologic units, the rock beds that define the _____ are well identified, but the exact start and end dates are uncertain by a few million years.

a. Mississippian
b. Dinantian
c. Pennsylvanian
d. Calciferous sandstone

17. A _____ is a natural depression or hole in the surface topography caused by the removal of soil or bedrock, often both, by water. They may vary in size from less than a meter to several hundred meters both in diameter and depth, and vary in form from soil-lined bowls to bedrock-edged chasms. They may be formed gradually or suddenly, and are found worldwide.

a. 1703 Genroku earthquake
b. Sinkhole
c. 1700 Cascadia earthquake
d. 1509 Istanbul earthquake

18. In geology a _____ is the smallest division of a geologic formation or stratigraphic rock series marked by well-defined divisional planes (bedding planes) separating it from layers above and below. A _____ is the smallest lithostratigraphic unit, usually ranging in thickness from a centimeter to several meters and distinguishable from _____ s above and below it. _____ s can be differentiated in various ways, including rock or mineral type and particle size.

a. Cyclostratigraphy
b. Sequence stratigraphy
c. Biozones
d. Bed

19. _____ are composed of sheetlike deposits of calcite formed where water flows down the walls or along the floors of a cave. They are typically found in 'solution', or limestone caves, where they are the most common speleothem. However, they may form in any type of cave where water enters that has picked up dissolved minerals.

a. Flowstones
b. 1703 Genroku earthquake
c. 1509 Istanbul earthquake
d. 1700 Cascadia earthquake

20. A _____ is a speleothem found in limestone caves that changes its axis from the vertical at one or more stages during its growth. They have a curving or angular form that looks as if they were grown in zero gravity. They are most likely the result of capillary forces acting on tiny water droplets, a force often strong enough at this scale to defy gravity.

a. 1700 Cascadia earthquake
b. 1509 Istanbul earthquake
c. 1703 Genroku earthquake
d. Helictite

21. A _____ is a type of speleothem (secondary mineral) that hangs from the ceiling or wall of limestone caves. It is sometimes referred to as dripstone.

They are formed by the deposition of calcium carbonate and other minerals, which is precipitated from mineralized water solutions.

a. 1703 Genroku earthquake
b. 1509 Istanbul earthquake
c. 1700 Cascadia earthquake
d. Stalactite

22. A _____ is a type of speleothem that rises from the floor of a limestone cave due to the dripping of mineralized solutions and the deposition of calcium carbonate.

The corresponding formation on the ceiling of a cave is known as a stalactite. If these formations grow together, the result is known as a column.

a. 1703 Genroku earthquake
b. 1700 Cascadia earthquake
c. 1509 Istanbul earthquake
d. Stalagmite

23. _____ is the decomposition of Earth rocks, soils and their minerals through direct contact with the planet's atmosphere. _____ occurs in situ, or 'with no movement', and thus should not be confused with erosion, which involves the movement of rocks and minerals by agents such as water, ice, wind and gravity.

Two important classifications of _____ processes exist -- physical and chemical _____.

a. Physical weathering
b. Weathering
c. 1700 Cascadia earthquake
d. 1509 Istanbul earthquake

24. The _____ is the earliest of three geologic eras of the Phanerozoic eon. The _____ spanned from roughly 542 to 251 million years ago (ICS, 2004), and is subdivided into six geologic periods; from oldest to youngest they are: the Cambrian, Ordovician, Silurian, Devonian, Carboniferous, and Permian.

The _____ covers the time from the first appearance of abundant, soft-shelled fossils to the time when the continents were beginning to be dominated by large, relatively sophisticated reptiles and modern plants. The lower (oldest) boundary was classically set at the first appearance of creatures known as trilobites and archeocyathids.

a. 1703 Genroku earthquake
c. Paleozoic
b. 1509 Istanbul earthquake
d. 1700 Cascadia earthquake

25. The _____ is a geologic subperiod and stratigraphic subsystem of the Carboniferous Period. It is the later subperiod of the Carboniferous, lasting from roughly 318.1>± 1.3 to 299>± 0.8 Ma (million years ago.) As with most other geochronologic units, the rock beds that define the _____ are well identified, but the exact date of the start and end are uncertain by a few million years.
   a. Dinantian
   b. Calciferous sandstone
   c. Mississippian
   d. Pennsylvanian

1. The _____ , usually abbreviated K for its German translation Kreide, is a geologic period and system from circa >145.5 >± 4 to >65.5 >± 0.3 million years ago . In the geologic timescale, the _____ follows on the Jurassic period and is followed by the Paleogene period. It is the youngest period of the Mesozoic era, and at 80 million years long, the longest period of the Phanerozoic eon. The end of the _____ defines the boundary between the Mesozoic and Cenozoic eras.
   a. Cretaceous
   b. Hauterivian
   c. Campanian
   d. Valanginian

2. The _____ is the earliest of three geologic eras of the Phanerozoic eon. The _____ spanned from roughly 542 to 251 million years ago (ICS, 2004), and is subdivided into six geologic periods; from oldest to youngest they are: the Cambrian, Ordovician, Silurian, Devonian, Carboniferous, and Permian.

   The _____ covers the time from the first appearance of abundant, soft-shelled fossils to the time when the continents were beginning to be dominated by large, relatively sophisticated reptiles and modern plants. The lower (oldest) boundary was classically set at the first appearance of creatures known as trilobites and archeocyathids.

   a. 1703 Genroku earthquake
   b. Paleozoic
   c. 1509 Istanbul earthquake
   d. 1700 Cascadia earthquake

3. _____ is a carbonate mineral, one of the two common, naturally occurring polymorphs of calcium carbonate, $CaCO_3$. The other polymorph is the mineral calcite. _____'s crystal lattice differs from that of calcite, resulting in a different crystal shape, an orthorhombic system with acicular crystals.
   a. Apatite
   b. AL 129-1
   c. Aragonite
   d. AASHTO Soil Classification System

4. _____ is a rock composed of angular fragments of minerals or rocks in a matrix (cementing material), that may be similar or different in composition to the fragments. A _____ may have a variety of different origins, as indicated by the named types including sedimentary _____, tectonic _____, igneous _____, impact _____ and hydrothermal _____.

   Sedimentary _____s are a type of clastic sedimentary rock which are composed of angular to subangular, randomly oriented clasts of other sedimentary rocks.

   a. 1509 Istanbul earthquake
   b. Ventifacts
   c. Breccia
   d. Fault breccia

5. The _____ Era is one of three geologic eras of the Phanerozoic eon. The division of time into eras dates back to Giovanni Arduino, in the 18th century, although his original name for the era now called the '_____' was 'Secondary' (making the modern era the 'Tertiary'.)

   The _____ was a time of tectonic, climatic and evolutionary activity. The continents gradually shifted from a state of connectedness into their present configuration; the drifting provided for speciation and other important evolutionary developments.

   a. Mesozoic
   b. 1700 Cascadia earthquake
   c. 1703 Genroku earthquake
   d. 1509 Istanbul earthquake

6. The _____ is a geologic subperiod and stratigraphic subsystem of the Carboniferous Period. It is the earliest/lowermost of two divisions of the Carboniferous, lasting from roughly 359 to 318 Ma (million years ago.) As with most other geochronologic units, the rock beds that define the _____ are well identified, but the exact start and end dates are uncertain by a few million years.

   a. Calciferous sandstone
   b. Pennsylvanian
   c. Dinantian
   d. Mississippian

7. The _____ is a geologic period and system that began 65.5 ± 0.3 and ended 23.03 ± 0.05 million years ago and comprises the first part of the Cenozoic era. Lasting 42 million years, the _____ is most notable as being the time in which mammals evolved from relatively small, simple forms into a plethora of diverse animals in the wake of the mass extinction that ended the preceding Cretaceous Period. Some of these mammals would evolve into large forms that would dominate the land, while others would become capable of living in marine, specialized terrestrial and even airborne environments.

   a. Paleogene
   b. Tabenbulakian
   c. Mustersan
   d. Riochican

8. _____ is the decomposition of Earth rocks, soils and their minerals through direct contact with the planet's atmosphere. _____ occurs in situ, or 'with no movement', and thus should not be confused with erosion, which involves the movement of rocks and minerals by agents such as water, ice, wind and gravity.

Two important classifications of _____ processes exist -- physical and chemical _____.

   a. Physical weathering
   b. 1509 Istanbul earthquake
   c. 1700 Cascadia earthquake
   d. Weathering

9. _____ is the removal of solids (sediment, soil, rock and other particles) in the natural environment. It usually occurs due to transport by wind, water, or ice; by down-slope creep of soil and other material under the force of gravity; or by living organisms, such as burrowing animals, in the case of bioerosion.

_____ is distinguished from weathering, which is the process of chemical or physical breakdown of the minerals in the rocks, although the two processes may occur concurrently.

   a. AL 333
   b. Erosion
   c. AASHTO Soil Classification System
   d. AL 129-1

1. The _____ is the epoch from 1.8 million to 11550 years BP covering the world's recent period of repeated glaciations. The _____ epoch follows the Pliocene epoch and is followed by the Holocene epoch. The _____ is the third epoch of the Neogene period or 6th epoch of the Cenozoic Era. The end of the _____ corresponds with the retreat of the last continental glacier. It also corresponds with the end of the Paleolithic age used in archaeology.
   a. Late Pleistocene
   b. Pleistocene
   c. Tyrrhenian
   d. Sicilian Stage

2. The _____ is a a term for a geologic period 65 million to 1.8 million years ago. The _____ covered the time span between the superseded Secondary period and an out-of-date definition of the Quaternary period. The period began with the demise of the non-avian dinosaurs in the Cretaceous-_____ extinction event, at start of the Cenozoic era, spanning to beginning of the most recent Ice Age, at the end of the Pliocene epoch.
   a. Historical geology
   b. Loihi Seamount
   c. Logarithmic Spiral Beach
   d. Tertiary

3. The _____ Era, is the most recent of the three classic geological eras and covers the period from 65.5 million years ago to the present. It is marked by the Cretaceous-Tertiary extinction event at the end of the Cretaceous that saw the demise of the last non-avian dinosaurs and the end of the Mesozoic Era. The _____ era is ongoing.
   a. Cenozoic
   b. 1703 Genroku earthquake
   c. 1700 Cascadia earthquake
   d. 1509 Istanbul earthquake

4. The _____ , usually abbreviated K for its German translation Kreide, is a geologic period and system from circa >145.5 >± 4 to >65.5 >± 0.3 million years ago . In the geologic timescale, the _____ follows on the Jurassic period and is followed by the Paleogene period. It is the youngest period of the Mesozoic era, and at 80 million years long, the longest period of the Phanerozoic eon. The end of the _____ defines the boundary between the Mesozoic and Cenozoic eras.
   a. Campanian
   b. Hauterivian
   c. Valanginian
   d. Cretaceous

5. _____ is a landscape shaped by the dissolution of a layer or layers of soluble bedrock, usually carbonate rock such as limestone or dolomite.

Due to subterranean drainage, there may be very limited surface water, even to the absence of all rivers and lakes. Many karst regions display distinctive surface features, with sinkholes or dolines being the most common.

   a. Amblypoda
   b. Andrija Mohorovićić
   c. Ambulocetus
   d. Karst topography

6. The _____ Era is one of three geologic eras of the Phanerozoic eon. The division of time into eras dates back to Giovanni Arduino, in the 18th century, although his original name for the era now called the '_____' was 'Secondary' (making the modern era the 'Tertiary'.)

The _____ was a time of tectonic, climatic and evolutionary activity. The continents gradually shifted from a state of connectedness into their present configuration; the drifting provided for speciation and other important evolutionary developments.

   a. 1700 Cascadia earthquake
   b. 1703 Genroku earthquake
   c. 1509 Istanbul earthquake
   d. Mesozoic

Chapter 16. Carlsbad Caverns National Park by Arthur N. Palmer

7. _____ is a carbonate mineral, one of the two common, naturally occurring polymorphs of calcium carbonate, $CaCO_3$. The other polymorph is the mineral calcite. _____'s crystal lattice differs from that of calcite, resulting in a different crystal shape, an orthorhombic system with acicular crystals.
   a. AASHTO Soil Classification System
   b. Apatite
   c. AL 129-1
   d. Aragonite

8. In geology the term _____ refers to a fracture in rock where there has been no lateral movement in the plane of the fracture (up, down or sideways) of one side relative to the other. This makes it different from a fault which is defined as a fracture in rock where one side slides laterally past to the other. _____s normally have a regular spacing related to either the mechanical properties of the individual rock or the thickness of the layer involved.
   a. 1703 Genroku earthquake
   b. Joint
   c. 1509 Istanbul earthquake
   d. 1700 Cascadia earthquake

9. _____ is a sedimentary rock composed largely of the mineral calcite (calcium carbonate: $CaCO_3$.) The deposition of _____ strata is often a by-product and indicator of biological activity in the geologic record. Calcium (along with nitrogen, phosphorus, and potassium) is a key mineral to plant nutrition: soils overlying _____ bedrock tend to be pre-fertilized with calcium.
   a. Limestone
   b. 1703 Genroku earthquake
   c. 1509 Istanbul earthquake
   d. 1700 Cascadia earthquake

10. The _____, also termed the unsaturated zone, is the portion of Earth between the land surface and the phreatic zone or zone of saturation . It extends from the top of the ground surface to the water table. Water in the _____ has a pressure head less than atmospheric pressure, and is retained by a combination of adhesion , and capillary action (capillary groundwater.)
    a. Water cycle
    b. Hydraulic conductivity
    c. Strahler stream order
    d. Vadose zone

11. A _____ is a type of speleothem (secondary mineral) that hangs from the ceiling or wall of limestone caves. It is sometimes referred to as dripstone.

They are formed by the deposition of calcium carbonate and other minerals, which is precipitated from mineralized water solutions.

   a. 1509 Istanbul earthquake
   b. 1700 Cascadia earthquake
   c. 1703 Genroku earthquake
   d. Stalactite

12. _____ is a sedimentary rock. It is a natural chemical precipitate of carbonate minerals; typically aragonite, but often recrystallized to, or primarily, calcite.

_____ forms as calcium carbonate is deposited from the water of mineral springs or rivulets that are saturated with dissolved calcium bicarbonate. The spring water from which the calcium carbonate precipitates can be hot, warm or cold. The rate of deposition increases with the temperature of the water, or alternatively, when biotic material accelerates the process of precipitation.

a. 1509 Istanbul earthquake
b. 1703 Genroku earthquake
c. 1700 Cascadia earthquake
d. Travertine

13. _____ is any particulate matter that can be transported by fluid flow, and which eventually is deposited.

They are most often transported by water (fluvial processes) transported by wind (aeolian processes) and glaciers. Beach sands and river channel deposits are examples of fluvial transport and deposition, though _____ also often settles out of slow-moving or standing water in lakes and oceans.

a. Fech fech
b. Brickearth
c. Sediment
d. Salt glacier

14. _____ is a very soft phyllosilicate mineral that typically forms in microscopic crystals, forming a clay. _____, a member of the smectite family, is a 2:1 clay, meaning that it has 2 tetrahedral sheets sandwiching a central octahedral sheet.

a. 1700 Cascadia earthquake
b. 1703 Genroku earthquake
c. Montmorillonite
d. 1509 Istanbul earthquake

15. A _____, commonly known as a cave formation, is a secondary mineral deposit formed in a cave. They are typically formed in limestone or dolostone solutional caves.

Water seeping through cracks in a cave's surrounding bedrock may dissolve certain compounds, usually calcite and aragonite, or gypsum (calcium sulfate.)

a. 1700 Cascadia earthquake
b. Speleothem
c. 1509 Istanbul earthquake
d. 1703 Genroku earthquake

16. In chronostratigraphy, a _____ is a succession of rock strata laid down in an single age on the geologic timescale, which usually represents millions of years of deposition. A given _____ of rock and the corresponding age of time will by convention have the same name, and the same boundaries.

a. Lichenometry
b. Relative dating
c. Paleomagnetism
d. Stage

1. In geography and geology, a _____ is a significant vertical, or near vertical, rock exposure. _____s are formed as erosion landforms due to the processes of erosion and weathering that produce them. _____s are common on coasts, in mountainous areas, escarpments and along rivers. _____s are usually formed by rock that is resistant to erosion and weathering. Sedimentary rocks are most likely to form sandstone, limestone, chalk, and dolomite. Igneous rocks, such as granite and basalt also often form _____s.
   a. Cliff
   b. 1509 Istanbul earthquake
   c. 1700 Cascadia earthquake
   d. 1703 Genroku earthquake

2. In chronostratigraphy, a _____ is a succession of rock strata laid down in an single age on the geologic timescale, which usually represents millions of years of deposition. A given _____ of rock and the corresponding age of time will by convention have the same name, and the same boundaries.
   a. Relative dating
   b. Lichenometry
   c. Paleomagnetism
   d. Stage

3. In geology, _____ are a body of rock with specified characteristics. Ideally, a _____ is a distinctive rock unit that forms under certain conditions of sedimentation, reflecting a particular process or environment.

The term _____ was introduced by the Swiss geologist Amanz Gressly in 1838 and was part of his significant contribution to the foundations of modern stratigraphy, [Cross and Homewood (1997)] which replaced the earlier notions of Neptunism.

   a. Greenstone belts
   b. Metamorphic facies
   c. Metaconglomerate
   d. Facies

4. _____ is a mineral - anhydrous calcium sulfate, $CaSO_4$. It is in the orthorhombic crystal system, with three directions of perfect cleavage parallel to the three planes of symmetry. It is not isomorphous with the orthorhombic barium (baryte) and strontium (celestine) sulfates, as might be expected from the chemical formulas.
   a. Anhydrite
   b. AASHTO Soil Classification System
   c. AL 129-1
   d. Aragonite

5. In chemistry, a _____ is a salt or ester of carbonic acid.

To test for the presence of the _____ anion in a salt, the addition of dilute mineral acid (e.g. hydrochloric acid) will yield carbon dioxide gas.

_____-containing salts are industrially and mineralogically ubiquitous.

   a. 1703 Genroku earthquake
   b. Carbonate
   c. 1509 Istanbul earthquake
   d. 1700 Cascadia earthquake

6. _____ rocks are composed of fragments of pre-existing rock. The term is most commonly, but not uniquely, applied to sedimentary rocks.

_____ metamorphic rocks include breccias formed in faults, as well as some protomylonite and pseudotachylite.

a. 1703 Genroku earthquake
c. 1509 Istanbul earthquake
b. Clastic
d. 1700 Cascadia earthquake

7. _____ is an incompletely consolidated sedimentary rock. _____ was formed in association with marine reefs and is a variety of 'coral rag', technically a subset of limestone.

_____ is mainly composed of mineral calcite, often including some phosphate, in the form of seashells or coral.

a. Mudstone
c. Coquina
b. Shale
d. Superficial deposits

8. _____ is the name of a sedimentary carbonate rock and a mineral, both composed of calcium magnesium carbonate $CaMg_2$ found in crystals.

_____ rock (also dolostone) is composed predominantly of the mineral _____. Limestone that is partially replaced by _____ is referred to as dolomitic limestone, or in old U.S. geologic literature as magnesian limestone.

a. Dolomite
c. Pelagic sediments
b. Superficial deposits
d. Dolostone

9. _____ is one of the three main rock types (the others being igneous and metamorphic rock.) _____ is formed by deposition and consolidation of mineral and organic material and from precipitation of minerals from solution. The processes that form _____ occur at the surface of the Earth and within bodies of water.

a. Large igneous provinces
c. Serpentinite
b. Felsic
d. Sedimentary rock

10. _____ is a rock composed of angular fragments of minerals or rocks in a matrix (cementing material), that may be similar or different in composition to the fragments. A _____ may have a variety of different origins, as indicated by the named types including sedimentary _____, tectonic _____, igneous _____, impact _____ and hydrothermal _____.

Sedimentary _____s are a type of clastic sedimentary rock which are composed of angular to subangular, randomly oriented clasts of other sedimentary rocks.

a. Fault breccia
c. Ventifacts
b. 1509 Istanbul earthquake
d. Breccia

11. _____ is a sedimentary rock which has a composition intermediate in grain size between the coarser sandstones and the finer mudstones and shales.

As its name implies, it is primarily composed (greater than 2/3) of silt sized particles, defined as grains between 3.9 and 62.5 micrometres or 4 to 8 on the Krumbein phi (>φ) scale. _____s differ significantly from sandstones due to their smaller pores and higher propensity for containing a significant clay fraction.

a. Keystone
b. Sedimentary deposits
c. Pelagic sediments
d. Siltstone

12. _____ is a term given to an accumulation of broken rock fragments at the base of crags, mountain cliffs, or valley shoulders. Landforms associated with these materials are sometimes called _____ slopes or talus piles. These deposits typically have a concave upwards form, while the maximum inclination of such deposits corresponds to the angle of repose of the mean debris size.
   a. 1703 Genroku earthquake
   b. Scree
   c. 1700 Cascadia earthquake
   d. 1509 Istanbul earthquake

13. The _____ Era, is the most recent of the three classic geological eras and covers the period from 65.5 million years ago to the present. It is marked by the Cretaceous-Tertiary extinction event at the end of the Cretaceous that saw the demise of the last non-avian dinosaurs and the end of the Mesozoic Era. The _____ era is ongoing.
   a. 1700 Cascadia earthquake
   b. Cenozoic
   c. 1509 Istanbul earthquake
   d. 1703 Genroku earthquake

14. The _____ Era is one of three geologic eras of the Phanerozoic eon. The division of time into eras dates back to Giovanni Arduino, in the 18th century, although his original name for the era now called the '_____' was 'Secondary' (making the modern era the 'Tertiary'.)

The _____ was a time of tectonic, climatic and evolutionary activity. The continents gradually shifted from a state of connectedness into their present configuration; the drifting provided for speciation and other important evolutionary developments.

   a. 1509 Istanbul earthquake
   b. 1700 Cascadia earthquake
   c. Mesozoic
   d. 1703 Genroku earthquake

1. An _____ is a chain or cluster of islands that are formed tectonically. They are usually found in the open sea; less commonly, a large land mass may neighbour them.
   a. Archipelago
   b. AL 333
   c. AASHTO Soil Classification System
   d. AL 129-1

2. The _____ , usually abbreviated K for its German translation Kreide, is a geologic period and system from circa >145.5 >± 4 to >65.5 >± 0.3 million years ago . In the geologic timescale, the _____ follows on the Jurassic period and is followed by the Paleogene period. It is the youngest period of the Mesozoic era, and at 80 million years long, the longest period of the Phanerozoic eon. The end of the _____ defines the boundary between the Mesozoic and Cenozoic eras.
   a. Hauterivian
   b. Cretaceous
   c. Valanginian
   d. Campanian

3. A _____ is a mountain rising from the ocean seafloor that does not reach to the water's surface (sea level), and thus is not an island. These are typically formed from extinct volcanoes, that rise abruptly and are usually found rising from a seafloor of 1,000-4,000 meters depth. They are defined by oceanographers as independent features that rise to at least 1,000 meters above the seafloor.
   a. 1509 Istanbul earthquake
   b. 1700 Cascadia earthquake
   c. 1703 Genroku earthquake
   d. Seamount

4. The _____ Period is the geologic time period after the Neogene Period, spanning 1.805 +/- 0.005 million years ago to the present. The _____ includes two geologic epochs: the Pleistocene and the Holocene Epoch.

There is an ongoing debate of the status of _____ -- a recent proposal from International Commission on Stratigraphy (ICS) was to make _____ a subperiod under Neogene, but that was retracted after criticism from International Union for _____ Research (INQUA), so instead ICS and INQUA agreed to erect _____ as an Era, above Neogene, and to place the base for _____ at 2.588 >± 3.005, the base for Gelasian Stage.

   a. Tributary
   b. Yilgarn Craton
   c. Geomorphology
   d. Quaternary

5. The _____ epoch (55.8 >± 0.2 - 33.9 >± 0.1 Ma) is a major division of the geologic timescale and the second epoch of the Palaeogene period in the Cenozoic era. The _____ spans the time from the end of the Paleocene epoch to the beginning of the Oligocene epoch. The start of the _____ is marked by the emergence of the first modern mammals.
   a. AL 333
   b. AASHTO Soil Classification System
   c. Eocene
   d. AL 129-1

6. _____ describes the large scale motions of Earth's lithosphere. The theory encompasses the older concepts of continental drift, developed during the first decades of the 20th century by Alfred Wegener, and seafloor spreading, understood during the 1960s.

The outermost part of the Earth's interior is made up of two layers: the lithosphere and the asthenosphere.

   a. Continental crust
   b. Nappe
   c. Mantle convection
   d. Plate tectonics

7. _____s is a field of study within geology concerned generally with the structures within the lithosphere of the Earth and particularly with the forces and movements that have operated in a region to create these structures.

_____s is concerned with the orogenies and _____ development of cratons and _____ terranes as well as the earthquake and volcanic belts which directly affect much of the global population. _____ studies are also important for understanding erosion patterns in geomorphology and as guides for the economic geologist searching for petroleum and metallic ores.

  a. Cocos Plate   b. Tectonic
  c. Rivera Plate   d. Fault trace

8. _____ is a field of study within geology concerned generally with the structures within the lithosphere of the Earth and particularly with the forces and movements that have operated in a region to create these structures.

_____ is concerned with the orogenies and tectonic development of cratons and tectonic terranes as well as the earthquake and volcanic belts which directly affect much of the global population. Tectonic studies are also important for understanding erosion patterns in geomorphology and as guides for the economic geologist searching for petroleum and metallic ores.

  a. Cocos Plate   b. Tectonics
  c. Rivera Plate   d. Fault trace

9. The _____ is the epoch from 1.8 million to 11550 years BP covering the world's recent period of repeated glaciations. The _____ epoch follows the Pliocene epoch and is followed by the Holocene epoch. The _____ is the third epoch of the Neogene period or 6th epoch of the Cenozoic Era. The end of the _____ corresponds with the retreat of the last continental glacier. It also corresponds with the end of the Paleolithic age used in archaeology.

  a. Sicilian Stage   b. Late Pleistocene
  c. Tyrrhenian   d. Pleistocene

10. _____ is a stage of the Cretaceous period.

_____ is a term proposed in 1842 by A. d'Orbigny for that stage of the Cretaceous system which comes above the Aptian and below (before) the Cenomanian (Pal. France. Cret. ii.). Approximate time range is 112.0 ± 1.0 Ma to 99.6 ± 0.9 Ma (million years ago).

  a. Albian   b. AL 129-1
  c. Aptian   d. AASHTO Soil Classification System

11. In geology, _____ was a name given to the lowest stage of the Cretaceous system. It was introduced by Jules Thurmann in 1835 on account of the development of these rocks at Neuchâtel (Neocomum), Switzerland. It has been employed in more than one sense.

  a. Juan Fernandez hotspot   b. Saint Helena hotspot
  c. Thrace Basin   d. Neocomian

12. _____ is molten rock expelled by a volcano during eruption. When first expelled from a volcanic vent, it is a liquid at temperatures from 700 >°C to 1,200 >°C (1,300 >°F to 2,200 >°F.) Although _____ is quite viscous, with about 100,000 times the viscosity of water, it can flow great distances before cooling and solidifying, because of both its thixotropic and shear thinning properties.

   a. Pyroclastic flow   b. Volcanic ash

   c. Cinder   d. Lava

13. The _____ is a geological epoch which began approximately 11â€‰700 years ago (10â€‰000 ^{14}C years ago). According to traditional geological thinking, the _____ continues to the present. The _____ is part of the Neogene and Quaternary periods.

   a. 1509 Istanbul earthquake   b. 1700 Cascadia earthquake

   c. Holocene   d. Neoglaciation

1. The _____ is a a term for a geologic period 65 million to 1.8 million years ago. The _____ covered the time span between the superseded Secondary period and an out-of-date definition of the Quaternary period. The period began with the demise of the non-avian dinosaurs in the Cretaceous-_____ extinction event, at start of the Cenozoic era, spanning to beginning of the most recent Ice Age, at the end of the Pliocene epoch.
   a. Loihi Seamount
   b. Logarithmic Spiral Beach
   c. Historical geology
   d. Tertiary

2. The _____, usually abbreviated K for its German translation Kreide, is a geologic period and system from circa >145.5 >± 4 to >65.5 >± 0.3 million years ago . In the geologic timescale, the _____ follows on the Jurassic period and is followed by the Paleogene period. It is the youngest period of the Mesozoic era, and at 80 million years long, the longest period of the Phanerozoic eon. The end of the _____ defines the boundary between the Mesozoic and Cenozoic eras.
   a. Hauterivian
   b. Campanian
   c. Valanginian
   d. Cretaceous

3. A _____ is a mountain rising from the ocean seafloor that does not reach to the water's surface (sea level), and thus is not an island. These are typically formed from extinct volcanoes, that rise abruptly and are usually found rising from a seafloor of 1,000-4,000 meters depth. They are defined by oceanographers as independent features that rise to at least 1,000 meters above the seafloor.
   a. Seamount
   b. 1703 Genroku earthquake
   c. 1700 Cascadia earthquake
   d. 1509 Istanbul earthquake

4. _____ or _____ stone is a calcium carbonate or lime-rich mud or mudstone which contains variable amounts of clays and aragonite. _____ is originally an old term loosely applied to a variety of materials, most of which occur as loose, earthy deposits consisting chiefly of an intimate mixture of clay and calcium carbonate, formed under freshwater conditions; specifically an earthy substance containing 35-65% clay and 65-35% carbonate. The term is today often used to describe indurated marine deposits and lacustrine (lake) sediments which more accurately should be named _____ stones.
   a. 1703 Genroku earthquake
   b. 1700 Cascadia earthquake
   c. Marl
   d. 1509 Istanbul earthquake

5. An _____ is an underground layer of water-bearing permeable rock or unconsolidated materials (gravel, sand, silt, or clay) from which groundwater can be usefully extracted using a water well. The study of water flow in _____ s and the characterization of _____ s is called hydrogeology. Related terms include: an aquitard, which is an impermeable layer along an _____, and an aquiclude (or aquifuge), which is a solid, impermeable area beneath an _____.
   a. AL 129-1
   b. AL 333
   c. AASHTO Soil Classification System
   d. Aquifer

6. _____ are small (< 2 mm), spheroidal, 'coated' (layered) sedimentary grains, usually composed of calcium carbonate, but sometimes made up of iron- or phosphate-based minerals. _____ usually form on the sea floor, most commonly in shallow tropical seas. After being buried under additional sediment, these _____ can be cemented together to form a sedimentary rock called an oolite.
   a. AASHTO Soil Classification System
   b. Ooids
   c. AL 333
   d. AL 129-1

7. The _____ is the epoch from 1.8 million to 11550 years BP covering the world's recent period of repeated glaciations. The _____ epoch follows the Pliocene epoch and is followed by the Holocene epoch. The _____ is the third epoch of the Neogene period or 6th epoch of the Cenozoic Era. The end of the _____ corresponds with the retreat of the last continental glacier. It also corresponds with the end of the Paleolithic age used in archaeology.

a. Sicilian Stage
b. Tyrrhenian
c. Late Pleistocene
d. Pleistocene

8. The _____ is a geological epoch which began approximately 11‰700 years ago (10‰000 ^{14}C years ago). According to traditional geological thinking, the _____ continues to the present. The _____ is part of the Neogene and Quaternary periods.

a. 1509 Istanbul earthquake
b. 1700 Cascadia earthquake
c. Neoglaciation
d. Holocene

Chapter 20. Biscayne National Park

1. In chemistry, a _____ is a salt or ester of carbonic acid.

To test for the presence of the _____ anion in a salt, the addition of dilute mineral acid (e.g. hydrochloric acid) will yield carbon dioxide gas.

_____-containing salts are industrially and mineralogically ubiquitous.

    a. 1703 Genroku earthquake
    b. 1700 Cascadia earthquake
    c. 1509 Istanbul earthquake
    d. Carbonate

2. _____ are a class of sedimentary rocks composed primarily of carbonate minerals. The two major types are limestone and dolomite, composed of calcite ($CaCO_3$) and the mineral dolomite ($CaMg(CO_3)_2$) respectively. Chalk and tufa are also minor sedimentary carbonates.
    a. Carbonate rocks
    b. Diatomaceous earth
    c. Shale
    d. Dolostone

3. The _____ is the epoch from 1.8 million to 11550 years BP covering the world's recent period of repeated glaciations. The _____ epoch follows the Pliocene epoch and is followed by the Holocene epoch. The _____ is the third epoch of the Neogene period or 6th epoch of the Cenozoic Era. The end of the _____ corresponds with the retreat of the last continental glacier. It also corresponds with the end of the Paleolithic age used in archaeology.
    a. Late Pleistocene
    b. Tyrrhenian
    c. Sicilian Stage
    d. Pleistocene

4. _____ are small (< 2 mm), spheroidal, 'coated' (layered) sedimentary grains, usually composed of calcium carbonate, but sometimes made up of iron- or phosphate-based minerals. _____ usually form on the sea floor, most commonly in shallow tropical seas. After being buried under additional sediment, these _____ can be cemented together to form a sedimentary rock called an oolite.
    a. AL 333
    b. AL 129-1
    c. AASHTO Soil Classification System
    d. Ooids

5. _____ is a sedimentary rock formed from ooids, spherical grains composed of concentric layers. The name derives from the Hellenic word >òoion for egg. Strictly, _____s consist of ooids of diameter 0.25-2 mm: rocks composed of ooids larger than 2 mm are called pisolites.
    a. Oolite
    b. AL 333
    c. AL 129-1
    d. AASHTO Soil Classification System

6. _____ are the preserved remains or traces of animals, plants, and other organisms from the remote past. The totality of _____, both discovered and undiscovered, and their placement in fossiliferous rock formations and sedimentary layers (strata) is known as the fossil record. The study of _____ across geological time, how they were formed, and the evolutionary relationships between taxa (phylogeny) are some of the most important functions of the science of paleontology.
    a. 1703 Genroku earthquake
    b. 1700 Cascadia earthquake
    c. 1509 Istanbul earthquake
    d. Fossils

1. In nuclear physics, a _____ is a nuclide produced by radioactive decay. Radioactive decay often involves a sequence of steps For example, U-238 decays to Th-234 which decays to Pa-234 which decays, and so on, to Pb-206:

>

In this example:

- Th-234, Pa-234,…,Pb-206 are the _____s of U-238.
- Th-234 is the daughter of the parent U-238.
- Pa-234 is the granddaughter of U-238.

Note that Th-234, Pa-234,…,Pb-206 might also be referred to as the daughter products of U-238.

_____s are extremely important in understanding radioactive decay and the management of radioactive waste.

a. Mass deficiency
b. Positron emission
c. Decay product
d. Mass excess

2. The _____ is a geological epoch which began approximately 11,700 years ago (10,000 ^{14}C years ago). According to traditional geological thinking, the _____ continues to the present. The _____ is part of the Neogene and Quaternary periods.
a. Neoglaciation
b. Holocene
c. 1509 Istanbul earthquake
d. 1700 Cascadia earthquake

3. The _____ is the epoch from 1.8 million to 11550 years BP covering the world's recent period of repeated glaciations. The _____ epoch follows the Pliocene epoch and is followed by the Holocene epoch. The _____ is the third epoch of the Neogene period or 6th epoch of the Cenozoic Era. The end of the _____ corresponds with the retreat of the last continental glacier. It also corresponds with the end of the Paleolithic age used in archaeology.
a. Pleistocene
b. Tyrrhenian
c. Late Pleistocene
d. Sicilian Stage

4. _____ is a colloid hydrogel consisting of fine granular matter (such as sand or silt), clay, and salt water. In the name, as in that of quicksilver (mercury), 'quick' does not mean 'fast,' but 'living' (cf. the expression the quick and the dead.)
a. Sediment
b. Brickearth
c. Fech fech
d. Quicksand

5. _____ is a fine-grained, foliated, homogeneous metamorphic rock derived from an original shale-type sedimentary rock composed of clay or volcanic ash through low grade regional metamorphism. The result is a foliated rock in which the foliation may not correspond to the original sedimentary layering. _____ is frequently grey in colour especially when seen en masse covering roofs.
a. Shock metamorphism
b. Talc carbonate
c. Cataclasite
d. Slate

6. The _____ -- also called the Laurentian Plateau, or Bouclier Canadien -- is a massive geological shield covered by a thin layer of soil that forms the nucleus of the North American or Laurentia craton. It has a deep, common, joined bedrock region in eastern and central Canada and stretches North from the Great Lakes to the Arctic Ocean, covering over half of Canada; it also extends south into the northern reaches of the United States. Population is scarce, and industrial development is minimal, although the region has a large hydroelectric power potential.
   a. Quaternary
   b. Canadian Shield
   c. Gawler craton
   d. Yilgarn Craton

7. A _____ is an old and stable part of the continental crust that has survived the merging and splitting of continents and supercontinents for at least 500 million years. Some are over two billion years old. They are generally found in the interiors of continents and are characteristically composed of ancient crystalline basement crust of lightweight felsic igneous rock such as granite.
   a. Wyoming craton
   b. Sebakwe proto-craton
   c. Superior craton
   d. Craton

8. A _____ is generally a large area of exposed Precambrian crystalline igneous and high-grade metamorphic rocks that form tectonically stable areas. In all cases, the age of these rocks is greater than 570 million years and sometimes dates back 2 to 3.5 billion years. They have been little affected by tectonic events following the end of the Precambrian Era, and are relatively flat regions where mountain building, faulting, and other tectonic processes are greatly diminished compared with the activity that occurs at the margins of the _____s and the boundaries between tectonic plates.
   a. 1509 Istanbul earthquake
   b. 1700 Cascadia earthquake
   c. 1703 Genroku earthquake
   d. Shield

9. _____ is an adjective describing a silicate mineral or rock that is rich in magnesium and iron; the term was derived by contracting 'magnesium' and 'ferric'. Most _____ minerals are dark in color and the specific gravity is greater than 3. Common rock-forming _____ minerals include olivine, pyroxene, amphibole, and biotite.

_____ lava, before cooling, has a low viscosity, in comparison to felsic lava, due to the lower silica content in _____ magma. Water and other volatiles can more easily and gradually escape from _____ lava, so eruptions of volcanoes made of _____ lavas are less explosively violent than felsic lava eruptions.

   a. 1703 Genroku earthquake
   b. 1700 Cascadia earthquake
   c. 1509 Istanbul earthquake
   d. Mafic

Chapter 22. Voyageurs National Park

1. _____ refers to natural mountain building, and may be studied as a tectonic structural event, (b) as a geographical event, and (c) a chronological event. Orogenic events (a) cause distinctive structural phenomena and related tectonic activity, (b) affect certain regions of rocks and crust, and (c) happen within a specific period of time.
   - a. Orogenesis
   - b. Alice Springs Orogeny
   - c. Antler orogeny
   - d. Orogeny

2. The _____ is the earliest of three geologic eras of the Phanerozoic eon. The _____ spanned from roughly 542 to 251 million years ago (ICS, 2004), and is subdivided into six geologic periods; from oldest to youngest they are: the Cambrian, Ordovician, Silurian, Devonian, Carboniferous, and Permian.

   The _____ covers the time from the first appearance of abundant, soft-shelled fossils to the time when the continents were beginning to be dominated by large, relatively sophisticated reptiles and modern plants. The lower (oldest) boundary was classically set at the first appearance of creatures known as trilobites and archeocyathids.

   - a. 1700 Cascadia earthquake
   - b. Paleozoic
   - c. 1703 Genroku earthquake
   - d. 1509 Istanbul earthquake

3. The _____ is the epoch from 1.8 million to 11550 years BP covering the world's recent period of repeated glaciations. The _____ epoch follows the Pliocene epoch and is followed by the Holocene epoch. The _____ is the third epoch of the Neogene period or 6th epoch of the Cenozoic Era. The end of the _____ corresponds with the retreat of the last continental glacier. It also corresponds with the end of the Paleolithic age used in archaeology.
   - a. Late Pleistocene
   - b. Tyrrhenian
   - c. Pleistocene
   - d. Sicilian Stage

4. The _____ forms the core of both the North American continent and the Canadian Shield. It extends from Quebec in the east to eastern Manitoba in the west. The western margin extends from northern Minnesota through eastern Manitoba to northwestern Ontario.

   The formation of the _____ is best explained within the context of 2.72-2.68 Ga accretion of small continental plates and trapped oceanic terranes in a tectonic regime resembling that of the rapidly changing southwestern Pacific Ocean. The craton is made up of a collage of small continental fragments of Mesoarchean age and Neoarchean oceanic plates and tracts of oceanic crust that consists of the following domains: Northern Superior, North Caribou, Winnipeg River, Marmion, Minnesota River Valley, Opatica, and Goudalie.

   - a. Wyoming craton
   - b. Kalahari craton
   - c. Craton
   - d. Superior craton

5. The _____, is a geologic eon before the Proterozoic and Paleoproterozoic, before 2.5 Ga (billion years ago, or 2,500 Ma.) Instead of being based on stratigraphy, this date is defined chronometrically. The lower boundary (starting point) has not been officially recognized by the International Commission on Stratigraphy, but it is usually set to 3.8 Ga, at the end of the Hadean eon.
   - a. AASHTO Soil Classification System
   - b. AL 129-1
   - c. Archean
   - d. AL 333

6. The _____ is an informal name for the supereon comprising the eons of the geologic timescale that came before the current Phanerozoic eon. It spans from the formation of Earth around 4500 Mya (million years ago) to the evolution of abundant macroscopic hard-shelled animals, which marked the beginning of the Cambrian, the first period of the first era of the Phanerozoic eon, some 542 Mya. It is named after the Roman name for Wales - Cambria - where rocks from this age were first studied.
   a. 1509 Istanbul earthquake
   b. Precambrian
   c. 1703 Genroku earthquake
   d. 1700 Cascadia earthquake

7. A _____ is generally a large area of exposed Precambrian crystalline igneous and high-grade metamorphic rocks that form tectonically stable areas. In all cases, the age of these rocks is greater than 570 million years and sometimes dates back 2 to 3.5 billion years. They have been little affected by tectonic events following the end of the Precambrian Era, and are relatively flat regions where mountain building, faulting, and other tectonic processes are greatly diminished compared with the activity that occurs at the margins of the _____ s and the boundaries between tectonic plates.
   a. 1509 Istanbul earthquake
   b. Shield
   c. 1703 Genroku earthquake
   d. 1700 Cascadia earthquake

8. _____ is a technique used to date materials, usually based on a comparison between the observed abundance of a naturally occurring radioactive isotope and its decay products, using known decay rates. It is the principal source of information about the absolute age of rocks and other geological features, including the age of the Earth itself, and can be used to date a wide range of natural and man-made materials. Together with stratigraphic principles, _____ methods are used in geochronology to establish the geological time scale.
   a. Stage
   b. Lichenometry
   c. Relative dating
   d. Radiometric dating

9. _____ - also known as greenstone - is a general field petrologic term applied to metamorphic and/or altered mafic volcanic rock. The green is due to abundant green chlorite, actinolite and epidote minerals that dominate the rock. However, basalts may remain quite black if primary pyroxene does not revert to chlorite or actinolite.
   a. Metasomatism
   b. Prehnite-pumpellyite facies
   c. Greenstone belts
   d. Greenschist

10. _____ are zones of variably metamorphosed mafic to ultramafic volcanic sequences with associated sedimentary rocks that occur within Archaean and Proterozoic cratons between granite and gneiss bodies.

The name comes from the green hue imparted by the colour of the metamorphic minerals within the mafic rocks. Chlorite, actinolite and other green amphiboles are the typical green minerals.

   a. Greenschist facies
   b. Porphyroclast
   c. Talc carbonate
   d. Greenstone belts

11. _____ is a common and widely distributed type of rock formed by high-grade regional metamorphic processes from pre-existing formations that were originally either igneous or sedimentary rocks. Gneissic rocks are usually medium to coarse foliated and largely recrystallized but do not carry large quantities of micas, chlorite or other platy minerals. _____ es that are metamorphosed igneous rocks or their equivalent are termed granite _____ es, diorite _____ es, etc.

a. 1703 Genroku earthquake
b. Gneiss
c. 1509 Istanbul earthquake
d. 1700 Cascadia earthquake

12. The terms _____ and icehouse Earth refer to the prevailing global climate on a timescale of millions of years.

During a _____ Earth period, the planet's atmosphere contains sufficient _____ gases such as carbon dioxide and methane for ice to be entirely absent from the planet's surface.

During icehouse periods, glaciers are present in fluctuating amounts; variations in the Earth's orbit may result in many ice ages, glacials, and interglacials.

a. 1700 Cascadia earthquake
b. 1703 Genroku earthquake
c. 1509 Istanbul earthquake
d. Greenhouse

13. A _____ is a moraine that forms at the end of the glacier called the snout.

They mark the maximum advance of the glacier. An end moraine is at the present boundary of the glacier. They are one of the most prominent types of moraines in the Arctic. One famous _____ is the Giant's Wall in Norway.

a. Terminal moraine
b. Glacial plucking
c. Bull Lake glaciation
d. Firn

14. A _____ is any glacially formed accumulation of unconsolidated glacial debris (soil and rock) which can occur in currently glaciated and formerly glaciated regions, such as those areas acted upon by a past ice age. This debris may have been plucked off the valley floor as a glacier advanced or it may have fallen off the valley walls as a result of frost wedging. _____s may be composed of silt like glacial flour to large boulders.

a. 1700 Cascadia earthquake
b. 1703 Genroku earthquake
c. 1509 Istanbul earthquake
d. Moraine

15. A _____ is a mountain rising from the ocean seafloor that does not reach to the water's surface (sea level), and thus is not an island. These are typically formed from extinct volcanoes, that rise abruptly and are usually found rising from a seafloor of 1,000-4,000 meters depth. They are defined by oceanographers as independent features that rise to at least 1,000 meters above the seafloor.

a. 1700 Cascadia earthquake
b. 1703 Genroku earthquake
c. 1509 Istanbul earthquake
d. Seamount

16. _____ is molten rock expelled by a volcano during eruption. When first expelled from a volcanic vent, it is a liquid at temperatures from 700 >°C to 1,200 >°C (1,300 >°F to 2,200 >°F.) Although _____ is quite viscous, with about 100,000 times the viscosity of water, it can flow great distances before cooling and solidifying, because of both its thixotropic and shear thinning properties.

a. Pyroclastic flow
b. Lava
c. Cinder
d. Volcanic ash

17. _____ forms a group of medium-grade metamorphic rocks, chiefly notable for the preponderance of lamellar minerals such as micas, chlorite, talc, hornblende, graphite, and others. Quartz often occurs in drawn-out grains to such an extent that a particular form called quartz _____ is produced. By definition, _____ contains more than 50% platy and elongated minerals, often finely interleaved with quartz and feldspar.
   a. Hornfels
   b. Porphyroblast
   c. Talc carbonate
   d. Schist

18. _____ is unsorted glacial sediment. Glacial drift is a general term for the coarsely graded and extremely heterogeneous sediments of glacial origin. Glacial _____ is that part of glacial drift which was deposited directly by the glacier. In cases where _____ has been indurated or lithified by subsequent burial into solid rock, it is known as the sedimentary rock tillite.
   a. 1509 Istanbul earthquake
   b. Till
   c. 1703 Genroku earthquake
   d. 1700 Cascadia earthquake

19. _____ is an accumulation of partially decayed vegetation matter. _____ forms in wetlands or peatlands, variously called bogs, moors, muskegs, pocosins, mires, and _____ swamp forests. By volume there are about 4 trillion mÂÂ³ of _____ in the world covering a total of around 2% of global land mass (about 3 million km^2), containing about 8 billion terajoules of energy.
   a. 1703 Genroku earthquake
   b. 1700 Cascadia earthquake
   c. Peat
   d. 1509 Istanbul earthquake

20. _____ is a characteristic of rock surfaces where glaciers have passed over bedrock, typically granite or other hard igneous or metamorphic rock. Moving ice will carry pebbles and sand grains removed from upper levels which in turn grind a smooth or groved surface upon the underlying rock. The presence of such polish indicates that the glaciation was relatively recent (in geologic time scale) or was subsequently protected by deposition, as such polish will be subsequently lost due to weathering processes (such as exfoliation).
   a. Glacial plucking
   b. Glacial polish
   c. Bull Lake glaciation
   d. Glaciolacustrine deposits

21. _____ consists of clay-sized particles of rock, generated by glacial erosion or by artificial grinding to a similar size. Because the material is very small, it becomes suspended in river water making the water appear cloudy.

If the river flows into a glacial lake, the lake may appear turquoise in color as a result.

   a. Snowball Earth
   b. Pastonian Stage
   c. Post-glacial rebound
   d. Rock flour

22. A _____ is a piece of rock that differs from the size and type of rock native to the area in which it rests. They are carried by glacial ice, often over distances of hundreds of kilometres and can range in size from pebbles to large boulders such as Big Rock (16,500 tons) in Alberta.
   a. 1700 Cascadia earthquake
   b. 1703 Genroku earthquake
   c. 1509 Istanbul earthquake
   d. Glacial erratic

23. The _____ Era, is the most recent of the three classic geological eras and covers the period from 65.5 million years ago to the present. It is marked by the Cretaceous-Tertiary extinction event at the end of the Cretaceous that saw the demise of the last non-avian dinosaurs and the end of the Mesozoic Era. The _____ era is ongoing.

| a. 1703 Genroku earthquake | b. 1700 Cascadia earthquake |
| c. 1509 Istanbul earthquake | d. Cenozoic |

24. The _____ Era is one of three geologic eras of the Phanerozoic eon. The division of time into eras dates back to Giovanni Arduino, in the 18th century, although his original name for the era now called the '_____' was 'Secondary' (making the modern era the 'Tertiary'.)

The _____ was a time of tectonic, climatic and evolutionary activity. The continents gradually shifted from a state of connectedness into their present configuration; the drifting provided for speciation and other important evolutionary developments.

| a. 1700 Cascadia earthquake | b. 1703 Genroku earthquake |
| c. 1509 Istanbul earthquake | d. Mesozoic |

25. The _____ is a geological eon representing a period before the first abundant complex life on Earth. The _____ extended from 2500 Ma to 542.0 >± 1.0 Ma (million years ago), and is the most recent part of the old, informally named 'e;Precambrian'e; time.

The Proterozoic consists of 3 geologic eras, from oldest to youngest:

- Paleoproterozoic
- Mesoproterozoic
- Neoproterozoic

The well-identified events were:

- The transition to an oxygenated atmosphere during the Mesoproterozoic.
- Several glaciations, including the hypothesized Snowball Earth during the Cryogenian period in the late Neoproterozoic.
- The Ediacaran Period (635 to 542 Ma) which is characterized by the evolution of abundant soft-bodied multicellular organisms.

The geoloic record of the Proterozoic is much better than that for the preceding Archean. In contrast to the deep-water deposits of the Archean, the Proterozoic features many strata that were laid down in extensive shallow epicontinental seas; furthermore, many of these rocks are less metamorphosed than Archean-age ones, and plenty are unaltered.

| a. 1509 Istanbul earthquake | b. 1700 Cascadia earthquake |
| c. 1703 Genroku earthquake | d. Proterozoic Eon |

1. _____ is a volcanic rock texture characterised by, or containing many vesicles. The texture is often found in extrusive aphanitic igneous rock. The vesicles are small cavities formed by the expansion of bubbles of gas or steam during the solidification of the rock.
   a. Vesicular texture
   b. Rock cycle
   c. Pluton
   d. Large igneous provinces

2. _____ form when the vesicular cavities (created by expanding gas bubbles in volcanic lava) are filled with a secondary mineral such as calcite, quartz, chlorite or one of the zeolites, which are deposited by having minerals 'wash' through the pores in the rock They are filled from the outside, making some _____ concentrically layered.
   a. Augen
   b. Igneous rock
   c. Amygdules
   d. Extrusive

3. The _____ is an informal name for the supereon comprising the eons of the geologic timescale that came before the current Phanerozoic eon. It spans from the formation of Earth around 4500 Mya (million years ago) to the evolution of abundant macroscopic hard-shelled animals, which marked the beginning of the Cambrian, the first period of the first era of the Phanerozoic eon, some 542 Mya. It is named after the Roman name for Wales - Cambria - where rocks from this age were first studied.
   a. Precambrian
   b. 1700 Cascadia earthquake
   c. 1703 Genroku earthquake
   d. 1509 Istanbul earthquake

4. The _____ -- also called the Laurentian Plateau, or Bouclier Canadien -- is a massive geological shield covered by a thin layer of soil that forms the nucleus of the North American or Laurentia craton. It has a deep, common, joined bedrock region in eastern and central Canada and stretches North from the Great Lakes to the Arctic Ocean, covering over half of Canada; it also extends south into the northern reaches of the United States. Population is scarce, and industrial development is minimal, although the region has a large hydroelectric power potential.
   a. Quaternary
   b. Gawler craton
   c. Canadian Shield
   d. Yilgarn Craton

5. The _____ is the earliest of three geologic eras of the Phanerozoic eon. The _____ spanned from roughly 542 to 251 million years ago (ICS, 2004), and is subdivided into six geologic periods; from oldest to youngest they are: the Cambrian, Ordovician, Silurian, Devonian, Carboniferous, and Permian.

The _____ covers the time from the first appearance of abundant, soft-shelled fossils to the time when the continents were beginning to be dominated by large, relatively sophisticated reptiles and modern plants. The lower (oldest) boundary was classically set at the first appearance of creatures known as trilobites and archeocyathids.

   a. 1700 Cascadia earthquake
   b. 1509 Istanbul earthquake
   c. 1703 Genroku earthquake
   d. Paleozoic

6. A _____ is generally a large area of exposed Precambrian crystalline igneous and high-grade metamorphic rocks that form tectonically stable areas. In all cases, the age of these rocks is greater than 570 million years and sometimes dates back 2 to 3.5 billion years. They have been little affected by tectonic events following the end of the Precambrian Era, and are relatively flat regions where mountain building, faulting, and other tectonic processes are greatly diminished compared with the activity that occurs at the margins of the _____s and the boundaries between tectonic plates.

| a. 1703 Genroku earthquake | b. 1700 Cascadia earthquake |
| c. 1509 Istanbul earthquake | d. Shield |

7. _____ is a microcrystalline variety of quartz, chiefly chalcedony, characterised by its fineness of grain and brightness of color. Although _____s may be found in various kinds of rock, they are classically associated with volcanic rocks but can be common in certain metamorphic rocks.

Colorful _____s and other chalcedonies were obtained over 3,000 years ago from the Achates River, now called Dirillo, in Sicily.

| a. AL 333 | b. AL 129-1 |
| c. AASHTO Soil Classification System | d. Agate |

8. A _____ is a rock consisting of individual stones that have become cemented together. They are sedimentary rocks consisting of rounded fragments and are thus differentiated from breccias, which consist of angular clasts. Both _____s and breccias are characterized by clasts larger than sand (>2 mm).
| a. Pelagic sediments | b. Keystone |
| c. Conglomerate | d. Concretion |

9. _____ is a term used in geology to refer to silicate minerals, magma, and rocks which are enriched in the lighter elements such as silicon, oxygen, aluminium, sodium, and potassium. _____ minerals are usually light in color and have specific gravities less than 3. Common _____ minerals include quartz, muscovite, orthoclase, and the sodium-rich plagioclase feldspars.
| a. Groundmass | b. Volcanic rock |
| c. Magma | d. Felsic |

10. _____ is an adjective describing a silicate mineral or rock that is rich in magnesium and iron; the term was derived by contracting 'magnesium' and 'ferric'. Most _____ minerals are dark in color and the specific gravity is greater than 3. Common rock-forming _____ minerals include olivine, pyroxene, amphibole, and biotite.

_____ lava, before cooling, has a low viscosity, in comparison to felsic lava, due to the lower silica content in _____ magma. Water and other volatiles can more easily and gradually escape from _____ lava, so eruptions of volcanoes made of _____ lavas are less explosively violent than felsic lava eruptions.

| a. 1700 Cascadia earthquake | b. 1703 Genroku earthquake |
| c. 1509 Istanbul earthquake | d. Mafic |

11. In materials science, _____ is the distribution of crystallographic orientations of a polycrystalline sample. A sample in which these orientations are fully random is said to have no _____. If the crystallographic orientations are not random, but have some preferred orientation, then the sample has a weak, strong, or moderate _____.
| a. Geothermal | b. Diamond Head |
| c. Platform | d. Texture |

12. A _____ is an elongated whale-shaped hill formed by glacial action. Its long axis is parallel with the movement of the ice, with the blunter end facing into the glacial movement. They may be more than 45 m (150 ft) high and more than 0.8 km (1/2 mile) long, and are often in _____ fields of similarly shaped, sized and oriented hills. They usually have layers indicating that the material was repeatedly added to a core, which may be of rock or glacial till.
    a. Drumlin
    b. Monadnock
    c. Sandur
    d. 1509 Istanbul earthquake

13. _____ - also known as greenstone - is a general field petrologic term applied to metamorphic and/or altered mafic volcanic rock. The green is due to abundant green chlorite, actinolite and epidote minerals that dominate the rock. However, basalts may remain quite black if primary pyroxene does not revert to chlorite or actinolite.
    a. Prehnite-pumpellyite facies
    b. Metasomatism
    c. Greenstone belts
    d. Greenschist

14. A _____ is a mountain rising from the ocean seafloor that does not reach to the water's surface (sea level), and thus is not an island. These are typically formed from extinct volcanoes, that rise abruptly and are usually found rising from a seafloor of 1,000-4,000 meters depth. They are defined by oceanographers as independent features that rise to at least 1,000 meters above the seafloor.
    a. Seamount
    b. 1509 Istanbul earthquake
    c. 1703 Genroku earthquake
    d. 1700 Cascadia earthquake

15. A _____ is a vector field which surrounds magnets and electric currents, and is detected by the force it exerts on moving electric charges and on magnetic materials. When placed in a _____, magnetic dipoles tend to align their axes parallel to the _____. Magnetic fields also have their own energy with an energy density proportional to the square of the field intensity.
    a. 1703 Genroku earthquake
    b. 1509 Istanbul earthquake
    c. 1700 Cascadia earthquake
    d. Magnetic field

16. In some natural sciences, _____ is the typical or representative location and is typically the first example of a newly discovered or described object. Often it is namesake for the term.

It is most commonly used in geology for formations, structures, rock types, minerals and fossils.

    a. Geostrophic current
    b. Pneumatolysis
    c. Medical geology
    d. Type locality

17. The _____ is the epoch from 1.8 million to 11550 years BP covering the world's recent period of repeated glaciations. The _____ epoch follows the Pliocene epoch and is followed by the Holocene epoch. The _____ is the third epoch of the Neogene period or 6th epoch of the Cenozoic Era. The end of the _____ corresponds with the retreat of the last continental glacier. It also corresponds with the end of the Paleolithic age used in archaeology.
    a. Sicilian Stage
    b. Tyrrhenian
    c. Late Pleistocene
    d. Pleistocene

18. _____, also known as the Pleistocene glaciation, the current ice age or simply the ice age, refers to the period of the last few million years in which permanent ice sheets were established in Antarctica and perhaps Greenland, and fluctuating ice sheets have occurred elsewhere The major effects of the ice age were erosion and deposition of material over large parts of the continents, modification of river systems, creation of millions of lakes, changes in sea level, development of pluvial lakes far from the ice margins, isostatic adjustment of the crust, and abnormal winds. It affected oceans, flooding, and biological communities.

a. Quaternary glaciation
b. Snowball Earth
c. Wolstonian Stage
d. Rock glaciers

Chapter 24. Acadia National Park

1. The _____ is a geologic period and system of the Paleozoic era spanning from >416 to 359.2 million years ago (ICS, 2004.).

During the _____ Period, which occurred in the Paleozoic era, the first fish evolved legsand started to walk on land as tetrapods around 365 Ma.

    a. Xitun Formation
    c. 1509 Istanbul earthquake
    b. Gogo Formation
    d. Devonian

2. The _____ is the epoch from 1.8 million to 11550 years BP covering the world's recent period of repeated glaciations. The _____ epoch follows the Pliocene epoch and is followed by the Holocene epoch. The _____ is the third epoch of the Neogene period or 6th epoch of the Cenozoic Era. The end of the _____ corresponds with the retreat of the last continental glacier. It also corresponds with the end of the Paleolithic age used in archaeology.

    a. Sicilian Stage
    c. Tyrrhenian
    b. Late Pleistocene
    d. Pleistocene

3. _____, also known as the Pleistocene glaciation, the current ice age or simply the ice age, refers to the period of the last few million years in which permanent ice sheets were established in Antarctica and perhaps Greenland, and fluctuating ice sheets have occurred elsewhere The major effects of the ice age were erosion and deposition of material over large parts of the continents, modification of river systems, creation of millions of lakes, changes in sea level, development of pluvial lakes far from the ice margins, isostatic adjustment of the crust, and abnormal winds. It affected oceans, flooding, and biological communities.

    a. Rock glaciers
    c. Wolstonian Stage
    b. Snowball Earth
    d. Quaternary glaciation

4. A _____ in geology is a fragment of crustal material formed on one tectonic plate and accreted -- 'sutured' -- to crust lying on another plate. The crustal block or fragment preserves its own distinctive geologic history, which is different from that of the surrounding areas (hence the term 'exotic' _____). The suture zone between a _____ and the crust it attaches to is usually identifiable as a fault.

    a. 1703 Genroku earthquake
    c. 1509 Istanbul earthquake
    b. 1700 Cascadia earthquake
    d. Terrane

5. The _____ is a a term for a geologic period 65 million to 1.8 million years ago. The _____ covered the time span between the superseded Secondary period and an out-of-date definition of the Quaternary period. The period began with the demise of the non-avian dinosaurs in the Cretaceous-_____ extinction event, at start of the Cenozoic era, spanning to beginning of the most recent Ice Age, at the end of the Pliocene epoch.

    a. Historical geology
    c. Tertiary
    b. Logarithmic Spiral Beach
    d. Loihi Seamount

6. _____ occurs typically around intrusive igneous rocks as a result of the temperature increase caused by the intrusion of magma into cooler country rock. The area surrounding the intrusion (called aureoles) where the _____ effects are present is called the metamorphic aureole. Contact metamorphic rocks are usually known as hornfels.

    a. Dispersion
    c. Sea-level curve
    b. Georeactor
    d. Contact metamorphism

7. _____ is any penetrative planar fabric present in rocks. _____ is common to rocks affected by regional metamorphic compression typical of orogenic belts. Rocks exhibiting _____ include the typical metamorphic rock sequence of slate, phyllite, schist and gneiss.
   a. Shock metamorphism
   b. Foliation
   c. Slate
   d. Supracrustal rocks

8. The _____ Era is one of three geologic eras of the Phanerozoic eon. The division of time into eras dates back to Giovanni Arduino, in the 18th century, although his original name for the era now called the '_____' was 'Secondary' (making the modern era the 'Tertiary'.)

The _____ was a time of tectonic, climatic and evolutionary activity. The continents gradually shifted from a state of connectedness into their present configuration; the drifting provided for speciation and other important evolutionary developments.

   a. 1703 Genroku earthquake
   b. 1509 Istanbul earthquake
   c. 1700 Cascadia earthquake
   d. Mesozoic

9. _____ forms a group of medium-grade metamorphic rocks, chiefly notable for the preponderance of lamellar minerals such as micas, chlorite, talc, hornblende, graphite, and others. Quartz often occurs in drawn-out grains to such an extent that a particular form called quartz _____ is produced. By definition, _____ contains more than 50% platy and elongated minerals, often finely interleaved with quartz and feldspar.
   a. Porphyroblast
   b. Talc carbonate
   c. Schist
   d. Hornfels

10. _____ is the result of the transformation of an existing rock type, the protolith, in a process called metamorphism, which means 'change in form'. The protolith is subjected to heat and pressure (temperatures greater than 150 to 200 >°C and pressures of 1500 bars) causing profound physical and/or chemical change. The protolith may be sedimentary rock, igneous rock or another older _____.
   a. Pluton
   b. Serpentinite
   c. Metamorphic rock
   d. Laccolith

11. _____ is the solid-state recrystallization of pre-existing rocks due to changes in physical and chemical conditions, primarily heat, pressure, and the introduction of chemically active fluids. Both mineralogical, chemical and crystallographic changes can occur during this process.

Three types of _____ exist: dynamic, contact and regional.

   a. Gibraltar Arc
   b. Pumice raft
   c. Lake capture
   d. Metamorphism

12. In materials science, _____ is the distribution of crystallographic orientations of a polycrystalline sample. A sample in which these orientations are fully random is said to have no _____. If the crystallographic orientations are not random, but have some preferred orientation, then the sample has a weak, strong, or moderate _____.
   a. Platform
   b. Geothermal
   c. Diamond Head
   d. Texture

Chapter 24. Acadia National Park

13. In geology, an _____ is a body of igneous rock that has crystallized from molten magma below the surface of the Earth. Bodies of magma that solidify underground before they reach the surface of the earth are called plutons the Roman god of the underworld. Correspondingly, rocks of this kind are also referred to as igneous plutonic rocks or igneous intrusive rocks.
   a. AL 129-1
   b. AASHTO Soil Classification System
   c. AL 333
   d. Intrusion

14. A _____ is a mountain rising from the ocean seafloor that does not reach to the water's surface (sea level), and thus is not an island. These are typically formed from extinct volcanoes, that rise abruptly and are usually found rising from a seafloor of 1,000-4,000 meters depth. They are defined by oceanographers as independent features that rise to at least 1,000 meters above the seafloor.
   a. 1703 Genroku earthquake
   b. Seamount
   c. 1509 Istanbul earthquake
   d. 1700 Cascadia earthquake

15. The _____ is a middle Paleozoic mountain building event (orogeny), especially in the northern Appalachians, between New York and Newfoundland. The _____ most greatly affected the Northern Appalachian region (New England northeastward into the Gasp>é region of Canada.) The _____ should not be regarded as a single tectonic event, but rather as an orogenic era.
   a. Orogenesis
   b. Acadian orogeny
   c. Alice Springs Orogeny
   d. Alpine orogeny

16. A _____ or dyke in geology is a type of sheet intrusion referring to any geologic body that cuts discordantly across

   - planar wall rock structures, such as bedding or foliation
   - massive rock formations, like igneous/magmatic intrusions and salt diapirs.

They can therefore be either intrusive or sedimentary in origin.

An intrusive _____ is an igneous body with a very high aspect ratio, which means that its thickness is usually much smaller than the other two dimensions. Thickness can vary from sub-centimeter scale to many meters and the lateral dimensions can extend over many kilometers. A _____ is an intrusion into an opening cross-cutting fissure, shouldering aside other pre-existing layers or bodies of rock; this implies that a _____ is always younger than the rocks that contain it.

   a. Type locality
   b. Detritus
   c. Gradualism
   d. Dike

17. _____ refers to natural mountain building, and may be studied as a tectonic structural event, (b) as a geographical event, and (c) a chronological event. Orogenic events (a) cause distinctive structural phenomena and related tectonic activity, (b) affect certain regions of rocks and crust, and (c) happen within a specific period of time.
   a. Orogeny
   b. Alice Springs Orogeny
   c. Orogenesis
   d. Antler orogeny

18. Geologically, a _____ is a long, narrow inlet with steep sides, created in a valley carved by glacial activity.

The seeds of a _____ are laid when a glacier cuts a U-shaped valley through abrasion of the surrounding bedrock by the sediment it carries. Many such valleys were formed during the recent ice age.

   a. 1700 Cascadia earthquake   b. 1509 Istanbul earthquake
   c. 1703 Genroku earthquake   d. Fjord

19. _____ is the removal of solids (sediment, soil, rock and other particles) in the natural environment. It usually occurs due to transport by wind, water, or ice; by down-slope creep of soil and other material under the force of gravity; or by living organisms, such as burrowing animals, in the case of bioerosion.

_____ is distinguished from weathering, which is the process of chemical or physical breakdown of the minerals in the rocks, although the two processes may occur concurrently.

   a. AL 129-1   b. AL 333
   c. AASHTO Soil Classification System   d. Erosion

20. _____ is the decomposition of Earth rocks, soils and their minerals through direct contact with the planet's atmosphere. _____ occurs in situ, or 'with no movement', and thus should not be confused with erosion, which involves the movement of rocks and minerals by agents such as water, ice, wind and gravity.

Two important classifications of _____ processes exist -- physical and chemical _____.

   a. Physical weathering   b. Weathering
   c. 1700 Cascadia earthquake   d. 1509 Istanbul earthquake

21. _____ is a naturally occurring granular material composed of finely divided rock and mineral particles.

As the term is used by geologists, _____ particles range in diameter from 0.0625 (or $>^1\!\!>\!\!/_{16}$ mm, or 62.5 micrometers) to 2 millimeters. An individual particle in this range size is termed a _____ grain.

   a. Sand   b. 1509 Istanbul earthquake
   c. 1700 Cascadia earthquake   d. 1703 Genroku earthquake

Chapter 25. Rocky Mountain National Park

1. The _____ was a period of mountain building in western North America, which started in the Late Cretaceous, 70 to 80 million years ago, and ended 35 to 55 million years ago. The exact duration and ages of beginning and end of the orogeny are in dispute, as is the cause. The _____ occurred in a series of pulses, with quiescent phases intervening. The major feature that was created by this orogeny was the Rocky Mountains, but evidence of this orogeny can be found from Alaska to northern Mexico, with the easternmost extent of the mountain-building represented by the Black Hills of South Dakota.
   a. Pan-African orogeny
   b. Kaikoura Orogeny
   c. Nevadan orogeny
   d. Laramide orogeny

2. _____ refers to natural mountain building, and may be studied as a tectonic structural event, (b) as a geographical event, and (c) a chronological event. Orogenic events (a) cause distinctive structural phenomena and related tectonic activity, (b) affect certain regions of rocks and crust, and (c) happen within a specific period of time.
   a. Antler orogeny
   b. Orogeny
   c. Orogenesis
   d. Alice Springs Orogeny

3. _____ refers to the mode of igneous volcanic rock formation in which hot magma from inside the Earth flows out (extrudes) onto the surface as lava or explodes violently into the atmosphere to fall back as pyroclastics or tuff. This is opposed to intrusive rock formation, in which magma does not reach the surface.
   a. Extrusive
   b. Ignimbrite
   c. Igneous rock
   d. Augen

4. _____ is one of the three main rock types (the others being sedimentary and metamorphic rock.) _____ is formed by magma (molten rock) being cooled and becoming solid . They may form with or without crystallization, either below the surface as intrusive (plutonic) rocks or on the surface as extrusive (volcanic) rocks. They make up approximately 95% of the upper part of the Earth's crust, but their great abundance is hidden on the Earth's surface by a relatively thin but widespread layer of sedimentary and metamorphic rocks.
   a. Ignimbrite
   b. Igneous rock
   c. Igneous differentiation
   d. Extrusive

5. In geology, an _____ is a body of igneous rock that has crystallized from molten magma below the surface of the Earth. Bodies of magma that solidify underground before they reach the surface of the earth are called plutons the Roman god of the underworld. Correspondingly, rocks of this kind are also referred to as igneous plutonic rocks or igneous intrusive rocks.
   a. AASHTO Soil Classification System
   b. AL 333
   c. AL 129-1
   d. Intrusion

6. _____ is a very coarse-grained igneous rock that has a grain size of 20 mm or more; such rocks are referred to as pegmatitic.

Most _____ is composed of quartz, feldspar and mica; in essence a 'granite'. Rarer 'intermediate' and 'mafic' _____ containing amphibole, Ca-plagioclase feldspar, pyroxene and other minerals are known, found in recrystallised zones and apophyses associated with large layered intrusions.

   a. Pegmatite
   b. 1509 Istanbul earthquake
   c. 1703 Genroku earthquake
   d. 1700 Cascadia earthquake

Chapter 25. Rocky Mountain National Park

7. _____ is a term used in geology to refer to silicate minerals, magma, and rocks which are enriched in the lighter elements such as silicon, oxygen, aluminium, sodium, and potassium. _____ minerals are usually light in color and have specific gravities less than 3. Common _____ minerals include quartz, muscovite, orthoclase, and the sodium-rich plagioclase feldspars.
   a. Felsic
   b. Groundmass
   c. Magma
   d. Volcanic rock

8. _____ is an adjective describing a silicate mineral or rock that is rich in magnesium and iron; the term was derived by contracting 'magnesium' and 'ferric'. Most _____ minerals are dark in color and the specific gravity is greater than 3. Common rock-forming _____ minerals include olivine, pyroxene, amphibole, and biotite.

_____ lava, before cooling, has a low viscosity, in comparison to felsic lava, due to the lower silica content in _____ magma. Water and other volatiles can more easily and gradually escape from _____ lava, so eruptions of volcanoes made of _____ lavas are less explosively violent than felsic lava eruptions.

   a. 1509 Istanbul earthquake
   b. 1700 Cascadia earthquake
   c. 1703 Genroku earthquake
   d. Mafic

9. _____ is molten rock that is found beneath the surface of the Earth, and may also exist on other terrestrial planets. Besides molten rock, _____ may also contain suspended crystals and gas bubbles. _____ often collects in a _____ chamber inside a volcano. _____ is capable of intrusion into adjacent rocks, extrusion onto the surface as lava, and explosive ejection as tephra to form pyroclastic rock.
   a. Groundmass
   b. Sedimentary rock
   c. Large igneous provinces
   d. Magma

10. In materials science, _____ is the distribution of crystallographic orientations of a polycrystalline sample. A sample in which these orientations are fully random is said to have no _____. If the crystallographic orientations are not random, but have some preferred orientation, then the sample has a weak, strong, or moderate _____.
   a. Diamond Head
   b. Geothermal
   c. Platform
   d. Texture

11. The _____ Era, is the most recent of the three classic geological eras and covers the period from 65.5 million years ago to the present. It is marked by the Cretaceous-Tertiary extinction event at the end of the Cretaceous that saw the demise of the last non-avian dinosaurs and the end of the Mesozoic Era. The _____ era is ongoing.
   a. 1509 Istanbul earthquake
   b. 1700 Cascadia earthquake
   c. 1703 Genroku earthquake
   d. Cenozoic

12. The _____ , usually abbreviated K for its German translation Kreide, is a geologic period and system from circa >145.5 >± 4 to >65.5 >± 0.3 million years ago . In the geologic timescale, the _____ follows on the Jurassic period and is followed by the Paleogene period. It is the youngest period of the Mesozoic era, and at 80 million years long, the longest period of the Phanerozoic eon. The end of the _____ defines the boundary between the Mesozoic and Cenozoic eras.
   a. Cretaceous
   b. Campanian
   c. Valanginian
   d. Hauterivian

13. In stratigraphy, _____ is the native consolidated rock underlying the surface of a terrestrial planet, usually the Earth. Above the _____ is usually an area of broken and weathered unconsolidated rock in the basal subsoil. The top of the _____ is known as rockhead and identifying this, via excavations, drilling or geophysical methods, is an important task in most civil engineering projects.

   a. Bedrock
   c. Sequence stratigraphy
   b. Polystrate
   d. Biozones

14. _____ is the solid-state recrystallization of pre-existing rocks due to changes in physical and chemical conditions, primarily heat, pressure, and the introduction of chemically active fluids. Both mineralogical, chemical and crystallographic changes can occur during this process.

Three types of _____ exist: dynamic, contact and regional.

   a. Pumice raft
   c. Metamorphism
   b. Lake capture
   d. Gibraltar Arc

15. _____ occurs typically around intrusive igneous rocks as a result of the temperature increase caused by the intrusion of magma into cooler country rock. The area surrounding the intrusion (called aureoles) where the _____ effects are present is called the metamorphic aureole. Contact metamorphic rocks are usually known as hornfels.

   a. Sea-level curve
   c. Georeactor
   b. Dispersion
   d. Contact metamorphism

16. The _____ Era is one of three geologic eras of the Phanerozoic eon. The division of time into eras dates back to Giovanni Arduino, in the 18th century, although his original name for the era now called the '_____' was 'Secondary' (making the modern era the 'Tertiary'.)

The _____ was a time of tectonic, climatic and evolutionary activity. The continents gradually shifted from a state of connectedness into their present configuration; the drifting provided for speciation and other important evolutionary developments.

   a. 1700 Cascadia earthquake
   c. 1703 Genroku earthquake
   b. 1509 Istanbul earthquake
   d. Mesozoic

17. The _____ is the earliest of three geologic eras of the Phanerozoic eon. The _____ spanned from roughly 542 to 251 million years ago (ICS, 2004), and is subdivided into six geologic periods; from oldest to youngest they are: the Cambrian, Ordovician, Silurian, Devonian, Carboniferous, and Permian.

The _____ covers the time from the first appearance of abundant, soft-shelled fossils to the time when the continents were beginning to be dominated by large, relatively sophisticated reptiles and modern plants. The lower (oldest) boundary was classically set at the first appearance of creatures known as trilobites and archeocyathids.

   a. 1700 Cascadia earthquake
   c. Paleozoic
   b. 1509 Istanbul earthquake
   d. 1703 Genroku earthquake

Chapter 25. Rocky Mountain National Park

18. The term _____ is used in geology when one or a stack of originally flat and planar surfaces, such as sedimentary strata, are bent or curved as a result of plastic (i.e. permanent) deformation. Synsedimentary _____s are those due to slumping of sedimentary material before it is lithified. _____s in rocks vary in size from microscopic crinkles to mountain-sized _____s.
  a. Fold
  b. 1703 Genroku earthquake
  c. 1509 Istanbul earthquake
  d. 1700 Cascadia earthquake

19. _____ is molten rock expelled by a volcano during eruption. When first expelled from a volcanic vent, it is a liquid at temperatures from 700 >°C to 1,200 >°C (1,300 >°F to 2,200 >°F.) Although _____ is quite viscous, with about 100,000 times the viscosity of water, it can flow great distances before cooling and solidifying, because of both its thixotropic and shear thinning properties.
  a. Pyroclastic flow
  b. Volcanic ash
  c. Cinder
  d. Lava

20. In geography and geology, a _____ is a significant vertical, or near vertical, rock exposure. _____s are formed as erosion landforms due to the processes of erosion and weathering that produce them. _____s are common on coasts, in mountainous areas, escarpments and along rivers. _____s are usually formed by rock that is resistant to erosion and weathering. Sedimentary rocks are most likely to form sandstone, limestone, chalk, and dolomite. Igneous rocks, such as granite and basalt also often form _____s.
  a. 1700 Cascadia earthquake
  b. 1703 Genroku earthquake
  c. 1509 Istanbul earthquake
  d. Cliff

21. _____ is a term used in geology to refer to the state of gravitational equilibrium between the earth's lithosphere and asthenosphere such that the tectonic plates 'float' at an elevation which depends on their thickness and density. This concept is invoked to explain how different topographic heights can exist at the Earth's surface. When a certain area of lithosphere reaches the state of _____, it is said to be in isostatic equilibrium.
  a. Economic geology
  b. Orientation Tensor
  c. Isograd
  d. Isostasy

22. _____ circulation in its most general sense is the circulation of hot water; 'hydros' in the Greek meaning water and 'thermos' meaning heat. _____ circulation occurs most often in the vicinity of sources of heat within the Earth's crust. This generally occurs near volcanic activity, but can occur in the deep crust related to the intrusion of granite, or as the result of orogeny or metamorphism.
  a. Transgression
  b. Headward erosion
  c. Seafloor spreading
  d. Hydrothermal

23. A _____ or inselberg is an isolated rock hill, knob, ridge, or small mountain that rises abruptly from a gently sloping or virtually level surrounding plain. The term '_____' is usually used in the United States, whereas 'inselberg' is the more common international term. In southern and southern-central Africa, a similar formation of granite is known as a kopje (in fact a Dutch word) from the Afrikaans word: koppie.

_____ is an originally Native American term for an isolated hill or a lone mountain that has risen above the surrounding area, typically by surviving erosion.

a. Monadnock
b. Rogen moraine
c. Sandur
d. 1509 Istanbul earthquake

24. The _____ is a a term for a geologic period 65 million to 1.8 million years ago. The _____ covered the time span between the superseded Secondary period and an out-of-date definition of the Quaternary period. The period began with the demise of the non-avian dinosaurs in the Cretaceous-_____ extinction event, at start of the Cenozoic era, spanning to beginning of the most recent Ice Age, at the end of the Pliocene epoch.
   a. Tertiary
   b. Logarithmic Spiral Beach
   c. Historical geology
   d. Loihi Seamount

25. The _____ is the epoch from 1.8 million to 11550 years BP covering the world's recent period of repeated glaciations. The _____ epoch follows the Pliocene epoch and is followed by the Holocene epoch. The _____ is the third epoch of the Neogene period or 6th epoch of the Cenozoic Era. The end of the _____ corresponds with the retreat of the last continental glacier. It also corresponds with the end of the Paleolithic age used in archaeology.
   a. Tyrrhenian
   b. Pleistocene
   c. Sicilian Stage
   d. Late Pleistocene

26. The _____ is an informal name for the supereon comprising the eons of the geologic timescale that came before the current Phanerozoic eon. It spans from the formation of Earth around 4500 Mya (million years ago) to the evolution of abundant macroscopic hard-shelled animals, which marked the beginning of the Cambrian, the first period of the first era of the Phanerozoic eon, some 542 Mya. It is named after the Roman name for Wales - Cambria - where rocks from this age were first studied.
   a. 1700 Cascadia earthquake
   b. 1703 Genroku earthquake
   c. Precambrian
   d. 1509 Istanbul earthquake

27. _____ are distinctive geomorphological landforms of blocky detritus which may extend outward and downslope from talus cones or from glaciers or the terminal moraines of glaciers. Their growth and formation is subject to some debate, with three main theories in prominence:

   - They originated from cirque glaciers and contain a glacial ice core or interstitial ice between the rocks which causes the formation to move downslope;

   - A permafrost origin, which implies that the features are related to permafrost action rather than glacial action;

   - A mass wasting or landslide origin which does not require the presence of ice and suggests a sudden catastrophic origin with little subsequent movement.

   _____ may move or creep at a very slow rate in part dependent on the amount of ice present.

   a. Pastonian Stage
   b. Rock glaciers
   c. Pressure melting point
   d. Pre-Pastonian Stage

28. In geology, _____ is transported rock debris overlying the solid bedrock. The term is also sometimes refers to organic debris so-transported. In the largest sense, it refers to the material left behind by retreating continental glaciers.

Chapter 25. Rocky Mountain National Park

a. Geomechanics
b. Metamorphic reaction
c. Riegel
d. Drift

29. A _____ is a large, slow-moving mass of ice, formed from compacted layers of snow, that slowly deforms and flows in response to gravity and high pressure.

_____ ice is the largest reservoir of fresh water on Earth, and second only to oceans as the largest reservoir of total water.

a. Little Ice Age
b. Deforestation
c. Keeling Curve
d. Glacier

30. A _____ is a piece of rock that differs from the size and type of rock native to the area in which it rests. They are carried by glacial ice, often over distances of hundreds of kilometres and can range in size from pebbles to large boulders such as Big Rock (16,500 tons) in Alberta.
a. 1509 Istanbul earthquake
b. 1700 Cascadia earthquake
c. 1703 Genroku earthquake
d. Glacial erratic

31. A _____ is a lake with origins in a melted glacier.

_____s can be green as a result of pulverized minerals (rock flour) that support a large population of algae.

A retreating glacier often leaves behind large deposits of ice in hollows between drumlins or hills. As the ice age ends, these will melt to create lakes.

a. Bergschrund
b. Pastonian Stage
c. Pressure melting point
d. Glacial lake

32. _____ is a term used to describe the distinct, and often symmetrical geometric shapes formed by ground material in periglacial regions. Typically found in remote regions of the Arctic, Antarctica, and the Australian outback, but also found anywhere that freezing and thawing of soil alternate, the geometric shapes and patterns associated with _____ are often mistaken as artistic human creations. The nature of _____ puzzled scientists for ages.
a. Gibraltar Arc
b. Megamullion
c. Pneumatolysis
d. Patterned ground

33. In geology, _____ is a type of mass wasting where waterlogged sediment slowly moves downslope over impermeable material. It can occur in any climate where the ground is saturated by water, though it is most often found in periglacial environments where the ground is permanently frozen, under which conditions the process is often called gelifluction. During warm seasonal periods the surface layer melts and slides over the frozen underlayer, slowly moving downslope due to frost heave that occurs normal to the slope.
a. Solifluction
b. Rockfall
c. Geohazard
d. Sturzstrom

34. _____ is the geomorphic process by which soil, regolith, and rock move downslope under the force of gravity. Types of _____ include creep, slides, flows, topples, and falls, each with its own characteristic features, and taking place over timescales from seconds to years. _____ occurs on both terrestrial and submarine slopes, and has been observed on Earth, Mars, and Venus.
   a. 1700 Cascadia earthquake
   b. 1509 Istanbul earthquake
   c. Soil liquefaction
   d. Mass wasting

35. A _____ or dyke in geology is a type of sheet intrusion referring to any geologic body that cuts discordantly across

   - planar wall rock structures, such as bedding or foliation
   - massive rock formations, like igneous/magmatic intrusions and salt diapirs.

They can therefore be either intrusive or sedimentary in origin.

An intrusive _____ is an igneous body with a very high aspect ratio, which means that its thickness is usually much smaller than the other two dimensions. Thickness can vary from sub-centimeter scale to many meters and the lateral dimensions can extend over many kilometers. A _____ is an intrusion into an opening cross-cutting fissure, shouldering aside other pre-existing layers or bodies of rock; this implies that a _____ is always younger than the rocks that contain it.

   a. Dike
   b. Gradualism
   c. Detritus
   d. Type locality

36. The _____ is a geologic subperiod and stratigraphic subsystem of the Carboniferous Period. It is the later subperiod of the Carboniferous, lasting from roughly 318.1>± 1.3 to 299>± 0.8 Ma (million years ago.) As with most other geochronologic units, the rock beds that define the _____ are well identified, but the exact date of the start and end are uncertain by a few million years.
   a. Calciferous sandstone
   b. Pennsylvanian
   c. Dinantian
   d. Mississippian

37. The _____ is a glacial period that began roughly 200,000 years ago and ended 130,000 years ago when several large sheets of ice moved down the Buffalo River valley from the north and from the Teton Range in the west. The name _____ itself is derived from the well-preserved moraines found in the vicinity of Bull Lake near the Wind River Mountains.

The glacial till from this period is most apparent around Jenny Lake.

   a. Firn
   b. Bull Lake glaciation
   c. Bramertonian Stage
   d. Glacial plucking

38. _____, also known as the Pleistocene glaciation, the current ice age or simply the ice age, refers to the period of the last few million years in which permanent ice sheets were established in Antarctica and perhaps Greenland, and fluctuating ice sheets have occurred elsewhere The major effects of the ice age were erosion and deposition of material over large parts of the continents, modification of river systems, creation of millions of lakes, changes in sea level, development of pluvial lakes far from the ice margins, isostatic adjustment of the crust, and abnormal winds. It affected oceans, flooding, and biological communities.

a. Wolstonian Stage
c. Snowball Earth
b. Rock glaciers
d. Quaternary glaciation

39. The general term '_____' or, more precisely, 'glacial age' denotes a geological period of long-term reduction in the temperature of the Earth's surface and atmosphere, resulting in an expansion of continental ice sheets, polar ice sheets and alpine glaciers. Within a long-term _____, individual pulses of extra cold climate are termed 'glaciations'. Glaciologically, _____ implies the presence of extensive ice sheets in the northern and southern hemispheres; by this definition we are still in an _____
   a. AASHTO Soil Classification System
   c. AL 333
   b. AL 129-1
   d. Ice Age

40. The _____ was a period of cooling occurring after a warmer North Atlantic era known as the Medieval Warm Period. While not a true ice age, the term was introduced into scientific literature by Fran>çois E. Matthes in 1939. Climatologists and historians working with local records no longer expect to agree on either the start or end dates of this period, which varied according to local conditions.
   a. Deforestation
   c. Glacier
   b. Little Ice Age
   d. Pacific Decadal Oscillation

41. The _____ describes the documented cooling trend in the Earth's climate during the Holocene, following the retreat of the Wisconsin glaciation, the most recent glacial period. _____ has followed the hypsithermal or Holocene Climatic Optimum, the warmest point in the Earth's climate during the current interglacial stage. The _____ has no well-marked universal beginning: local conditions and ecological inertia affected the onset of detectably cooler (and wetter) conditions.
   a. 1700 Cascadia earthquake
   c. Holocene glacial retreat
   b. Neoglaciation
   d. 1509 Istanbul earthquake

Chapter 26. Waterton-Glacier International Peace Park

1. A _____ is an amphitheatre-like valley formed at the head of a glacier by erosion. A _____ is also known as a coombe or coomb in England, a combe or comb in America, a corrie in Scotland and Ireland, and a cwm in Wales, although these terms apply to a specific feature of which several may be found in a _____. The term 'comb' is often found at the end of placenames such as Newcomb and Maycomb, where it is pronounced /kÉ™m/.
   a. 1703 Genroku earthquake
   b. 1700 Cascadia earthquake
   c. 1509 Istanbul earthquake
   d. Cirque

2. A _____ is a drainage divide on a continent such that the drainage basin on one side of the divide feeds into one ocean or sea and the basin on the other side either feeds into a different ocean or sea, or else is endorheic, not connected to the open sea. The endpoints where a _____ meets the coast are not always definite, because the exact border between adjacent bodies of water is usually not clearly defined. The International Hydrographic Organization's publication Limits of Oceans and Seas defines exact boundaries of oceans, but it is not universally recognized.
   a. 1509 Istanbul earthquake
   b. 1700 Cascadia earthquake
   c. 1703 Genroku earthquake
   d. Continental Divide

3. _____ is caused by movement of ice, typically as glaciers. Glaciers erode predominantly by three different processes: abrasion/scouring, plucking, and ice thrusting. In an abrasion process, debris in the basal ice scrapes along the bed, polishing and gouging the underlying rocks, similar to sandpaper on wood. Glaciers can also cause pieces of bedrock to crack off in the process of plucking. In ice thrusting, the glacier freezes to its bed, then as it surges forward, it moves large sheets of frozen sediment at the base along with the glacier. This method produced some of the many thousands of lake basins that dot the edge of the Canadian Shield. These processes, combined with erosion and transport by the water network beneath the glacier, leave moraines, drumlins, eskers, ground moraine (till), kames, kame deltas, moulins, and glacial erratics in their wake, typically at the terminus or during glacier retreat.
   a. Ice erosion
   b. AL 333
   c. AASHTO Soil Classification System
   d. AL 129-1

4. The general term '_____' or, more precisely, 'glacial age' denotes a geological period of long-term reduction in the temperature of the Earth's surface and atmosphere, resulting in an expansion of continental ice sheets, polar ice sheets and alpine glaciers. Within a long-term _____, individual pulses of extra cold climate are termed 'glaciations'. Glaciologically, _____ implies the presence of extensive ice sheets in the northern and southern hemispheres; by this definition we are still in an _____
   a. AL 333
   b. Ice Age
   c. AL 129-1
   d. AASHTO Soil Classification System

5. The _____ was a period of cooling occurring after a warmer North Atlantic era known as the Medieval Warm Period. While not a true ice age, the term was introduced into scientific literature by Fran>çois E. Matthes in 1939. Climatologists and historians working with local records no longer expect to agree on either the start or end dates of this period, which varied according to local conditions.
   a. Deforestation
   b. Pacific Decadal Oscillation
   c. Glacier
   d. Little Ice Age

6. The _____ is the epoch from 1.8 million to 11550 years BP covering the world's recent period of repeated glaciations. The _____ epoch follows the Pliocene epoch and is followed by the Holocene epoch. The _____ is the third epoch of the Neogene period or 6th epoch of the Cenozoic Era. The end of the _____ corresponds with the retreat of the last continental glacier. It also corresponds with the end of the Paleolithic age used in archaeology.
   a. Sicilian Stage
   b. Late Pleistocene
   c. Pleistocene
   d. Tyrrhenian

7. The _____ is a geological eon representing a period before the first abundant complex life on Earth. The _____ extended from 2500 Ma to 542.0 >± 1.0 Ma (million years ago), and is the most recent part of the old, informally named 'e;Precambrian'e; time.

The Proterozoic consists of 3 geologic eras, from oldest to youngest:

- Paleoproterozoic
- Mesoproterozoic
- Neoproterozoic

The well-identified events were:

- The transition to an oxygenated atmosphere during the Mesoproterozoic.
- Several glaciations, including the hypothesized Snowball Earth during the Cryogenian period in the late Neoproterozoic.
- The Ediacaran Period (635 to 542 Ma) which is characterized by the evolution of abundant soft-bodied multicellular organisms.

The geoloic record of the Proterozoic is much better than that for the preceding Archean. In contrast to the deep-water deposits of the Archean, the Proterozoic features many strata that were laid down in extensive shallow epicontinental seas; furthermore, many of these rocks are less metamorphosed than Archean-age ones, and plenty are unaltered.

a. 1703 Genroku earthquake
b. 1700 Cascadia earthquake
c. Proterozoic Eon
d. 1509 Istanbul earthquake

8. _____ is located in Glacier National Park, Montana, United States. It is a hydrologic apex of the North American continent (the other is Snow Dome in Jasper National Park, on the border between Alberta and British Columbia, Canada.) The Continental (Great) Divide and the Laurentian Divide meet at the summit of the peak, and all water that falls at this point can flow to the Pacific and Atlantic Oceans and to Hudson Bay, which opens into the North Atlantic to the north of Labrador.

a. 1703 Genroku earthquake
b. 1700 Cascadia earthquake
c. 1509 Istanbul earthquake
d. Triple Divide Peak

9. _____ is the removal of solids (sediment, soil, rock and other particles) in the natural environment. It usually occurs due to transport by wind, water, or ice; by down-slope creep of soil and other material under the force of gravity; or by living organisms, such as burrowing animals, in the case of bioerosion.

_____ is distinguished from weathering, which is the process of chemical or physical breakdown of the minerals in the rocks, although the two processes may occur concurrently.

a. AASHTO Soil Classification System
b. AL 129-1
c. AL 333
d. Erosion

Chapter 26. Waterton-Glacier International Peace Park

10. A _____ is a tributary valley with the floor at a higher relief than the main channel into which it flows. They are most commonly associated with U-shaped valleys when a tributary glacier flows into a glacier of larger volume. The main glacier erodes a deep U-shaped valley with nearly vertical sides while the tributary glacier, with a smaller volume of ice, makes a shallower U-shaped valley.
   a. 1703 Genroku earthquake
   b. 1509 Istanbul earthquake
   c. 1700 Cascadia earthquake
   d. Hanging valley

11. _____ consists of clay-sized particles of rock, generated by glacial erosion or by artificial grinding to a similar size. Because the material is very small, it becomes suspended in river water making the water appear cloudy.

If the river flows into a glacial lake, the lake may appear turquoise in color as a result.

   a. Snowball Earth
   b. Post-glacial rebound
   c. Pastonian Stage
   d. Rock flour

12. _____ is unsorted glacial sediment. Glacial drift is a general term for the coarsely graded and extremely heterogeneous sediments of glacial origin. Glacial _____ is that part of glacial drift which was deposited directly by the glacier. In cases where _____ has been indurated or lithified by subsequent burial into solid rock, it is known as the sedimentary rock tillite.
   a. 1703 Genroku earthquake
   b. Till
   c. 1700 Cascadia earthquake
   d. 1509 Istanbul earthquake

13. A _____ is a glacial outwash plain formed of sediments deposited by meltwater at the terminus of a glacier.

_____ are found in glaciated areas, such as Svalbard, Kerguelen Islands, and Iceland. Glaciers and icecaps contain large amounts of silt and sediment, picked up as they erode the underlying rocks when they move slowly downhill, and at the snout of the glacier, meltwater can carry this sediment away from the glacier and deposit it on a broad plain.

   a. Rogen moraine
   b. Monadnock
   c. 1509 Istanbul earthquake
   d. Sandur

14. An _____ is a rapid flow of snow down a slope, from either natural triggers or human activity. Typically occurring in mountainous terrain, an _____ can mix air and water with the descending snow. Powerful _____ s have the capability to entrain ice, rocks, trees, and other material on the slope; however _____ s are always initiated in snow, are primarily composed of flowing snow, and are distinct from mudslides, rock slides, rock _____ s, and serac collapses from an icefall.
   a. AASHTO Soil Classification System
   b. AL 333
   c. AL 129-1
   d. Avalanche

15. A _____ is a large, slow-moving mass of ice, formed from compacted layers of snow, that slowly deforms and flows in response to gravity and high pressure.

_____ ice is the largest reservoir of fresh water on Earth, and second only to oceans as the largest reservoir of total water.

a. Keeling Curve
b. Glacier
c. Deforestation
d. Little Ice Age

16. _____ is a term for a formation in rivers caused by a whirlpool eroding a hole into rock. The abrasion is mainly caused by the circular motion of small sediments such as small stones in the river. The interiors of _____s tend to be smooth and regular, unlike a plunge pool.
   a. Subsidence
   b. 1700 Cascadia earthquake
   c. 1509 Istanbul earthquake
   d. Pothole

17. The _____ is an informal name for the supereon comprising the eons of the geologic timescale that came before the current Phanerozoic eon. It spans from the formation of Earth around 4500 Mya (million years ago) to the evolution of abundant macroscopic hard-shelled animals, which marked the beginning of the Cambrian, the first period of the first era of the Phanerozoic eon, some 542 Mya. It is named after the Roman name for Wales - Cambria - where rocks from this age were first studied.
   a. 1700 Cascadia earthquake
   b. 1509 Istanbul earthquake
   c. Precambrian
   d. 1703 Genroku earthquake

18. _____ is one of the three main rock types (the others being sedimentary and metamorphic rock.) _____ is formed by magma (molten rock) being cooled and becoming solid . They may form with or without crystallization, either below the surface as intrusive (plutonic) rocks or on the surface as extrusive (volcanic) rocks. They make up approximately 95% of the upper part of the Earth's crust, but their great abundance is hidden on the Earth's surface by a relatively thin but widespread layer of sedimentary and metamorphic rocks.
   a. Igneous rock
   b. Igneous differentiation
   c. Ignimbrite
   d. Extrusive

19. _____ are pillow-shaped structures sometimes seen in lavas and are attributed to the congealment of lava under water, or subaqeous extrusion. A pillow structure in certain extrusive igneous rock is characterized by discontinuous pillow-shaped masses, commonly up to 1 metre in diameter. _____ commonly occur at Constructive plate boundaries, forming part of a mid-ocean ridge.
   a. Duricrust
   b. Patterned ground
   c. Fabric
   d. Pillow lava

20. _____ is molten rock expelled by a volcano during eruption. When first expelled from a volcanic vent, it is a liquid at temperatures from 700 >°C to 1,200 >°C (1,300 >°F to 2,200 >°F.) Although _____ is quite viscous, with about 100,000 times the viscosity of water, it can flow great distances before cooling and solidifying, because of both its thixotropic and shear thinning properties.
   a. Volcanic ash
   b. Cinder
   c. Pyroclastic flow
   d. Lava

21. _____ refers to a sediment, sedimentary rock, or soil type which is formed from or contains a high proportion of calcium carbonate in the form of calcite or aragonite.

It can also be used as an adjectival term applied to anatomical structures which are made of calcium carbonate in animals such as gastropods, when referring to such structures as the operculum, the clausilium, and the love dart.

_____ sediments are usually deposited in shallow water near land, since the carbonate is precipitated by marine organisms that need land-derived nutrients.

- a. Calcareous
- b. 1703 Genroku earthquake
- c. 1700 Cascadia earthquake
- d. 1509 Istanbul earthquake

22. _____ is a common and widely occurring type of intrusive, felsic, igneous rock. _____ has a medium to coarse texture, occasionally with some individual crystals larger than the groundmass forming a rock known as porphyry. _____s can be pink to dark gray or even black, depending on their chemistry and mineralogy.
- a. 1703 Genroku earthquake
- b. 1509 Istanbul earthquake
- c. 1700 Cascadia earthquake
- d. Granite

23. The _____ is a geologic fault structure of the Rocky Mountains within Glacier National Park in Montana, USA and Waterton Lakes National Park in Alberta, Canada, as well as into Lewis and Clark National Forest. It provides scientific insight into geologic processes happening in other parts of the world, like the Andes and the Himalaya Mountains. Scientific study of this region is practical because the original rock characteristics were well-preserved and recently sculptured by glaciers.
- a. 1509 Istanbul earthquake
- b. Lewis overthrust
- c. 1703 Genroku earthquake
- d. 1700 Cascadia earthquake

24. _____ is a liquid or semi-liquid mixture of water and some combination of soil, silt, and clay. Ancient _____ deposits harden over geological time to form sedimentary rock such as siltstone or solid, mudrock lutites. When geological deposits of _____ are formed in estuaries the resultant layers are termed bay _____s.
- a. Surface runoff
- b. Thermal pollution
- c. Continental slope
- d. Mud

25. In geology, _____ are sedimentary structures that indicate agitation by water (current or waves) or wind. _____ formed by water consist of two basic types:

1. Current _____ are asymmetrical in profile, with a gentle up-current slope and a steeper down-current slope. The down-current slope depends on the shape of the sediment, with 33>° being typical.
2. Wave-formed _____ have a symmetrical, almost sinusoidal profile; they indicate an environment with weak currents where water motion is dominated by wave oscillations.

Ripples will not form in sediment larger than course sand.

- a. 1509 Istanbul earthquake
- b. Ripple marks
- c. 1700 Cascadia earthquake
- d. 1703 Genroku earthquake

26. _____ are layered accretionary structures formed in shallow water by the trapping, binding and cementation of sedimentary grains by biofilms of microorganisms, especially cyanobacteria (commonly known as blue-green algae.)

A variety of stromatolite morphologies exist including conical, stratiform, branching, domal, and columnar types. _____ occur widely in the fossil record of the Precambrian, but are rare today.

a. 1509 Istanbul earthquake
c. 1700 Cascadia earthquake
b. 1703 Genroku earthquake
d. Stromatolites

27. _____ form when the vesicular cavities (created by expanding gas bubbles in volcanic lava) are filled with a secondary mineral such as calcite, quartz, chlorite or one of the zeolites, which are deposited by having minerals 'wash' through the pores in the rock They are filled from the outside, making some _____ concentrically layered.
   a. Amygdules
   b. Extrusive
   c. Augen
   d. Igneous rock

28. _____ is a common extrusive volcanic rock. It is usually grey to black and fine-grained due to rapid cooling of lava at the surface of a planet. It may be porphyritic containing larger crystals in a fine matrix, or vesicular, or frothy scoria.
   a. 1509 Istanbul earthquake
   b. 1700 Cascadia earthquake
   c. 1703 Genroku earthquake
   d. Basalt

29. _____ is a volcanic rock texture characterised by, or containing many vesicles. The texture is often found in extrusive aphanitic igneous rock. The vesicles are small cavities formed by the expansion of bubbles of gas or steam during the solidification of the rock.
   a. Rock cycle
   b. Pluton
   c. Large igneous provinces
   d. Vesicular texture

Chapter 27. Gates of the Arctic National Park and Preserve

1. In geology, _____ or _____ soil is soil at or below the freezing point of water (0 >°C or 32 >°F) for two or more years. Ice is not always present, as may be in the case of nonporous bedrock, but it frequently occurs and it may be in amounts exceeding the potential hydraulic saturation of the ground material. Most _____ is located in high latitudes (i.e. land in close proximity to the North and South poles), but alpine _____ may exist at high altitudes in much lower latitudes.
   a. 1703 Genroku earthquake
   b. 1700 Cascadia earthquake
   c. 1509 Istanbul earthquake
   d. Permafrost

2. The _____ is a a term for a geologic period 65 million to 1.8 million years ago. The _____ covered the time span between the superseded Secondary period and an out-of-date definition of the Quaternary period. The period began with the demise of the non-avian dinosaurs in the Cretaceous-_____ extinction event, at start of the Cenozoic era, spanning to beginning of the most recent Ice Age, at the end of the Pliocene epoch.
   a. Loihi Seamount
   b. Logarithmic Spiral Beach
   c. Historical geology
   d. Tertiary

3. _____ consists of clay-sized particles of rock, generated by glacial erosion or by artificial grinding to a similar size. Because the material is very small, it becomes suspended in river water making the water appear cloudy.

   If the river flows into a glacial lake, the lake may appear turquoise in color as a result.
   a. Snowball Earth
   b. Rock flour
   c. Post-glacial rebound
   d. Pastonian Stage

4. A _____ is a rock consisting of individual stones that have become cemented together. They are sedimentary rocks consisting of rounded fragments and are thus differentiated from breccias, which consist of angular clasts. Both _____ s and breccias are characterized by clasts larger than sand (>2 mm).
   a. Concretion
   b. Keystone
   c. Conglomerate
   d. Pelagic sediments

5. The _____ is the earliest of three geologic eras of the Phanerozoic eon. The _____ spanned from roughly 542 to 251 million years ago (ICS, 2004), and is subdivided into six geologic periods; from oldest to youngest they are: the Cambrian, Ordovician, Silurian, Devonian, Carboniferous, and Permian.

   The _____ covers the time from the first appearance of abundant, soft-shelled fossils to the time when the continents were beginning to be dominated by large, relatively sophisticated reptiles and modern plants. The lower (oldest) boundary was classically set at the first appearance of creatures known as trilobites and archeocyathids.
   a. 1703 Genroku earthquake
   b. 1509 Istanbul earthquake
   c. 1700 Cascadia earthquake
   d. Paleozoic

6. The _____ is an informal name for the supereon comprising the eons of the geologic timescale that came before the current Phanerozoic eon. It spans from the formation of Earth around 4500 Mya (million years ago) to the evolution of abundant macroscopic hard-shelled animals, which marked the beginning of the Cambrian, the first period of the first era of the Phanerozoic eon, some 542 Mya. It is named after the Roman name for Wales - Cambria - where rocks from this age were first studied.

a. Precambrian
b. 1703 Genroku earthquake
c. 1700 Cascadia earthquake
d. 1509 Istanbul earthquake

7. The _____ Era is one of three geologic eras of the Phanerozoic eon. The division of time into eras dates back to Giovanni Arduino, in the 18th century, although his original name for the era now called the '_____' was 'Secondary' (making the modern era the 'Tertiary'.)

The _____ was a time of tectonic, climatic and evolutionary activity. The continents gradually shifted from a state of connectedness into their present configuration; the drifting provided for speciation and other important evolutionary developments.

a. 1509 Istanbul earthquake
b. 1703 Genroku earthquake
c. 1700 Cascadia earthquake
d. Mesozoic

8. The _____ Period is the geologic time period after the Neogene Period, spanning 1.805 +/- 0.005 million years ago to the present. The _____ includes two geologic epochs: the Pleistocene and the Holocene Epoch.

There is an ongoing debate of the status of _____ -- a recent proposal from International Commission on Stratigraphy (ICS) was to make _____ a subperiod under Neogene, but that was retracted after criticism from International Union for _____ Research (INQUA), so instead ICS and INQUA agreed to erect _____ as an Era, above Neogene, and to place the base for _____ at 2.588 >± 3.005, the base for Gelasian Stage.

a. Geomorphology
b. Yilgarn Craton
c. Tributary
d. Quaternary

1. The _____ is the first geological period of the Phanerozoic eon, lasting from 542 ± 0.3 million years ago to 488.3 ± 1.7 million years ago (ICS, 2004); it is succeeded by the Ordovician. Its subdivisions, and indeed its base, are somewhat in flux. The period was established by Adam Sedgwick, who named it after Cambria, the classical name for Wales, where Britain's _____ rocks are best exposed.
   a. Cambrian
   b. 1703 Genroku earthquake
   c. 1509 Istanbul earthquake
   d. 1700 Cascadia earthquake

2. A _____ or sometimes ayre is a deposition landform in which an island is attached to the mainland by a narrow piece of land such as a spit or bar. They usually form because the island causes wave refraction, depositing sand and shingle moved by longshore drift in each direction around the island where the waves meet. Eustatic sea level rise may also contribute to accretion as material is pushed up with rising sea levels.
   a. 1700 Cascadia earthquake
   b. 1509 Istanbul earthquake
   c. Ria
   d. Tombolo

3. The _____, usually abbreviated K for its German translation Kreide, is a geologic period and system from circa >145.5 >± 4 to >65.5 >± 0.3 million years ago. In the geologic timescale, the _____ follows on the Jurassic period and is followed by the Paleogene period. It is the youngest period of the Mesozoic era, and at 80 million years long, the longest period of the Phanerozoic eon. The end of the _____ defines the boundary between the Mesozoic and Cenozoic eras.
   a. Hauterivian
   b. Campanian
   c. Cretaceous
   d. Valanginian

4. In stratigraphy, _____ is the native consolidated rock underlying the surface of a terrestrial planet, usually the Earth. Above the _____ is usually an area of broken and weathered unconsolidated rock in the basal subsoil. The top of the _____ is known as rockhead and identifying this, via excavations, drilling or geophysical methods, is an important task in most civil engineering projects.
   a. Bedrock
   b. Biozones
   c. Polystrate
   d. Sequence stratigraphy

5. The _____ is the earliest of three geologic eras of the Phanerozoic eon. The _____ spanned from roughly 542 to 251 million years ago (ICS, 2004), and is subdivided into six geologic periods; from oldest to youngest they are: the Cambrian, Ordovician, Silurian, Devonian, Carboniferous, and Permian.

   The _____ covers the time from the first appearance of abundant, soft-shelled fossils to the time when the continents were beginning to be dominated by large, relatively sophisticated reptiles and modern plants. The lower (oldest) boundary was classically set at the first appearance of creatures known as trilobites and archeocyathids.

   a. 1700 Cascadia earthquake
   b. 1703 Genroku earthquake
   c. 1509 Istanbul earthquake
   d. Paleozoic

6. The _____ is a geological eon representing a period before the first abundant complex life on Earth. The _____ extended from 2500 Ma to 542.0 >± 1.0 Ma (million years ago), and is the most recent part of the old, informally named 'e;Precambrian'e; time.

The Proterozoic consists of 3 geologic eras, from oldest to youngest:

- Paleoproterozoic
- Mesoproterozoic
- Neoproterozoic

The well-identified events were:

- The transition to an oxygenated atmosphere during the Mesoproterozoic.
- Several glaciations, including the hypothesized Snowball Earth during the Cryogenian period in the late Neoproterozoic.
- The Ediacaran Period (635 to 542 Ma) which is characterized by the evolution of abundant soft-bodied multicellular organisms.

The geoloic record of the Proterozoic is much better than that for the preceding Archean. In contrast to the deep-water deposits of the Archean, the Proterozoic features many strata that were laid down in extensive shallow epicontinental seas; furthermore, many of these rocks are less metamorphosed than Archean-age ones, and plenty are unaltered.

a. 1509 Istanbul earthquake
b. 1703 Genroku earthquake
c. 1700 Cascadia earthquake
d. Proterozoic Eon

7. A _____ is a large emplacement of igneous intrusive rock that forms from cooled magma deep in the Earth's crust. they are almost always made mostly of felsic or intermediate rock-types, such as granite, quartz monzonite, or diorite

Although they may appear uniform, _____s are in fact structures with complex histories and compositions.

a. Welded tuff
b. Litchfieldite
c. Batholith
d. Country rock

8. _____ is a common and widely occurring type of intrusive, felsic, igneous rock. _____ has a medium to coarse texture, occasionally with some individual crystals larger than the groundmass forming a rock known as porphyry. _____s can be pink to dark gray or even black, depending on their chemistry and mineralogy.

a. Granite
b. 1509 Istanbul earthquake
c. 1703 Genroku earthquake
d. 1700 Cascadia earthquake

9. In geology, an _____ is a body of igneous rock that has crystallized from molten magma below the surface of the Earth. Bodies of magma that solidify underground before they reach the surface of the earth are called plutons the Roman god of the underworld. Correspondingly, rocks of this kind are also referred to as igneous plutonic rocks or igneous intrusive rocks.

a. AASHTO Soil Classification System
b. AL 333
c. Intrusion
d. AL 129-1

10. The _____ Era is one of three geologic eras of the Phanerozoic eon. The division of time into eras dates back to Giovanni Arduino, in the 18th century, although his original name for the era now called the '_____' was 'Secondary' (making the modern era the 'Tertiary'.)

The _____ was a time of tectonic, climatic and evolutionary activity. The continents gradually shifted from a state of connectedness into their present configuration; the drifting provided for speciation and other important evolutionary developments.

   a. 1509 Istanbul earthquake   b. 1700 Cascadia earthquake
   c. Mesozoic   d. 1703 Genroku earthquake

11. A _____ in geology is an intrusive igneous rock body that crystallized from a magma slowly cooling below the surface of the Earth. _____s include batholiths, dikes, sills, laccoliths, lopoliths, and other igneous bodies. In practice, '_____' usually refers to a distinctive mass of igneous rock, typically kilometers in dimension, without a tabular shape like those of dikes and sills.
   a. Matrix   b. Tephra
   c. Petrology   d. Pluton

12. The _____ Era, is the most recent of the three classic geological eras and covers the period from 65.5 million years ago to the present. It is marked by the Cretaceous-Tertiary extinction event at the end of the Cretaceous that saw the demise of the last non-avian dinosaurs and the end of the Mesozoic Era. The _____ era is ongoing.
   a. 1703 Genroku earthquake   b. 1509 Istanbul earthquake
   c. 1700 Cascadia earthquake   d. Cenozoic

13. _____ is one of the most important geochemical and physical processes operating within the Earth's crust and mantle. _____ is the removal and segregation from a melt of mineral precipitates; except in special cases, removal of the crystals changes the composition of the magma. _____ in silicate melts (magmas) is complex compared to crystallization in chemical systems at constant pressure and composition, because changes in pressure and composition can have dramatic effects on magma evolution.
   a. Combe   b. Texture
   c. Deformation   d. Fractional crystallization

14. _____ is the (natural or artificial) process of formation of solid crystals precipitating from a solution, melt or more rarely deposited directly from a gas. _____ is also a chemical solid-liquid separation technique, in which mass transfer of a solute from the liquid solution to a pure solid crystalline phase occurs.

The _____ process consists of two major events, nucleation and crystal growth.

   a. 1509 Istanbul earthquake   b. 1700 Cascadia earthquake
   c. Crystallization   d. 1703 Genroku earthquake

15. In the earth sciences and geology sub-fields, a _____ or physical feature comprises a geomorphological unit, and is largely defined by its surface form and location in the landscape, as part of the terrain, and as such, is typically an element of topography. _____ elements also include seascape and oceanic waterbody interface features such as bays, peninsulas, seas and so forth, including sub-surface terrain features such as submersed mountain ranges, volcanoes, and the great ocean basins under the thin skin of water, for the whole earth is the province and domain of geology. This panorama in Great Smoky Mountains National Park has the readily identifiable physical features of a rolling plain, actually part of a broad valley, distant foothills, and a backdrop of the old much weathered Appalachian mountain range.

_____s are categorised by characteristic physical attributes such as elevation, slope, orientation, stratification, rock exposure, and soil type.

- a. Polar deserts
- b. 1509 Istanbul earthquake
- c. 1700 Cascadia earthquake
- d. Landform

16. In materials science, _____ is the distribution of crystallographic orientations of a polycrystalline sample. A sample in which these orientations are fully random is said to have no _____. If the crystallographic orientations are not random, but have some preferred orientation, then the sample has a weak, strong, or moderate _____.
- a. Diamond Head
- b. Platform
- c. Geothermal
- d. Texture

17. A _____ is a large, slow-moving mass of ice, formed from compacted layers of snow, that slowly deforms and flows in response to gravity and high pressure.

_____ ice is the largest reservoir of fresh water on Earth, and second only to oceans as the largest reservoir of total water.

- a. Deforestation
- b. Little Ice Age
- c. Keeling Curve
- d. Glacier

18. In geology the term _____ refers to a fracture in rock where there has been no lateral movement in the plane of the fracture (up, down or sideways) of one side relative to the other. This makes it different from a fault which is defined as a fracture in rock where one side slides laterally past to the other. _____s normally have a regular spacing related to either the mechanical properties of the individual rock or the thickness of the layer involved.
- a. 1703 Genroku earthquake
- b. 1700 Cascadia earthquake
- c. 1509 Istanbul earthquake
- d. Joint

19. _____ is the decomposition of Earth rocks, soils and their minerals through direct contact with the planet's atmosphere. _____ occurs in situ, or 'with no movement', and thus should not be confused with erosion, which involves the movement of rocks and minerals by agents such as water, ice, wind and gravity.

Two important classifications of _____ processes exist -- physical and chemical _____.

- a. 1700 Cascadia earthquake
- b. Weathering
- c. Physical weathering
- d. 1509 Istanbul earthquake

20. A _____ is a lake with origins in a melted glacier.

_____s can be green as a result of pulverized minerals (rock flour) that support a large population of algae.

A retreating glacier often leaves behind large deposits of ice in hollows between drumlins or hills. As the ice age ends, these will melt to create lakes.

a. Bergschrund
b. Glacial Lake
c. Pressure melting point
d. Pastonian Stage

21. A _____ is a piece of rock that differs from the size and type of rock native to the area in which it rests. They are carried by glacial ice, often over distances of hundreds of kilometres and can range in size from pebbles to large boulders such as Big Rock (16,500 tons) in Alberta.

a. 1703 Genroku earthquake
b. Glacial erratic
c. 1700 Cascadia earthquake
d. 1509 Istanbul earthquake

22. _____ is the removal of solids (sediment, soil, rock and other particles) in the natural environment. It usually occurs due to transport by wind, water, or ice; by down-slope creep of soil and other material under the force of gravity; or by living organisms, such as burrowing animals, in the case of bioerosion.

_____ is distinguished from weathering, which is the process of chemical or physical breakdown of the minerals in the rocks, although the two processes may occur concurrently.

a. AL 333
b. AL 129-1
c. Erosion
d. AASHTO Soil Classification System

23. _____ is caused by movement of ice, typically as glaciers. Glaciers erode predominantly by three different processes: abrasion/scouring, plucking, and ice thrusting. In an abrasion process, debris in the basal ice scrapes along the bed, polishing and gouging the underlying rocks, similar to sandpaper on wood. Glaciers can also cause pieces of bedrock to crack off in the process of plucking. In ice thrusting, the glacier freezes to its bed, then as it surges forward, it moves large sheets of frozen sediment at the base along with the glacier. This method produced some of the many thousands of lake basins that dot the edge of the Canadian Shield. These processes, combined with erosion and transport by the water network beneath the glacier, leave moraines, drumlins, eskers, ground moraine (till), kames, kame deltas, moulins, and glacial erratics in their wake, typically at the terminus or during glacier retreat.

a. AASHTO Soil Classification System
b. AL 129-1
c. AL 333
d. Ice erosion

24. A _____ is a mountain rising from the ocean seafloor that does not reach to the water's surface (sea level), and thus is not an island. These are typically formed from extinct volcanoes, that rise abruptly and are usually found rising from a seafloor of 1,000-4,000 meters depth. They are defined by oceanographers as independent features that rise to at least 1,000 meters above the seafloor.

a. 1509 Istanbul earthquake
b. 1700 Cascadia earthquake
c. 1703 Genroku earthquake
d. Seamount

25. The _____ is an informal name for the supereon comprising the eons of the geologic timescale that came before the current Phanerozoic eon. It spans from the formation of Earth around 4500 Mya (million years ago) to the evolution of abundant macroscopic hard-shelled animals, which marked the beginning of the Cambrian, the first period of the first era of the Phanerozoic eon, some 542 Mya. It is named after the Roman name for Wales - Cambria - where rocks from this age were first studied.
   a. Precambrian
   b. 1703 Genroku earthquake
   c. 1509 Istanbul earthquake
   d. 1700 Cascadia earthquake

26. The _____ is the epoch from 1.8 million to 11550 years BP covering the world's recent period of repeated glaciations. The _____ epoch follows the Pliocene epoch and is followed by the Holocene epoch. The _____ is the third epoch of the Neogene period or 6th epoch of the Cenozoic Era. The end of the _____ corresponds with the retreat of the last continental glacier. It also corresponds with the end of the Paleolithic age used in archaeology.
   a. Late Pleistocene
   b. Tyrrhenian
   c. Sicilian Stage
   d. Pleistocene

27. _____, also known as the Pleistocene glaciation, the current ice age or simply the ice age, refers to the period of the last few million years in which permanent ice sheets were established in Antarctica and perhaps Greenland, and fluctuating ice sheets have occurred elsewhere The major effects of the ice age were erosion and deposition of material over large parts of the continents, modification of river systems, creation of millions of lakes, changes in sea level, development of pluvial lakes far from the ice margins, isostatic adjustment of the crust, and abnormal winds. It affected oceans, flooding, and biological communities.
   a. Rock glaciers
   b. Quaternary glaciation
   c. Wolstonian Stage
   d. Snowball Earth

28. The general term '_____' or, more precisely, 'glacial age' denotes a geological period of long-term reduction in the temperature of the Earth's surface and atmosphere, resulting in an expansion of continental ice sheets, polar ice sheets and alpine glaciers. Within a long-term _____, individual pulses of extra cold climate are termed 'glaciations'. Glaciologically, _____ implies the presence of extensive ice sheets in the northern and southern hemispheres; by this definition we are still in an _____
   a. AASHTO Soil Classification System
   b. AL 129-1
   c. AL 333
   d. Ice Age

29. The _____ was a period of cooling occurring after a warmer North Atlantic era known as the Medieval Warm Period. While not a true ice age, the term was introduced into scientific literature by Fran>çois E. Matthes in 1939. Climatologists and historians working with local records no longer expect to agree on either the start or end dates of this period, which varied according to local conditions.
   a. Deforestation
   b. Pacific Decadal Oscillation
   c. Glacier
   d. Little Ice Age

Chapter 29. North Cascades National Park

1. The _____ is a geological epoch which began approximately 11‰700 years ago (10‰000 ^{14}C years ago). According to traditional geological thinking, the _____ continues to the present. The _____ is part of the Neogene and Quaternary periods.
   a. 1509 Istanbul earthquake
   b. 1700 Cascadia earthquake
   c. Neoglaciation
   d. Holocene

2. The _____ Era, is the most recent of the three classic geological eras and covers the period from 65.5 million years ago to the present. It is marked by the Cretaceous-Tertiary extinction event at the end of the Cretaceous that saw the demise of the last non-avian dinosaurs and the end of the Mesozoic Era. The _____ era is ongoing.
   a. 1509 Istanbul earthquake
   b. 1703 Genroku earthquake
   c. Cenozoic
   d. 1700 Cascadia earthquake

3. A _____ is a large, slow-moving mass of ice, formed from compacted layers of snow, that slowly deforms and flows in response to gravity and high pressure.

   _____ ice is the largest reservoir of fresh water on Earth, and second only to oceans as the largest reservoir of total water.

   a. Deforestation
   b. Glacier
   c. Little Ice Age
   d. Keeling Curve

4. _____ is an active glaciated andesitic stratovolcano in the Cascade Volcanic Arc and the North Cascades of Washington State in the United States. It is the second-most active volcano in the range after Mount Saint Helens. It is about 31 miles (50 km) due east of the city of Bellingham, Whatcom County, making it the northernmost volcano in the Cascade Range but not the northernmost of the Cascade Volcanic Arc, which extends north into the Coast Mountains.
   a. Mount Overlord
   b. Stratovolcano
   c. Broken Top
   d. Mount Baker

5. The _____ is an informal name for the supereon comprising the eons of the geologic timescale that came before the current Phanerozoic eon. It spans from the formation of Earth around 4500 Mya (million years ago) to the evolution of abundant macroscopic hard-shelled animals, which marked the beginning of the Cambrian, the first period of the first era of the Phanerozoic eon, some 542 Mya. It is named after the Roman name for Wales - Cambria - where rocks from this age were first studied.
   a. 1700 Cascadia earthquake
   b. 1509 Istanbul earthquake
   c. Precambrian
   d. 1703 Genroku earthquake

6. A _____ is the shadow a rain drop has before it lands on the ground, with respect to prevailing wind direction. In a more geographical sense, a _____ is an area of land that has suffered desertification from proximity to mountain ranges. The mountains block the passage of rain-producing weather systems, casting a 'shadow' of dryness behind them.
   a. 1509 Istanbul earthquake
   b. Rain shadow
   c. 1703 Genroku earthquake
   d. 1700 Cascadia earthquake

7. The _____ is a a term for a geologic period 65 million to 1.8 million years ago. The _____ covered the time span between the superseded Secondary period and an out-of-date definition of the Quaternary period. The period began with the demise of the non-avian dinosaurs in the Cretaceous-_____ extinction event, at start of the Cenozoic era, spanning to beginning of the most recent Ice Age, at the end of the Pliocene epoch.

a. Historical geology
b. Logarithmic Spiral Beach
c. Loihi Seamount
d. Tertiary

8. A _____, sometimes called a composite volcano, is a tall, conical volcano with many layers (strata) of hardened lava, tephra, and volcanic ash. They are characterized by a steep profile and periodic, explosive eruptions. The lava that flows from a _____ tends to be viscous; it cools and hardens before spreading far.
a. Broken Top
b. Mount Baker
c. Mount Overlord
d. Stratovolcano

9. The _____ Era is one of three geologic eras of the Phanerozoic eon. The division of time into eras dates back to Giovanni Arduino, in the 18th century, although his original name for the era now called the '_____' was 'Secondary' (making the modern era the 'Tertiary'.)

The _____ was a time of tectonic, climatic and evolutionary activity. The continents gradually shifted from a state of connectedness into their present configuration; the drifting provided for speciation and other important evolutionary developments.

a. 1509 Istanbul earthquake
b. 1700 Cascadia earthquake
c. 1703 Genroku earthquake
d. Mesozoic

10. A _____ is an opening in a planet's surface or crust, which allows hot, molten rock, ash, and gases to escape from below the surface. Volcanic activity involving the extrusion of rock tends to form mountains or features like mountains over a period of time.
a. 1700 Cascadia earthquake
b. Volcano
c. 1509 Istanbul earthquake
d. 1703 Genroku earthquake

11. A _____ in geology is a fragment of crustal material formed on one tectonic plate and accreted -- 'sutured' -- to crust lying on another plate. The crustal block or fragment preserves its own distinctive geologic history, which is different from that of the surrounding areas (hence the term 'exotic' _____). The suture zone between a _____ and the crust it attaches to is usually identifiable as a fault.
a. Terrane
b. 1509 Istanbul earthquake
c. 1703 Genroku earthquake
d. 1700 Cascadia earthquake

12. A _____ is a large emplacement of igneous intrusive rock that forms from cooled magma deep in the Earth's crust. they are almost always made mostly of felsic or intermediate rock-types, such as granite, quartz monzonite, or diorite

Although they may appear uniform, _____s are in fact structures with complex histories and compositions.

a. Country rock
b. Litchfieldite
c. Batholith
d. Welded tuff

13. _____ is the result of the transformation of an existing rock type, the protolith, in a process called metamorphism, which means 'change in form'. The protolith is subjected to heat and pressure (temperatures greater than 150 to 200 >°C and pressures of 1500 bars) causing profound physical and/or chemical change. The protolith may be sedimentary rock, igneous rock or another older _____.

a. Pluton
b. Laccolith
c. Serpentinite
d. Metamorphic rock

14. The _____ are groups of mineral compositions in metamorphic rocks, that are typical for a certain field in pressure-temperature space. Rocks which contain certain minerals can therefore be linked to certain tectonic settings.

The name facies was first used for specific sedimentary environments in sedimentary rocks by Swiss geologist Amanz Gressly in 1838.

a. Prehnite-pumpellyite facies
b. Metamorphic facies
c. Mylonite
d. Facies

15. The 10-km-wide _____ system is part of a 500-km-long zone of high-angle faults in the northern Cordillera. The _____ System consists of two major sets of faults. The eastern set of the Hozameen and Slate Creek faults and more southerly North Creek fault form the western boundary of the Jura-Cretaceous Methow basin and in part separate it from metamorphic equivalents of Methow strata.

a. Magallanes-Fagnano Fault
b. Macquarie Fault Zone
c. Sorong Fault
d. Ross Lake fault

16. In geology, _____ are a body of rock with specified characteristics. Ideally, a _____ is a distinctive rock unit that forms under certain conditions of sedimentation, reflecting a particular process or environment.

The term _____ was introduced by the Swiss geologist Amanz Gressly in 1838 and was part of his significant contribution to the foundations of modern stratigraphy, [Cross and Homewood (1997)] which replaced the earlier notions of Neptunism.

a. Metamorphic facies
b. Metaconglomerate
c. Facies
d. Greenstone belts

17. In geology, a _____ or _____ line is a planar fracture in rock in which the rock on one side of the fracture has moved with respect to the rock on the other side. Large _____s within the Earth's crust are the result of differential or shear motion and active _____ zones are the causal locations of most earthquakes. Earthquakes are caused by energy release during rapid slippage along a _____.

a. Cleavage
b. Compaction
c. Drainage system
d. Fault

18. _____ is a common extrusive volcanic rock. It is usually grey to black and fine-grained due to rapid cooling of lava at the surface of a planet. It may be porphyritic containing larger crystals in a fine matrix, or vesicular, or frothy scoria.

a. 1509 Istanbul earthquake
b. Basalt
c. 1700 Cascadia earthquake
d. 1703 Genroku earthquake

19. _____ is a common and widely distributed type of rock formed by high-grade regional metamorphic processes from pre-existing formations that were originally either igneous or sedimentary rocks. Gneissic rocks are usually medium to coarse foliated and largely recrystallized but do not carry large quantities of micas, chlorite or other platy minerals. _____es that are metamorphosed igneous rocks or their equivalent are termed granite _____es, diorite _____es, etc.

a. 1509 Istanbul earthquake
c. 1700 Cascadia earthquake
b. 1703 Genroku earthquake
d. Gneiss

20. A _____ is a type of mudflow or landslide composed of pyroclastic material and water that flows down from a volcano, typically along a river valley. The term '_____' originated in the Javanese language of Indonesia. They can be best described as volcanic mudflows. They may not necessarily be caused by volcanic activity, but at the very least do originate from some type of volcanism.
    a. Lahar
    b. 1509 Istanbul earthquake
    c. 1703 Genroku earthquake
    d. 1700 Cascadia earthquake

21. _____ is molten rock expelled by a volcano during eruption. When first expelled from a volcanic vent, it is a liquid at temperatures from 700 >°C to 1,200 >°C (1,300 >°F to 2,200 >°F.) Although _____ is quite viscous, with about 100,000 times the viscosity of water, it can flow great distances before cooling and solidifying, because of both its thixotropic and shear thinning properties.
    a. Cinder
    b. Volcanic ash
    c. Pyroclastic flow
    d. Lava

22. _____ is a measure of the resistance of a fluid which is being deformed by either shear stress or extensional stress. In everyday terms (and for fluids only), _____ is 'thickness'. Thus, water is 'thin', having a lower _____, while honey is 'thick' having a higher _____.
    a. Viscosity
    b. Shear stress
    c. Tensile stress
    d. Thixotropy

23. _____ is an igneous, volcanic rock, of intermediate composition, with aphanitic to porphyritic texture. The mineral assemblage is typically dominated by plagioclase plus pyroxene and/or hornblende. Magnetite, zircon, apatite, ilmenite, biotite, and garnet are common accessory minerals.
    a. AL 333
    b. AASHTO Soil Classification System
    c. AL 129-1
    d. Andesite

24. In geology, a _____ deposit or _____ is an accumulation of valuable minerals formed by deposition of dense mineral phases in a trap site. Types of _____ deposits include alluvium, eluvium, beach _____s, and paleoplacers.

Typical locations for alluvial _____ deposits are on the inside bends of rivers and creeks, in natural hollows, at the break of slope on a stream, the base of an escarpment, waterfall or other barrier, within sand dunes, beach profiles or in gravel beds.

    a. Placer
    b. 1509 Istanbul earthquake
    c. 1703 Genroku earthquake
    d. 1700 Cascadia earthquake

25. _____ is a common and widely occurring type of intrusive, felsic, igneous rock. _____ has a medium to coarse texture, occasionally with some individual crystals larger than the groundmass forming a rock known as porphyry. _____s can be pink to dark gray or even black, depending on their chemistry and mineralogy.
    a. 1700 Cascadia earthquake
    b. 1703 Genroku earthquake
    c. Granite
    d. 1509 Istanbul earthquake

26. The _____ is the earliest of three geologic eras of the Phanerozoic eon. The _____ spanned from roughly 542 to 251 million years ago (ICS, 2004), and is subdivided into six geologic periods; from oldest to youngest they are: the Cambrian, Ordovician, Silurian, Devonian, Carboniferous, and Permian.

The _____ covers the time from the first appearance of abundant, soft-shelled fossils to the time when the continents were beginning to be dominated by large, relatively sophisticated reptiles and modern plants. The lower (oldest) boundary was classically set at the first appearance of creatures known as trilobites and archeocyathids.

a. 1509 Istanbul earthquake
b. 1703 Genroku earthquake
c. 1700 Cascadia earthquake
d. Paleozoic

27. In geology, an _____ is a body of igneous rock that has crystallized from molten magma below the surface of the Earth. Bodies of magma that solidify underground before they reach the surface of the earth are called plutons the Roman god of the underworld. Correspondingly, rocks of this kind are also referred to as igneous plutonic rocks or igneous intrusive rocks.

a. AL 333
b. Intrusion
c. AASHTO Soil Classification System
d. AL 129-1

28. The _____ is the epoch from 1.8 million to 11550 years BP covering the world's recent period of repeated glaciations. The _____ epoch follows the Pliocene epoch and is followed by the Holocene epoch. The _____ is the third epoch of the Neogene period or 6th epoch of the Cenozoic Era. The end of the _____ corresponds with the retreat of the last continental glacier. It also corresponds with the end of the Paleolithic age used in archaeology.

a. Sicilian Stage
b. Pleistocene
c. Late Pleistocene
d. Tyrrhenian

29. _____, also known as the Pleistocene glaciation, the current ice age or simply the ice age, refers to the period of the last few million years in which permanent ice sheets were established in Antarctica and perhaps Greenland, and fluctuating ice sheets have occurred elsewhere The major effects of the ice age were erosion and deposition of material over large parts of the continents, modification of river systems, creation of millions of lakes, changes in sea level, development of pluvial lakes far from the ice margins, isostatic adjustment of the crust, and abnormal winds. It affected oceans, flooding, and biological communities.

a. Snowball Earth
b. Wolstonian Stage
c. Rock glaciers
d. Quaternary glaciation

Chapter 30. Olympic National Park

1. The _____ are a mountain range on the Olympic Peninsula of western Washington in the United States.

The _____ are made up of an obducted clastic wedge material and oceanic crust. They are primarily Eocene sandstones, turbidites, and basaltic oceanic crust.

Millions of years ago, vents and fissures opened under the Pacific ocean and lava flowed forth, creating huge underwater mountains and ranges called seamounts. The plates that formed the ocean floor inched toward North America about 35 million years ago and most of the sea floor went beneath the continental land mass. Some of the sea floor, however, was scraped off and jammed against the mainland, creating the dome that was the forerunner of today's _____.

   a. AL 129-1
   b. AASHTO Soil Classification System
   c. Olympic Mountains
   d. AL 333

2. The _____ is a geological epoch which began approximately 11 700 years ago (10 000 ^{14}C years ago). According to traditional geological thinking, the _____ continues to the present. The _____ is part of the Neogene and Quaternary periods.
   a. Neoglaciation
   b. 1509 Istanbul earthquake
   c. 1700 Cascadia earthquake
   d. Holocene

3. The _____ epoch (55.8 >± 0.2 - 33.9 >± 0.1 Ma) is a major division of the geologic timescale and the second epoch of the Palaeogene period in the Cenozoic era. The _____ spans the time from the end of the Paleocene epoch to the beginning of the Oligocene epoch. The start of the _____ is marked by the emergence of the first modern mammals.
   a. AASHTO Soil Classification System
   b. AL 333
   c. AL 129-1
   d. Eocene

4. A _____ is a special-purpose map made to show geological features.

The stratigraphic contour lines are drawn on the surface of a selected deep stratum, so that they can show the topographic trends of the strata under the ground. It is not always possible to properly show this when the strata are extremely fractured, mixed, in some discontinuities, or where they are otherwise disturbed.

   a. Geologic map
   b. 1703 Genroku earthquake
   c. 1700 Cascadia earthquake
   d. 1509 Istanbul earthquake

5. An _____ is a section of the Earth's oceanic crust and the underlying upper mantle that has been uplifted or emplaced to be exposed within continental crustal rocks. Ophio is Greek for 'snake', lite means 'stone' from the Greek lithos.

The term _____ was originally used by Alexandre Brongniart for an assemblage of green rocks (serpentine, diabase) in the Alps; Steinmann (1927) later modified its use to include serpentine, pillow lava, and chert ('Steinmann's trinity'), again based on occurrences in the Alps.

   a. AL 333
   b. AL 129-1
   c. AASHTO Soil Classification System
   d. Ophiolite

Chapter 30. Olympic National Park

6. _____s is a field of study within geology concerned generally with the structures within the lithosphere of the Earth and particularly with the forces and movements that have operated in a region to create these structures.

_____s is concerned with the orogenies and _____ development of cratons and _____ terranes as well as the earthquake and volcanic belts which directly affect much of the global population. _____ studies are also important for understanding erosion patterns in geomorphology and as guides for the economic geologist searching for petroleum and metallic ores.

    a. Fault trace
    b. Tectonic
    c. Cocos Plate
    d. Rivera Plate

7. _____ geological formations have their origins in turbidity current deposits, which are deposits from a form of underwater avalanche that are responsible for distributing vast amounts of clastic sediment into the deep ocean.

They were first properly described by Bouma (1962), who studied deepwater sediments and recognized particular fining up intervals within deep water, fine grained shales, which were anomalous because they started at pebble conglomerates and terminated in shales.

This was anomalous because within the deep ocean it had historically been assumed that there was no mechanism by which tractional flow could carry and deposit coarse-grained sediments into the abyssal depths.

    a. 1703 Genroku earthquake
    b. Turbidite
    c. 1509 Istanbul earthquake
    d. 1700 Cascadia earthquake

8. A _____ is a change in the orientation of Earth's magnetic field such that the positions of magnetic north and magnetic south become interchanged. These events often involve an extended decline in field strength followed by a rapid recovery after the new orientation has been established. These events occur on a scale of thousands of years or longer.
    a. Geomagnetic reversal
    b. 1703 Genroku earthquake
    c. 1509 Istanbul earthquake
    d. 1700 Cascadia earthquake

9. _____ is the study of the record of the Earth's magnetic field preserved in various magnetic minerals through time. The study of _____ has demonstrated that the Earth's magnetic field varies substantially in both orientation and intensity through time. <
    a. Chronozone
    b. Global Standard Stratigraphic Age
    c. Relative dating
    d. Paleomagnetism

10. A _____ is a geological phenomenon which includes a wide range of ground movement, such as rock falls, deep failure of slopes and shallow debris flows, which can occur in offshore, coastal and onshore environments. Although the action of gravity is the primary driving force for a _____ to occur, there are other contributing factors affecting the original slope stability. Typically, pre-conditional factors build up specific sub-surface conditions that make the area/slope prone to failure, whereas the actual _____ often requires a trigger before being released.
    a. Landslide
    b. 1700 Cascadia earthquake
    c. 1509 Istanbul earthquake
    d. Mass wasting

11. _____ is the geomorphic process by which soil, regolith, and rock move downslope under the force of gravity. Types of _____ include creep, slides, flows, topples, and falls, each with its own characteristic features, and taking place over timescales from seconds to years. _____ occurs on both terrestrial and submarine slopes, and has been observed on Earth, Mars, and Venus.

   a. 1700 Cascadia earthquake   b. 1509 Istanbul earthquake
   c. Soil liquefaction   d. Mass wasting

12. The _____ of any physical feature such as a hill, stream, roof, railroad, or road refers to the amount of inclination of that surface where zero indicates level (with respect to gravity) and larger numbers indicate higher degrees of 'tilt'. Often slope is calculated as a ratio of 'rise over run' in which run is the horizontal distance and rise is the vertical distance.

There are several systems for expressing slope:

1. as an angle of inclination from the horizontal of a right triangle. (This is the angle >α opposite the 'rise' side of the triangle.)
2. as a percentage (also known as the _____), the formula for which is $\boxed{\times}$> which could also be expressed as the tangent of the angle of inclination times 100. In the U.S., the _____ is the most commonly used unit for communicating slopes in transportation, surveying, construction, and civil engineering.
3. as a per mille figure, the formula for which is $\boxed{\times}$> which could also be expressed as the tangent of the angle of inclination times 1000. This is commonly used in Europe to denote the incline of a railway.
4. as a ratio of one part rise per so many parts run. For example, a slope that has a rise of 5 feet for every 100 feet of run would have a slope ratio of 1 in 20.

Any one of these expressions may be used interchangeably to express the characteristics of a slope. _____ is usually expressed as a percentage, but this may easily be converted to the angle >α from horizontal since that carries the same information.

   a. Compaction   b. Diamond Head
   c. Heavy metal   d. Grade

13. A _____ is a large, slow-moving mass of ice, formed from compacted layers of snow, that slowly deforms and flows in response to gravity and high pressure.

_____ ice is the largest reservoir of fresh water on Earth, and second only to oceans as the largest reservoir of total water.

   a. Little Ice Age   b. Keeling Curve
   c. Deforestation   d. Glacier

14. The _____ zone is the area that is exposed to the air at low tide and submerged at high tide, for example, the area between tide marks. This area can include many different types of habitats, including steep rocky cliffs, sandy beaches, or wetlands The area can be a narrow strip, as in Pacific islands that have only a narrow tidal range, or can include many meters of shoreline where shallow beach slope interacts with high tidal excursion.

a. Overland flow
b. Upwelling
c. Intertidal
d. Eutrophication

15. _____ is a homogeneous, typically nonstratified, porous, friable, slightly coherent, often calcareous, fine-grained, silty, pale yellow or buff, windblown (aeolian) sediment. It generally occurs as a widespread blanket deposit that covers areas of hundreds of square kilometers and tens of meters thick. _____ often stands in either steep or vertical faces.
 a. 1509 Istanbul earthquake
 b. 1703 Genroku earthquake
 c. Loess
 d. 1700 Cascadia earthquake

16. _____, sometimes known as shore drift, is a geological process by which sediments such as sand or other materials, move along a beach shore. It uses the process of swash to push the material up the beach and backwash down the beach; until it reaches a groyne or another obstacle.

Where waves approach the coastline at an angle, when they break their swash pushes beach material up the beach at the same angle.

 a. Longshore drift
 b. Swash
 c. 1509 Istanbul earthquake
 d. Cuspate forelands

17. As ocean surface waves come closer to shore they break, forming the foamy, bubbly surface we call surf. The region of breaking waves defines the _____. After breaking in the _____, the waves (now reduced in height) continue to move in, and they run up onto the sloping front of the beach, forming an uprush of water called swash.
 a. 1703 Genroku earthquake
 b. 1700 Cascadia earthquake
 c. 1509 Istanbul earthquake
 d. Surf zone

18. In geology, _____ is transported rock debris overlying the solid bedrock. The term is also sometimes refers to organic debris so-transported. In the largest sense, it refers to the material left behind by retreating continental glaciers.
 a. Riegel
 b. Drift
 c. Metamorphic reaction
 d. Geomechanics

19. _____, is the water that washes up on shore after an incoming wave has broken. This action will cause sand and other light particles to be transported up the beach. The direction of the _____ varies with the prevailing wind, whereas the backwash is always perpendicular to the coastline.
 a. Longshore drift
 b. Cuspate forelands
 c. 1509 Istanbul earthquake
 d. Swash

20. The _____ is the epoch from 1.8 million to 11550 years BP covering the world's recent period of repeated glaciations. The _____ epoch follows the Pliocene epoch and is followed by the Holocene epoch. The _____ is the third epoch of the Neogene period or 6th epoch of the Cenozoic Era. The end of the _____ corresponds with the retreat of the last continental glacier. It also corresponds with the end of the Paleolithic age used in archaeology.
 a. Sicilian Stage
 b. Tyrrhenian
 c. Pleistocene
 d. Late Pleistocene

Chapter 31. Glacier Bay National Park and Preserve

1. The _____ Era, is the most recent of the three classic geological eras and covers the period from 65.5 million years ago to the present. It is marked by the Cretaceous-Tertiary extinction event at the end of the Cretaceous that saw the demise of the last non-avian dinosaurs and the end of the Mesozoic Era. The _____ era is ongoing.
   a. Cenozoic
   b. 1703 Genroku earthquake
   c. 1509 Istanbul earthquake
   d. 1700 Cascadia earthquake

2. A _____ is a large, slow-moving mass of ice, formed from compacted layers of snow, that slowly deforms and flows in response to gravity and high pressure.

   _____ ice is the largest reservoir of fresh water on Earth, and second only to oceans as the largest reservoir of total water.

   a. Glacier
   b. Deforestation
   c. Keeling Curve
   d. Little Ice Age

3. In nuclear physics, a _____ is a nuclide produced by radioactive decay. Radioactive decay often involves a sequence of steps For example, U-238 decays to Th-234 which decays to Pa-234 which decays, and so on, to Pb-206:

   In this example:

   - Th-234, Pa-234,â€¦,Pb-206 are the _____s of U-238.
   - Th-234 is the daughter of the parent U-238.
   - Pa-234 is the granddaughter of U-238.

   Note that Th-234, Pa-234,â€¦,Pb-206 might also be referred to as the daughter products of U-238.

   _____s are extremely important in understanding radioactive decay and the management of radioactive waste.

   a. Mass deficiency
   b. Positron emission
   c. Mass excess
   d. Decay product

4. The _____ is a a term for a geologic period 65 million to 1.8 million years ago. The _____ covered the time span between the superseded Secondary period and an out-of-date definition of the Quaternary period. The period began with the demise of the non-avian dinosaurs in the Cretaceous-_____ extinction event, at start of the Cenozoic era, spanning to beginning of the most recent Ice Age, at the end of the Pliocene epoch.
   a. Historical geology
   b. Tertiary
   c. Loihi Seamount
   d. Logarithmic Spiral Beach

5. A _____ in geology is a fragment of crustal material formed on one tectonic plate and accreted -- 'sutured' -- to crust lying on another plate. The crustal block or fragment preserves its own distinctive geologic history, which is different from that of the surrounding areas (hence the term 'exotic' _____). The suture zone between a _____ and the crust it attaches to is usually identifiable as a fault.

a. 1700 Cascadia earthquake
b. 1703 Genroku earthquake
c. 1509 Istanbul earthquake
d. Terrane

6. _____ are the largest glaciers, enormous masses of ice that are not visibly affected by the landscape and that cover the entire surface beneath them, except possibly on the margins where they are thinnest. Antarctica and Greenland are the only places where continental _____ currently exist. These regions contain vast quantities of fresh water.
   a. AL 333
   b. AL 129-1
   c. AASHTO Soil Classification System
   d. Ice sheets

7. In geology, a _____ or _____ line is a planar fracture in rock in which the rock on one side of the fracture has moved with respect to the rock on the other side. Large _____s within the Earth's crust are the result of differential or shear motion and active _____ zones are the causal locations of most earthquakes. Earthquakes are caused by energy release during rapid slippage along a _____.
   a. Fault
   b. Drainage system
   c. Cleavage
   d. Compaction

8. A _____ is an elongated whale-shaped hill formed by glacial action. Its long axis is parallel with the movement of the ice, with the blunter end facing into the glacial movement. They may be more than 45 m (150 ft) high and more than 0.8 km (1/2 mile) long, and are often in _____ fields of similarly shaped, sized and oriented hills. They usually have layers indicating that the material was repeatedly added to a core, which may be of rock or glacial till.
   a. Sandur
   b. 1509 Istanbul earthquake
   c. Drumlin
   d. Monadnock

9. An _____ is a long winding ridge of stratified sand and gravel, examples of which occur in glaciated and formerly glaciated regions of Europe and North America. They are frequently several miles long and, because of their peculiar uniform shape, are somewhat like railroad embankments.

Most are believed to form in ice-walled tunnels by streams which flowed within (englacial) and under (subglacial) glaciers.

   a. AASHTO Soil Classification System
   b. AL 333
   c. AL 129-1
   d. Esker

10. _____ is caused by movement of ice, typically as glaciers. Glaciers erode predominantly by three different processes: abrasion/scouring, plucking, and ice thrusting. In an abrasion process, debris in the basal ice scrapes along the bed, polishing and gouging the underlying rocks, similar to sandpaper on wood. Glaciers can also cause pieces of bedrock to crack off in the process of plucking. In ice thrusting, the glacier freezes to its bed, then as it surges forward, it moves large sheets of frozen sediment at the base along with the glacier. This method produced some of the many thousands of lake basins that dot the edge of the Canadian Shield. These processes, combined with erosion and transport by the water network beneath the glacier, leave moraines, drumlins, eskers, ground moraine (till), kames, kame deltas, moulins, and glacial erratics in their wake, typically at the terminus or during glacier retreat.
    a. AL 129-1
    b. AL 333
    c. AASHTO Soil Classification System
    d. Ice erosion

Chapter 31. Glacier Bay National Park and Preserve

11. _____ is the removal of solids (sediment, soil, rock and other particles) in the natural environment. It usually occurs due to transport by wind, water, or ice; by down-slope creep of soil and other material under the force of gravity; or by living organisms, such as burrowing animals, in the case of bioerosion.

_____ is distinguished from weathering, which is the process of chemical or physical breakdown of the minerals in the rocks, although the two processes may occur concurrently.

   a. AL 129-1
   b. AL 333
   c. AASHTO Soil Classification System
   d. Erosion

12. The _____ is the earliest of three geologic eras of the Phanerozoic eon. The _____ spanned from roughly 542 to 251 million years ago (ICS, 2004), and is subdivided into six geologic periods; from oldest to youngest they are: the Cambrian, Ordovician, Silurian, Devonian, Carboniferous, and Permian.

The _____ covers the time from the first appearance of abundant, soft-shelled fossils to the time when the continents were beginning to be dominated by large, relatively sophisticated reptiles and modern plants. The lower (oldest) boundary was classically set at the first appearance of creatures known as trilobites and archeocyathids.

   a. 1703 Genroku earthquake
   b. Paleozoic
   c. 1509 Istanbul earthquake
   d. 1700 Cascadia earthquake

13. The _____ is an informal name for the supereon comprising the eons of the geologic timescale that came before the current Phanerozoic eon. It spans from the formation of Earth around 4500 Mya (million years ago) to the evolution of abundant macroscopic hard-shelled animals, which marked the beginning of the Cambrian, the first period of the first era of the Phanerozoic eon, some 542 Mya. It is named after the Roman name for Wales - Cambria - where rocks from this age were first studied.
   a. 1509 Istanbul earthquake
   b. Precambrian
   c. 1700 Cascadia earthquake
   d. 1703 Genroku earthquake

14. In stratigraphy, _____ is the native consolidated rock underlying the surface of a terrestrial planet, usually the Earth. Above the _____ is usually an area of broken and weathered unconsolidated rock in the basal subsoil. The top of the _____ is known as rockhead and identifying this, via excavations, drilling or geophysical methods, is an important task in most civil engineering projects.
   a. Polystrate
   b. Biozones
   c. Sequence stratigraphy
   d. Bedrock

15. The _____ Era is one of three geologic eras of the Phanerozoic eon. The division of time into eras dates back to Giovanni Arduino, in the 18th century, although his original name for the era now called the '_____' was 'Secondary' (making the modern era the 'Tertiary'.)

The _____ was a time of tectonic, climatic and evolutionary activity. The continents gradually shifted from a state of connectedness into their present configuration; the drifting provided for speciation and other important evolutionary developments.

a. 1703 Genroku earthquake
b. 1700 Cascadia earthquake
c. Mesozoic
d. 1509 Istanbul earthquake

16. The _____ Period is the geologic time period after the Neogene Period, spanning 1.805 +/- 0.005 million years ago to the present. The _____ includes two geologic epochs: the Pleistocene and the Holocene Epoch.

There is an ongoing debate of the status of _____ -- a recent proposal from International Commission on Stratigraphy (ICS) was to make _____ a subperiod under Neogene, but that was retracted after criticism from International Union for _____ Research (INQUA), so instead ICS and INQUA agreed to erect _____ as an Era, above Neogene, and to place the base for _____ at 2.588 >± 3.005, the base for Gelasian Stage.

a. Quaternary
b. Tributary
c. Geomorphology
d. Yilgarn Craton

17. The _____ is the epoch from 1.8 million to 11550 years BP covering the world's recent period of repeated glaciations. The _____ epoch follows the Pliocene epoch and is followed by the Holocene epoch. The _____ is the third epoch of the Neogene period or 6th epoch of the Cenozoic Era. The end of the _____ corresponds with the retreat of the last continental glacier. It also corresponds with the end of the Paleolithic age used in archaeology.

a. Pleistocene
b. Late Pleistocene
c. Tyrrhenian
d. Sicilian Stage

18. _____, also known as the Pleistocene glaciation, the current ice age or simply the ice age, refers to the period of the last few million years in which permanent ice sheets were established in Antarctica and perhaps Greenland, and fluctuating ice sheets have occurred elsewhere The major effects of the ice age were erosion and deposition of material over large parts of the continents, modification of river systems, creation of millions of lakes, changes in sea level, development of pluvial lakes far from the ice margins, isostatic adjustment of the crust, and abnormal winds. It affected oceans, flooding, and biological communities.

a. Wolstonian Stage
b. Snowball Earth
c. Quaternary glaciation
d. Rock glaciers

19. The _____ is a geological epoch which began approximately 11‰700 years ago (10‰000 ^{14}C years ago). According to traditional geological thinking, the _____ continues to the present. The _____ is part of the Neogene and Quaternary periods.

a. Neoglaciation
b. 1509 Istanbul earthquake
c. 1700 Cascadia earthquake
d. Holocene

1. _____ describes the large scale motions of Earth's lithosphere. The theory encompasses the older concepts of continental drift, developed during the first decades of the 20th century by Alfred Wegener, and seafloor spreading, understood during the 1960s.

The outermost part of the Earth's interior is made up of two layers: the lithosphere and the asthenosphere.

   a. Plate tectonics   b. Mantle convection
   c. Continental crust   d. Nappe

2. A _____ in geology is a fragment of crustal material formed on one tectonic plate and accreted -- 'sutured' -- to crust lying on another plate. The crustal block or fragment preserves its own distinctive geologic history, which is different from that of the surrounding areas (hence the term 'exotic' _____). The suture zone between a _____ and the crust it attaches to is usually identifiable as a fault.

   a. 1700 Cascadia earthquake   b. 1509 Istanbul earthquake
   c. Terrane   d. 1703 Genroku earthquake

3. _____s is a field of study within geology concerned generally with the structures within the lithosphere of the Earth and particularly with the forces and movements that have operated in a region to create these structures.

_____s is concerned with the orogenies and _____ development of cratons and _____ terranes as well as the earthquake and volcanic belts which directly affect much of the global population. _____ studies are also important for understanding erosion patterns in geomorphology and as guides for the economic geologist searching for petroleum and metallic ores.

   a. Rivera Plate   b. Cocos Plate
   c. Tectonic   d. Fault trace

4. _____ is a field of study within geology concerned generally with the structures within the lithosphere of the Earth and particularly with the forces and movements that have operated in a region to create these structures.

_____ is concerned with the orogenies and tectonic development of cratons and tectonic terranes as well as the earthquake and volcanic belts which directly affect much of the global population. Tectonic studies are also important for understanding erosion patterns in geomorphology and as guides for the economic geologist searching for petroleum and metallic ores.

   a. Fault trace   b. Cocos Plate
   c. Tectonics   d. Rivera Plate

5. The _____ Era, is the most recent of the three classic geological eras and covers the period from 65.5 million years ago to the present. It is marked by the Cretaceous-Tertiary extinction event at the end of the Cretaceous that saw the demise of the last non-avian dinosaurs and the end of the Mesozoic Era. The _____ era is ongoing.
   a. 1700 Cascadia earthquake   b. Cenozoic
   c. 1703 Genroku earthquake   d. 1509 Istanbul earthquake

6. The _____ Era is one of three geologic eras of the Phanerozoic eon. The division of time into eras dates back to Giovanni Arduino, in the 18th century, although his original name for the era now called the '_____' was 'Secondary' (making the modern era the 'Tertiary'.)

The _____ was a time of tectonic, climatic and evolutionary activity. The continents gradually shifted from a state of connectedness into their present configuration; the drifting provided for speciation and other important evolutionary developments.

   a. 1509 Istanbul earthquake
   b. Mesozoic
   c. 1700 Cascadia earthquake
   d. 1703 Genroku earthquake

7. An _____ is the result of a sudden release of energy in the Earth's crust that creates seismic waves. They are recorded with a seismometer or the related and mostly obsolete Richter magnitude, with a magnitude 3 or lower _____ being mostly imperceptible and magnitude 7 causing serious damage over large areas.
   a. AASHTO Soil Classification System
   b. AL 333
   c. Earthquake
   d. AL 129-1

8. A _____ is an opening in a planet's surface or crust, which allows hot, molten rock, ash, and gases to escape from below the surface. Volcanic activity involving the extrusion of rock tends to form mountains or features like mountains over a period of time.
   a. 1703 Genroku earthquake
   b. 1700 Cascadia earthquake
   c. 1509 Istanbul earthquake
   d. Volcano

9. A _____ is a type of arid terrain where softer sedimentary rocks and clay-rich soils have been extensively eroded by wind and water. It can resemble malpa>ís, a terrain of volcanic rocks. Canyons, ravines, gullies, hoodoos and other such geological forms are common in _____.
   a. 1703 Genroku earthquake
   b. 1700 Cascadia earthquake
   c. Badlands
   d. 1509 Istanbul earthquake

10. A _____ is a large, slow-moving mass of ice, formed from compacted layers of snow, that slowly deforms and flows in response to gravity and high pressure.

_____ ice is the largest reservoir of fresh water on Earth, and second only to oceans as the largest reservoir of total water.

   a. Deforestation
   b. Glacier
   c. Keeling Curve
   d. Little Ice Age

11. _____ is a tidewater glacier in the U.S. state of Alaska and the Yukon Territory of Canada. From its source in the Yukon, the glacier stretches 122 km (76 mi) to the sea at Yakutat Bay and Disenchantment Bay. It is the longest tidewater glacier in Alaska, with an open calving face over ten kilometers (6 mi) wide.
   a. Hubbard Glacier
   b. 1703 Genroku earthquake
   c. 1509 Istanbul earthquake
   d. 1700 Cascadia earthquake

12. The _____ Period is the geologic time period after the Neogene Period, spanning 1.805 +/- 0.005 million years ago to the present. The _____ includes two geologic epochs: the Pleistocene and the Holocene Epoch.

Chapter 32. Wrangell-St. Elias National Park and Preserve by Monte D. Wilson

There is an ongoing debate of the status of _____ -- a recent proposal from International Commission on Stratigraphy (ICS) was to make _____ a subperiod under Neogene, but that was retracted after criticism from International Union for _____ Research (INQUA), so instead ICS and INQUA agreed to erect _____ as an Era, above Neogene, and to place the base for _____ at 2.588 >± 3.005, the base for Gelasian Stage.

a. Tributary
b. Yilgarn Craton
c. Geomorphology
d. Quaternary

13. The _____ is the earliest of three geologic eras of the Phanerozoic eon. The _____ spanned from roughly 542 to 251 million years ago (ICS, 2004), and is subdivided into six geologic periods; from oldest to youngest they are: the Cambrian, Ordovician, Silurian, Devonian, Carboniferous, and Permian.

The _____ covers the time from the first appearance of abundant, soft-shelled fossils to the time when the continents were beginning to be dominated by large, relatively sophisticated reptiles and modern plants. The lower (oldest) boundary was classically set at the first appearance of creatures known as trilobites and archeocyathids.

a. 1509 Istanbul earthquake
b. Paleozoic
c. 1703 Genroku earthquake
d. 1700 Cascadia earthquake

14. In geology, _____ or _____ soil is soil at or below the freezing point of water (0 >°C or 32 >°F) for two or more years. Ice is not always present, as may be in the case of nonporous bedrock, but it frequently occurs and it may be in amounts exceeding the potential hydraulic saturation of the ground material. Most _____ is located in high latitudes (i.e. land in close proximity to the North and South poles), but alpine _____ may exist at high altitudes in much lower latitudes.

a. 1700 Cascadia earthquake
b. 1509 Istanbul earthquake
c. 1703 Genroku earthquake
d. Permafrost

15. The _____ is an informal name for the supereon comprising the eons of the geologic timescale that came before the current Phanerozoic eon. It spans from the formation of Earth around 4500 Mya (million years ago) to the evolution of abundant macroscopic hard-shelled animals, which marked the beginning of the Cambrian, the first period of the first era of the Phanerozoic eon, some 542 Mya. It is named after the Roman name for Wales - Cambria - where rocks from this age were first studied.

a. 1509 Istanbul earthquake
b. 1700 Cascadia earthquake
c. 1703 Genroku earthquake
d. Precambrian

Chapter 33. Kenai Fjords National Park by Donald S. Follows

1. Geologically, a _____ is a long, narrow inlet with steep sides, created in a valley carved by glacial activity.

The seeds of a _____ are laid when a glacier cuts a U-shaped valley through abrasion of the surrounding bedrock by the sediment it carries. Many such valleys were formed during the recent ice age.

    a. Fjord
    b. 1509 Istanbul earthquake
    c. 1703 Genroku earthquake
    d. 1700 Cascadia earthquake

2. The _____ epoch (55.8 >± 0.2 - 33.9 >± 0.1 Ma) is a major division of the geologic timescale and the second epoch of the Palaeogene period in the Cenozoic era. The _____ spans the time from the end of the Paleocene epoch to the beginning of the Oligocene epoch. The start of the _____ is marked by the emergence of the first modern mammals.
    a. AASHTO Soil Classification System
    b. AL 333
    c. AL 129-1
    d. Eocene

3. The _____ is a a term for a geologic period 65 million to 1.8 million years ago. The _____ covered the time span between the superseded Secondary period and an out-of-date definition of the Quaternary period. The period began with the demise of the non-avian dinosaurs in the Cretaceous-_____ extinction event, at start of the Cenozoic era, spanning to beginning of the most recent Ice Age, at the end of the Pliocene epoch.
    a. Tertiary
    b. Logarithmic Spiral Beach
    c. Historical geology
    d. Loihi Seamount

4. A _____ is a large, slow-moving mass of ice, formed from compacted layers of snow, that slowly deforms and flows in response to gravity and high pressure.

_____ ice is the largest reservoir of fresh water on Earth, and second only to oceans as the largest reservoir of total water.

    a. Deforestation
    b. Keeling Curve
    c. Little Ice Age
    d. Glacier

5. In geology, a _____ is a large scale breccia, a mappable body of rock characterized by a lack of continuous bedding and the inclusion of fragments of rock of all sizes, contained in a fine-grained deformed matrix. The _____ typically consists of a jumble of large blocks of varied lithologies of altered oceanic crustal material and blocks of continental slope sediments in a sheared mudstone matrix. Some larger blocks of rock may be as much as 1 km across.
    a. Stratification
    b. Melange
    c. Diamond Head
    d. Leaching

6. The _____ Era is one of three geologic eras of the Phanerozoic eon. The division of time into eras dates back to Giovanni Arduino, in the 18th century, although his original name for the era now called the '_____' was 'Secondary' (making the modern era the 'Tertiary'.)

The _____ was a time of tectonic, climatic and evolutionary activity. The continents gradually shifted from a state of connectedness into their present configuration; the drifting provided for speciation and other important evolutionary developments.

a. 1700 Cascadia earthquake
b. 1703 Genroku earthquake
c. 1509 Istanbul earthquake
d. Mesozoic

7. The _____ is a geologic period and system that began 65.5 ± 0.3 and ended 23.03 ± 0.05 million years ago and comprises the first part of the Cenozoic era. Lasting 42 million years, the _____ is most notable as being the time in which mammals evolved from relatively small, simple forms into a plethora of diverse animals in the wake of the mass extinction that ended the preceding Cretaceous Period. Some of these mammals would evolve into large forms that would dominate the land, while others would become capable of living in marine, specialized terrestrial and even airborne environments.
   a. Riochican
   b. Mustersan
   c. Tabenbulakian
   d. Paleogene

8. A _____ in geology is a fragment of crustal material formed on one tectonic plate and accreted -- 'sutured' -- to crust lying on another plate. The crustal block or fragment preserves its own distinctive geologic history, which is different from that of the surrounding areas (hence the term 'exotic' _____). The suture zone between a _____ and the crust it attaches to is usually identifiable as a fault.
   a. 1509 Istanbul earthquake
   b. 1700 Cascadia earthquake
   c. 1703 Genroku earthquake
   d. Terrane

9. _____ is a common and widely occurring type of intrusive, felsic, igneous rock. _____ has a medium to coarse texture, occasionally with some individual crystals larger than the groundmass forming a rock known as porphyry. _____s can be pink to dark gray or even black, depending on their chemistry and mineralogy.
   a. 1700 Cascadia earthquake
   b. 1703 Genroku earthquake
   c. 1509 Istanbul earthquake
   d. Granite

10. A _____ is a mountain rising from the ocean seafloor that does not reach to the water's surface (sea level), and thus is not an island. These are typically formed from extinct volcanoes, that rise abruptly and are usually found rising from a seafloor of 1,000-4,000 meters depth. They are defined by oceanographers as independent features that rise to at least 1,000 meters above the seafloor.
    a. 1703 Genroku earthquake
    b. 1700 Cascadia earthquake
    c. 1509 Istanbul earthquake
    d. Seamount

11. An _____ is the result of a sudden release of energy in the Earth's crust that creates seismic waves. They are recorded with a seismometer or the related and mostly obsolete Richter magnitude, with a magnitude 3 or lower _____ being mostly imperceptible and magnitude 7 causing serious damage over large areas.
    a. AL 333
    b. Earthquake
    c. AASHTO Soil Classification System
    d. AL 129-1

Chapter 34. Denali National Park and Preserve by Phillip Brease

1. The _____ is an informal name for the supereon comprising the eons of the geologic timescale that came before the current Phanerozoic eon. It spans from the formation of Earth around 4500 Mya (million years ago) to the evolution of abundant macroscopic hard-shelled animals, which marked the beginning of the Cambrian, the first period of the first era of the Phanerozoic eon, some 542 Mya. It is named after the Roman name for Wales - Cambria - where rocks from this age were first studied.
   - a. 1509 Istanbul earthquake
   - b. 1700 Cascadia earthquake
   - c. 1703 Genroku earthquake
   - d. Precambrian

2. _____ usually refers to the thick foundation of ancient, and oldest metamorphic and igneous rock that forms the crust of continents, often in the form of granite. _____ is contrasted to overlying sedimentary rocks which are laid down on top of the _____s after the continent was formed, such as sandstone and limestone. The sedimentary rocks which may be deposited on top of the basement usually form a relatively thin veneer, but can be more than 3 miles thick.
   - a. Polystrate
   - b. Key bed
   - c. Bed
   - d. Basement rock

3. _____ - also known as greenstone - is a general field petrologic term applied to metamorphic and/or altered mafic volcanic rock. The green is due to abundant green chlorite, actinolite and epidote minerals that dominate the rock. However, basalts may remain quite black if primary pyroxene does not revert to chlorite or actinolite.
   - a. Greenstone belts
   - b. Metasomatism
   - c. Prehnite-pumpellyite facies
   - d. Greenschist

4. _____ is determined by the particular T-P conditions required to metamorphose basalt to form the typical _____ minerals chlorite, actinolite, and albite. _____ results from low temperature, moderate pressure metamorphism. Metamorphic conditions which create typical _____ assemblages are called the Barrovian Facies Sequence, and the lower-pressure Abukuma Facies Series.
   - a. Cataclasite
   - b. Prehnite-pumpellyite facies
   - c. Metaconglomerate
   - d. Greenschist facies

5. A _____ in geology is a fragment of crustal material formed on one tectonic plate and accreted -- 'sutured' -- to crust lying on another plate. The crustal block or fragment preserves its own distinctive geologic history, which is different from that of the surrounding areas (hence the term 'exotic' _____). The suture zone between a _____ and the crust it attaches to is usually identifiable as a fault.
   - a. 1700 Cascadia earthquake
   - b. 1509 Istanbul earthquake
   - c. 1703 Genroku earthquake
   - d. Terrane

6. In geology, _____ are a body of rock with specified characteristics. Ideally, a _____ is a distinctive rock unit that forms under certain conditions of sedimentation, reflecting a particular process or environment.

   The term _____ was introduced by the Swiss geologist Amanz Gressly in 1838 and was part of his significant contribution to the foundations of modern stratigraphy, [Cross and Homewood (1997)] which replaced the earlier notions of Neptunism.

   - a. Facies
   - b. Greenstone belts
   - c. Metaconglomerate
   - d. Metamorphic facies

7. _____ forms a group of medium-grade metamorphic rocks, chiefly notable for the preponderance of lamellar minerals such as micas, chlorite, talc, hornblende, graphite, and others. Quartz often occurs in drawn-out grains to such an extent that a particular form called quartz _____ is produced. By definition, _____ contains more than 50% platy and elongated minerals, often finely interleaved with quartz and feldspar.
   a. Hornfels
   b. Schist
   c. Porphyroblast
   d. Talc carbonate

8. A _____ is a rock consisting of individual stones that have become cemented together. They are sedimentary rocks consisting of rounded fragments and are thus differentiated from breccias, which consist of angular clasts. Both _____s and breccias are characterized by clasts larger than sand (>2 mm).
   a. Concretion
   b. Pelagic sediments
   c. Keystone
   d. Conglomerate

9. _____s (also radiolaria) are amoeboid protozoa that produce intricate mineral skeletons, typically with a central capsule dividing the cell into inner and outer portions, called endoplasm and ectoplasm. They are found as zooplankton throughout the ocean, and their skeletal remains cover large portions of the ocean bottom as _____ ooze. Due to their rapid turn-over of species, they represent an important diagnostic fossil found from the Cambrian onwards.
   a. Radiolarian
   b. 1700 Cascadia earthquake
   c. 1703 Genroku earthquake
   d. 1509 Istanbul earthquake

10. An _____ is a section of the Earth's oceanic crust and the underlying upper mantle that has been uplifted or emplaced to be exposed within continental crustal rocks. Ophio is Greek for 'snake', lite means 'stone' from the Greek lithos.

The term _____ was originally used by Alexandre Brongniart for an assemblage of green rocks (serpentine, diabase) in the Alps; Steinmann (1927) later modified its use to include serpentine, pillow lava, and chert ('Steinmann's trinity'), again based on occurrences in the Alps.

   a. AL 333
   b. AL 129-1
   c. AASHTO Soil Classification System
   d. Ophiolite

11. _____ describes a sediment or rock that can be found at its site of formation or deposition, as opposed to an allochthon, which has moved from that site.
   a. AASHTO Soil Classification System
   b. AL 129-1
   c. AL 333
   d. Autochthonous

12. _____ is any particulate matter that can be transported by fluid flow, and which eventually is deposited.

They are most often transported by water (fluvial processes) transported by wind (aeolian processes) and glaciers. Beach sands and river channel deposits are examples of fluvial transport and deposition, though _____ also often settles out of slow-moving or standing water in lakes and oceans.

   a. Brickearth
   b. Sediment
   c. Fech fech
   d. Salt glacier

Chapter 34. Denali National Park and Preserve by Phillip Brease

13. A marine _____ is a geologic event during which sea level rises relative to the land and the shoreline moves toward higher ground, resulting in flooding. They can be caused either by the land sinking or the ocean basins filling with water (or decreasing in capacity.) Transgresssions and regressions may be caused by tectonic events such as orogenies, severe climate change such as ice ages or isostatic adjustments following removal of ice or sediment load.
    a. Mid-ocean ridge
    b. Transgression
    c. Seafloor spreading
    d. Headward erosion

14. In geology, an _____ is a body of igneous rock that has crystallized from molten magma below the surface of the Earth. Bodies of magma that solidify underground before they reach the surface of the earth are called plutons the Roman god of the underworld. Correspondingly, rocks of this kind are also referred to as igneous plutonic rocks or igneous intrusive rocks.
    a. AASHTO Soil Classification System
    b. AL 333
    c. Intrusion
    d. AL 129-1

15. A _____ in geology is an intrusive igneous rock body that crystallized from a magma slowly cooling below the surface of the Earth. _____s include batholiths, dikes, sills, laccoliths, lopoliths, and other igneous bodies. In practice, '_____' usually refers to a distinctive mass of igneous rock, typically kilometers in dimension, without a tabular shape like those of dikes and sills.
    a. Matrix
    b. Pluton
    c. Petrology
    d. Tephra

16. An _____ is the result of a sudden release of energy in the Earth's crust that creates seismic waves. They are recorded with a seismometer or the related and mostly obsolete Richter magnitude, with a magnitude 3 or lower _____ being mostly imperceptible and magnitude 7 causing serious damage over large areas.
    a. AL 129-1
    b. AL 333
    c. Earthquake
    d. AASHTO Soil Classification System

17. The _____ of an earthquake describes the inelastic deformation in the source region that generates the seismic waves. In the case of a fault-related event it refers to the orientation of the fault plane that slipped and the slip vector and is also known as a fault-plane solution. _____s are derived from a solution of the moment tensor for the earthquake, which itself is estimated by an analysis of observed seismic waveforms.
    a. Seismotectonics
    b. 1509 Istanbul earthquake
    c. Morley-Vine-Matthews hypothesis
    d. Focal mechanism

18. A _____ is a large, slow-moving mass of ice, formed from compacted layers of snow, that slowly deforms and flows in response to gravity and high pressure.

    _____ ice is the largest reservoir of fresh water on Earth, and second only to oceans as the largest reservoir of total water.

    a. Little Ice Age
    b. Glacier
    c. Deforestation
    d. Keeling Curve

19. In geology, _____ or _____ soil is soil at or below the freezing point of water (0 >°C or 32 >°F) for two or more years. Ice is not always present, as may be in the case of nonporous bedrock, but it frequently occurs and it may be in amounts exceeding the potential hydraulic saturation of the ground material. Most _____ is located in high latitudes (i.e. land in close proximity to the North and South poles), but alpine _____ may exist at high altitudes in much lower latitudes.
   a. 1703 Genroku earthquake
   b. 1700 Cascadia earthquake
   c. Permafrost
   d. 1509 Istanbul earthquake

20. The _____ is the earliest of three geologic eras of the Phanerozoic eon. The _____ spanned from roughly 542 to 251 million years ago (ICS, 2004), and is subdivided into six geologic periods; from oldest to youngest they are: the Cambrian, Ordovician, Silurian, Devonian, Carboniferous, and Permian.

The _____ covers the time from the first appearance of abundant, soft-shelled fossils to the time when the continents were beginning to be dominated by large, relatively sophisticated reptiles and modern plants. The lower (oldest) boundary was classically set at the first appearance of creatures known as trilobites and archeocyathids.

   a. 1700 Cascadia earthquake
   b. Paleozoic
   c. 1509 Istanbul earthquake
   d. 1703 Genroku earthquake

21. In geology, _____ is a type of mass wasting where waterlogged sediment slowly moves downslope over impermeable material. It can occur in any climate where the ground is saturated by water, though it is most often found in periglacial environments where the ground is permanently frozen, under which conditions the process is often called gelifluction. During warm seasonal periods the surface layer melts and slides over the frozen underlayer, slowly moving downslope due to frost heave that occurs normal to the slope.
   a. Geohazard
   b. Sturzstrom
   c. Rockfall
   d. Solifluction

22. The _____ Era is one of three geologic eras of the Phanerozoic eon. The division of time into eras dates back to Giovanni Arduino, in the 18th century, although his original name for the era now called the '_____' was 'Secondary' (making the modern era the 'Tertiary'.)

The _____ was a time of tectonic, climatic and evolutionary activity. The continents gradually shifted from a state of connectedness into their present configuration; the drifting provided for speciation and other important evolutionary developments.

   a. 1509 Istanbul earthquake
   b. 1703 Genroku earthquake
   c. 1700 Cascadia earthquake
   d. Mesozoic

23. The _____ or Palaeocene, 'early dawn of the recent' is a geologic epoch that lasted from 65.5 >± 0.3 Ma to 55.8 >± 0.2 Ma (million years ago.) It is the first epoch of the Palaeogene Period in the modern Cenozoic era. As with most other older geologic periods, the strata that define the epoch's beginning and end are well identified but the exact date of the end is uncertain.
   a. Paleocene
   b. 1703 Genroku earthquake
   c. 1509 Istanbul earthquake
   d. 1700 Cascadia earthquake

24. The _____ is the epoch from 1.8 million to 11550 years BP covering the world's recent period of repeated glaciations. The _____ epoch follows the Pliocene epoch and is followed by the Holocene epoch. The _____ is the third epoch of the Neogene period or 6th epoch of the Cenozoic Era. The end of the _____ corresponds with the retreat of the last continental glacier. It also corresponds with the end of the Paleolithic age used in archaeology.
   a. Sicilian Stage
   b. Pleistocene
   c. Tyrrhenian
   d. Late Pleistocene

25. _____, also known as the Pleistocene glaciation, the current ice age or simply the ice age, refers to the period of the last few million years in which permanent ice sheets were established in Antarctica and perhaps Greenland, and fluctuating ice sheets have occurred elsewhere The major effects of the ice age were erosion and deposition of material over large parts of the continents, modification of river systems, creation of millions of lakes, changes in sea level, development of pluvial lakes far from the ice margins, isostatic adjustment of the crust, and abnormal winds. It affected oceans, flooding, and biological communities.
   a. Snowball Earth
   b. Wolstonian Stage
   c. Rock glaciers
   d. Quaternary glaciation

26. _____ is the tendency for particles in suspension or molecules in solution to settle out of the fluid in which they are entrained, and come to rest against a wall. This is due to their motion through the fluid in response to the forces acting on them: these forces can be due to gravity, centrifugal acceleration or electromagnetism.

   _____ may pertain to objects of various sizes, ranging from large rocks in flowing water to suspensions of dust and pollen particles to cellular suspensions to solutions of single molecules such as proteins and peptides.
   a. 1703 Genroku earthquake
   b. 1509 Istanbul earthquake
   c. Sedimentation
   d. 1700 Cascadia earthquake

27. _____ refers to the mode of igneous volcanic rock formation in which hot magma from inside the Earth flows out (extrudes) onto the surface as lava or explodes violently into the atmosphere to fall back as pyroclastics or tuff. This is opposed to intrusive rock formation, in which magma does not reach the surface.
   a. Augen
   b. Ignimbrite
   c. Igneous rock
   d. Extrusive

28. _____ is molten rock that is found beneath the surface of the Earth, and may also exist on other terrestrial planets. Besides molten rock, _____ may also contain suspended crystals and gas bubbles. _____ often collects in a _____ chamber inside a volcano. _____ is capable of intrusion into adjacent rocks, extrusion onto the surface as lava, and explosive ejection as tephra to form pyroclastic rock.
   a. Large igneous provinces
   b. Sedimentary rock
   c. Groundmass
   d. Magma

29. _____ is air-fall material produced by a volcanic eruption regardless of composition or fragment size. _____ is typically rhyolitic in composition, as most explosive volcanoes are the product of the more viscous felsic or high silica magmas.

Volcanologists also refer to airborne fragments as pyroclasts.

a. Sedimentary rock
b. Large igneous provinces
c. Laccolith
d. Tephra

30. _____ is a common extrusive volcanic rock. It is usually grey to black and fine-grained due to rapid cooling of lava at the surface of a planet. It may be porphyritic containing larger crystals in a fine matrix, or vesicular, or frothy scoria.
a. Basalt
b. 1700 Cascadia earthquake
c. 1509 Istanbul earthquake
d. 1703 Genroku earthquake

31. _____ is one of the three main rock types (the others being sedimentary and metamorphic rock.) _____ is formed by magma (molten rock) being cooled and becoming solid . They may form with or without crystallization, either below the surface as intrusive (plutonic) rocks or on the surface as extrusive (volcanic) rocks. They make up approximately 95% of the upper part of the Earth's crust, but their great abundance is hidden on the Earth's surface by a relatively thin but widespread layer of sedimentary and metamorphic rocks.
a. Igneous differentiation
b. Igneous rock
c. Ignimbrite
d. Extrusive

32. _____ are distinctive geomorphological landforms of blocky detritus which may extend outward and downslope from talus cones or from glaciers or the terminal moraines of glaciers. Their growth and formation is subject to some debate, with three main theories in prominence:

- They originated from cirque glaciers and contain a glacial ice core or interstitial ice between the rocks which causes the formation to move downslope;

- A permafrost origin, which implies that the features are related to permafrost action rather than glacial action;

- A mass wasting or landslide origin which does not require the presence of ice and suggests a sudden catastrophic origin with little subsequent movement.

_____ may move or creep at a very slow rate in part dependent on the amount of ice present.

a. Pastonian Stage
b. Pressure melting point
c. Pre-Pastonian Stage
d. Rock glaciers

33. _____ is molten rock expelled by a volcano during eruption. When first expelled from a volcanic vent, it is a liquid at temperatures from 700 >°C to 1,200 >°C (1,300 >°F to 2,200 >°F.) Although _____ is quite viscous, with about 100,000 times the viscosity of water, it can flow great distances before cooling and solidifying, because of both its thixotropic and shear thinning properties.
a. Cinder
b. Pyroclastic flow
c. Volcanic ash
d. Lava

34. A _____ is a pyroclastic material. They are extrusive igneous rocks, and are similar to pumice, which has so many cavities and is such low-density that it can float on water.
a. Volcanic gases
b. Supervolcano
c. Volcanic pipes
d. Cinder

35. A _____ or scoria cone is a steep conical hill of volcanic fragments that accumulate around and downwind from a volcanic vent. The rock fragments, often called cinders or scoria, are glassy and contain numerous gas bubbles 'frozen' into place as magma exploded into the air and then cooled quickly. _____s range in size from tens to hundreds of meters tall.
   a. 1703 Genroku earthquake
   b. 1700 Cascadia earthquake
   c. 1509 Istanbul earthquake
   d. Cinder cone

36. A _____, sometimes called a composite volcano, is a tall, conical volcano with many layers (strata) of hardened lava, tephra, and volcanic ash. They are characterized by a steep profile and periodic, explosive eruptions. The lava that flows from a _____ tends to be viscous; it cools and hardens before spreading far.
   a. Mount Baker
   b. Mount Overlord
   c. Broken Top
   d. Stratovolcano

37. A _____ is generally a large area of exposed Precambrian crystalline igneous and high-grade metamorphic rocks that form tectonically stable areas. In all cases, the age of these rocks is greater than 570 million years and sometimes dates back 2 to 3.5 billion years. They have been little affected by tectonic events following the end of the Precambrian Era, and are relatively flat regions where mountain building, faulting, and other tectonic processes are greatly diminished compared with the activity that occurs at the margins of the _____s and the boundaries between tectonic plates.
   a. Shield
   b. 1703 Genroku earthquake
   c. 1509 Istanbul earthquake
   d. 1700 Cascadia earthquake

38. A _____ is a large volcano with shallow-sloping sides.

They are formed by lava flows of low viscosity - lava that flows easily. Consequently, a volcanic mountain having a broad profile is built up over time by flow after flow of relatively fluid basaltic lava issuing from vents or fissures on the surface of the volcano

   a. Shield volcano
   b. 1700 Cascadia earthquake
   c. 1703 Genroku earthquake
   d. 1509 Istanbul earthquake

39. _____ is an igneous rock of volcanic origin.

They are usually fine-grained or aphanitic to glassy in texture. They often contain clasts of other rocks and phenocrysts.

   a. Petrology
   b. Large igneous provinces
   c. Vesicular texture
   d. Volcanic rock

40. A _____ is an opening in a planet's surface or crust, which allows hot, molten rock, ash, and gases to escape from below the surface. Volcanic activity involving the extrusion of rock tends to form mountains or features like mountains over a period of time.
   a. 1700 Cascadia earthquake
   b. 1703 Genroku earthquake
   c. Volcano
   d. 1509 Istanbul earthquake

41. _____ is an igneous, volcanic rock, of intermediate composition, with aphanitic to porphyritic texture. The mineral assemblage is typically dominated by plagioclase plus pyroxene and/or hornblende. Magnetite, zircon, apatite, ilmenite, biotite, and garnet are common accessory minerals.
   a. Andesite
   b. AL 129-1
   c. AL 333
   d. AASHTO Soil Classification System

42. _____ is a term used in geology to refer to silicate minerals, magma, and rocks which are enriched in the lighter elements such as silicon, oxygen, aluminium, sodium, and potassium. _____ minerals are usually light in color and have specific gravities less than 3. Common _____ minerals include quartz, muscovite, orthoclase, and the sodium-rich plagioclase feldspars.
   a. Magma
   b. Groundmass
   c. Volcanic rock
   d. Felsic

43. _____ is an adjective describing a silicate mineral or rock that is rich in magnesium and iron; the term was derived by contracting 'magnesium' and 'ferric'. Most _____ minerals are dark in color and the specific gravity is greater than 3. Common rock-forming _____ minerals include olivine, pyroxene, amphibole, and biotite.

   _____ lava, before cooling, has a low viscosity, in comparison to felsic lava, due to the lower silica content in _____ magma. Water and other volatiles can more easily and gradually escape from _____ lava, so eruptions of volcanoes made of _____ lavas are less explosively violent than felsic lava eruptions.

   a. 1700 Cascadia earthquake
   b. 1509 Istanbul earthquake
   c. 1703 Genroku earthquake
   d. Mafic

44. _____ is an igneous, volcanic (extrusive) rock, of felsic (silicon-rich) composition. It may have any texture from aphanitic to porphyritic. The mineral assemblage is usually quartz, alkali feldspar and plagioclase. Biotite and hornblende are common accessory minerals.

   _____ can be considered as the extrusive equivalent to the plutonic granite rock, and consequently, outcroppings of it often bear a resemblance to granite. Due to their high content of silica and low iron and magnesium contents, _____ melts are highly polymerized and form highly viscous lavas.

   a. 1703 Genroku earthquake
   b. 1700 Cascadia earthquake
   c. 1509 Istanbul earthquake
   d. Rhyolite

45. In chronostratigraphy, a _____ is a succession of rock strata laid down in an single age on the geologic timescale, which usually represents millions of years of deposition. A given _____ of rock and the corresponding age of time will by convention have the same name, and the same boundaries.
   a. Stage
   b. Relative dating
   c. Lichenometry
   d. Paleomagnetism

46. _____s is a field of study within geology concerned generally with the structures within the lithosphere of the Earth and particularly with the forces and movements that have operated in a region to create these structures.

_____s is concerned with the orogenies and _____ development of cratons and _____ terranes as well as the earthquake and volcanic belts which directly affect much of the global population. _____ studies are also important for understanding erosion patterns in geomorphology and as guides for the economic geologist searching for petroleum and metallic ores.

- a. Rivera Plate
- b. Tectonic
- c. Fault trace
- d. Cocos Plate

47. The lithosphere is broken up into what are called _____. In the case of Earth, there are eight major and many minor plates The lithospheric plates ride on the asthenosphere. These plates move in relation to one another at one of three types of plate boundaries: convergent, or collisional boundaries; divergent boundaries, also called spreading centers; and transform boundaries.
- a. Supercontinent cycle
- b. Continental drift
- c. Nappe
- d. Tectonic plates

48. In geology, a _____ is a location on the Earth's surface that has experienced active volcanism for a long period of time.

J. Tuzo Wilson came up with the idea in 1963 that volcanic chains like the Hawaiian Islands result from the slow movement of a tectonic plate across a 'fixed' _____ deep beneath the surface of the planet.

- a. 1703 Genroku earthquake
- b. 1700 Cascadia earthquake
- c. 1509 Istanbul earthquake
- d. Hotspot

Chapter 35. Mount Rainier National Park

1. The _____ Era, is the most recent of the three classic geological eras and covers the period from 65.5 million years ago to the present. It is marked by the Cretaceous-Tertiary extinction event at the end of the Cretaceous that saw the demise of the last non-avian dinosaurs and the end of the Mesozoic Era. The _____ era is ongoing.
   a. 1509 Istanbul earthquake
   b. Cenozoic
   c. 1703 Genroku earthquake
   d. 1700 Cascadia earthquake

2. A _____ is an opening in a planet's surface or crust, which allows hot, molten rock, ash, and gases to escape from below the surface. Volcanic activity involving the extrusion of rock tends to form mountains or features like mountains over a period of time.
   a. Volcano
   b. 1700 Cascadia earthquake
   c. 1509 Istanbul earthquake
   d. 1703 Genroku earthquake

3. A _____ is a cauldron-like volcanic feature usually formed by the collapse of land following a volcanic eruption such as the one at Yellowstone National Park. They are sometimes confused with volcanic craters.
   a. 1700 Cascadia earthquake
   b. 1703 Genroku earthquake
   c. 1509 Istanbul earthquake
   d. Caldera

4. _____ is a destroyed stratovolcano in the Oregon part of the Cascade Volcanic Arc and the Cascade Range. The volcano's collapsed caldera holds Crater Lake, and the entire mountain is located within Crater Lake National Park.

Mazama is most famous for a catastrophic volcanic eruption that occurred around 5,677 (± 150) BC.

   a. 1700 Cascadia earthquake
   b. 1509 Istanbul earthquake
   c. 1703 Genroku earthquake
   d. Mount Mazama

5. _____ is a textural term for a volcanic rock that is a solidified frothy lava typically created when super-heated, highly pressurized rock is violently ejected from a volcano. It can be formed when lava and water are mixed. This unusual formation is due to the simultaneous actions of rapid cooling and rapid depressurization.
   a. Pyroclastic flow
   b. Wadati-Benioff zone
   c. Pumice
   d. Fissure vent

6. _____ is an igneous, volcanic rock, of intermediate composition, with aphanitic to porphyritic texture. The mineral assemblage is typically dominated by plagioclase plus pyroxene and/or hornblende. Magnetite, zircon, apatite, ilmenite, biotite, and garnet are common accessory minerals.
   a. AL 333
   b. AASHTO Soil Classification System
   c. Andesite
   d. AL 129-1

7. In geology, _____ refers to heat sources within the planet. _____ is technically an adjective (e.g., _____ energy) but in U.S. English the word has attained frequent use as a noun.

The planet's internal heat was originally generated during its accretion, due to gravitational binding energy, and since then additional heat has continued to be generated by decay heat from the radioactive decay of elements.

   a. Grade
   b. Cleavage
   c. Geothermal
   d. Tarn

8. The _____ is the rate of increase in temperature per unit depth in the Earth. It varies with location and is typically measured by determining the bottom open-hole temperature after borehole drilling. To achieve accuracy the drilling fluid needs time to reach the ambient temperature.
   a. Hot Dry Rock Geothermal Energy
   b. Geothermal power
   c. Geothermal desalination
   d. Geothermal gradient

9. The _____ is an area where large numbers of earthquakes and volcanic eruptions occur in the basin of the Pacific Ocean. In a 40,000 km horseshoe shape, it is associated with a nearly continuous series of oceanic trenches, volcanic arcs, and volcanic belts and/or plate movements. The _____ has 452 volcanoes and is home to over 75% of the world's active and dormant volcanoes.
   a. 1703 Genroku earthquake
   b. 1700 Cascadia earthquake
   c. 1509 Istanbul earthquake
   d. Pacific Ring of Fire

10. The _____ of any physical feature such as a hill, stream, roof, railroad, or road refers to the amount of inclination of that surface where zero indicates level (with respect to gravity) and larger numbers indicate higher degrees of 'tilt'. Often slope is calculated as a ratio of 'rise over run' in which run is the horizontal distance and rise is the vertical distance.

There are several systems for expressing slope:

1. as an angle of inclination from the horizontal of a right triangle. (This is the angle >α opposite the 'rise' side of the triangle.)
2. as a percentage (also known as the _____), the formula for which is [×]> which could also be expressed as the tangent of the angle of inclination times 100. In the U.S., the _____ is the most commonly used unit for communicating slopes in transportation, surveying, construction, and civil engineering.
3. as a per mille figure, the formula for which is [×]> which could also be expressed as the tangent of the angle of inclination times 1000. This is commonly used in Europe to denote the incline of a railway.
4. as a ratio of one part rise per so many parts run. For example, a slope that has a rise of 5 feet for every 100 feet of run would have a slope ratio of 1 in 20.

Any one of these expressions may be used interchangeably to express the characteristics of a slope. _____ is usually expressed as a percentage, but this may easily be converted to the angle >α from horizontal since that carries the same information.

   a. Compaction
   b. Heavy metal
   c. Diamond Head
   d. Grade

11. _____ is one of the three main rock types (the others being sedimentary and metamorphic rock.) _____ is formed by magma (molten rock) being cooled and becoming solid. They may form with or without crystallization, either below the surface as intrusive (plutonic) rocks or on the surface as extrusive (volcanic) rocks. They make up approximately 95% of the upper part of the Earth's crust, but their great abundance is hidden on the Earth's surface by a relatively thin but widespread layer of sedimentary and metamorphic rocks.

a. Ignimbrite
b. Extrusive
c. Igneous differentiation
d. Igneous rock

12. _____ is the removal of solids (sediment, soil, rock and other particles) in the natural environment. It usually occurs due to transport by wind, water, or ice; by down-slope creep of soil and other material under the force of gravity; or by living organisms, such as burrowing animals, in the case of bioerosion.

_____ is distinguished from weathering, which is the process of chemical or physical breakdown of the minerals in the rocks, although the two processes may occur concurrently.

a. AL 129-1
b. AASHTO Soil Classification System
c. Erosion
d. AL 333

13. _____ is caused by movement of ice, typically as glaciers. Glaciers erode predominantly by three different processes: abrasion/scouring, plucking, and ice thrusting. In an abrasion process, debris in the basal ice scrapes along the bed, polishing and gouging the underlying rocks, similar to sandpaper on wood. Glaciers can also cause pieces of bedrock to crack off in the process of plucking. In ice thrusting, the glacier freezes to its bed, then as it surges forward, it moves large sheets of frozen sediment at the base along with the glacier. This method produced some of the many thousands of lake basins that dot the edge of the Canadian Shield. These processes, combined with erosion and transport by the water network beneath the glacier, leave moraines, drumlins, eskers, ground moraine (till), kames, kame deltas, moulins, and glacial erratics in their wake, typically at the terminus or during glacier retreat.

a. Ice erosion
b. AL 129-1
c. AASHTO Soil Classification System
d. AL 333

14. A _____ is a large, slow-moving mass of ice, formed from compacted layers of snow, that slowly deforms and flows in response to gravity and high pressure.

_____ ice is the largest reservoir of fresh water on Earth, and second only to oceans as the largest reservoir of total water.

a. Deforestation
b. Little Ice Age
c. Keeling Curve
d. Glacier

15. _____ are distinctive geomorphological landforms of blocky detritus which may extend outward and downslope from talus cones or from glaciers or the terminal moraines of glaciers. Their growth and formation is subject to some debate, with three main theories in prominence:

- They originated from cirque glaciers and contain a glacial ice core or interstitial ice between the rocks which causes the formation to move downslope;

- A permafrost origin, which implies that the features are related to permafrost action rather than glacial action;

- A mass wasting or landslide origin which does not require the presence of ice and suggests a sudden catastrophic origin with little subsequent movement.

_____ may move or creep at a very slow rate in part dependent on the amount of ice present.

a. Pre-Pastonian Stage
b. Pastonian Stage
c. Pressure melting point
d. Rock glaciers

16. A _____ is a type of mudflow or landslide composed of pyroclastic material and water that flows down from a volcano, typically along a river valley. The term '_____' originated in the Javanese language of Indonesia. They can be best described as volcanic mudflows. They may not necessarily be caused by volcanic activity, but at the very least do originate from some type of volcanism.
   a. 1700 Cascadia earthquake
   b. 1703 Genroku earthquake
   c. 1509 Istanbul earthquake
   d. Lahar

17. _____ is the geomorphic process by which soil, regolith, and rock move downslope under the force of gravity. Types of _____ include creep, slides, flows, topples, and falls, each with its own characteristic features, and taking place over timescales from seconds to years. _____ occurs on both terrestrial and submarine slopes, and has been observed on Earth, Mars, and Venus.
   a. Soil liquefaction
   b. 1509 Istanbul earthquake
   c. Mass wasting
   d. 1700 Cascadia earthquake

18. A _____ is a fast moving mass of unconsolidated, saturated debris that looks like flowing concrete. They differentiate from a mudflow by terms of the viscosity of the flow. Flows can carry clasts ranging in size from clay particles to boulders, and also often contains a large amount of woody debris.
   a. Geohazard
   b. Cryoseism
   c. Sturzstrom
   d. Debris flow

19. A _____ or mudslide is the most rapid (up to 80 km/h, or 50 mph) and fluid type of downhill mass wasting. It is a rapid movement of a large mass of mud formed from loose earth and water. Similar terms are mudslide (not very liquid), mud stream, debris flow (e.g. in high mountains), j>ökulhlaup, and lahar
   a. 1509 Istanbul earthquake
   b. 1700 Cascadia earthquake
   c. 1703 Genroku earthquake
   d. Mudflow

20. The _____ is the epoch from 1.8 million to 11550 years BP covering the world's recent period of repeated glaciations. The _____ epoch follows the Pliocene epoch and is followed by the Holocene epoch. The _____ is the third epoch of the Neogene period or 6th epoch of the Cenozoic Era. The end of the _____ corresponds with the retreat of the last continental glacier. It also corresponds with the end of the Paleolithic age used in archaeology.
   a. Tyrrhenian
   b. Sicilian Stage
   c. Late Pleistocene
   d. Pleistocene

21. _____, also known as the Pleistocene glaciation, the current ice age or simply the ice age, refers to the period of the last few million years in which permanent ice sheets were established in Antarctica and perhaps Greenland, and fluctuating ice sheets have occurred elsewhere The major effects of the ice age were erosion and deposition of material over large parts of the continents, modification of river systems, creation of millions of lakes, changes in sea level, development of pluvial lakes far from the ice margins, isostatic adjustment of the crust, and abnormal winds. It affected oceans, flooding, and biological communities.
   a. Wolstonian Stage
   b. Rock glaciers
   c. Snowball Earth
   d. Quaternary glaciation

Chapter 35. Mount Rainier National Park

22. A _____ is an opening in Earth's crust, often in the neighborhood of volcanoes, which emits steam and gases such as carbon dioxide, sulfur dioxide, hydrochloric acid, and hydrogen sulfide.

They may occur along tiny cracks or long fissures, in chaotic clusters or fields, and on the surfaces of lava flows and thick deposits of pyroclastic flows. A _____ field is an area of thermal springs and gas vents where magma or hot igneous rocks at shallow depth are releasing gases or interacting with groundwater.

- a. 1509 Istanbul earthquake
- c. 1700 Cascadia earthquake
- b. 1703 Genroku earthquake
- d. Fumarole

23. A _____ is defined as a faint earth tremor caused by natural phenomena, such as winds and ocean waves. Thus a _____ is a small and long-continuing oscillation of the ground. The term is most commonly used to refer to the dominant background seismic noise signal on Earth, which arises from wave action in the oceans.
- a. Seismotectonics
- c. Morley-Vine-Matthews hypothesis
- b. Microseism
- d. Supershear earthquake

Chapter 36. Crater Lake National Park

1. _____ is a caldera lake located in the U.S. state of Oregon. It is the main feature of _____ National Park and famous for its deep blue color and water clarity. The lake partly fills a nearly 1,958 foot (597 m) deep caldera that was formed around 7,700 (>± 150) BC by the collapse of the volcano Mount Mazama.
   a. 1509 Istanbul earthquake
   b. 1700 Cascadia earthquake
   c. 1703 Genroku earthquake
   d. Crater Lake

2. The _____ is a a term for a geologic period 65 million to 1.8 million years ago. The _____ covered the time span between the superseded Secondary period and an out-of-date definition of the Quaternary period. The period began with the demise of the non-avian dinosaurs in the Cretaceous-_____ extinction event, at start of the Cenozoic era, spanning to beginning of the most recent Ice Age, at the end of the Pliocene epoch.
   a. Historical geology
   b. Tertiary
   c. Loihi Seamount
   d. Logarithmic Spiral Beach

3. _____ is a textural term for macrovesicular volcanic rock. It is commonly, but not exclusively, basaltic or andesitic in composition. _____ is light as a result of numerous macroscopic ellipsoidal vesicles, but most _____ has a specific gravity greater than 1, and sinks in water.
   a. Charnockite
   b. Coldwell Complex
   c. Scoria
   d. Lopolith

4. _____ is a type of rock consisting of consolidated volcanic ash ejected from vents during a volcanic eruption. _____ is sometimes called tufa, particularly when used as construction material, although tufa also refers to a quite different rock.

The products of a volcanic eruption are volcanic gases, lava, steam, and tephra. Magma is blown apart when it interacts violently with volcanic gases and steam. Solid material produced and thrown into the air by such volcanic eruptions is called tephra, regardless of composition or fragment size. If the resulting pieces of ejecta are small enough, the material is called volcanic ash, defined as such particles less than 2 mm in diameter, sand-sized or smaller.

   a. Pyroclastic rocks
   b. Lopolith
   c. Phanerite
   d. Tuff

5. _____ is a pyroclastic rock, of any origin, that was sufficiently hot at the time of deposition to weld together. Strictly speaking, if the rock contains scattered pea-sized fragments or fiamme in it, it is called a welded lapilli-tuff. They (and welded lapilli-tuffs) can be of fallout origin, or deposited from pyroclastic density currents, as in the case of ignimbrites.
   a. Flood basalt
   b. Country rock
   c. Pyroclastic rocks
   d. Welded tuff

6. _____ is a rock composed of angular fragments of minerals or rocks in a matrix (cementing material), that may be similar or different in composition to the fragments. A _____ may have a variety of different origins, as indicated by the named types including sedimentary _____, tectonic _____, igneous _____, impact _____ and hydrothermal _____.

Sedimentary _____s are a type of clastic sedimentary rock which are composed of angular to subangular, randomly oriented clasts of other sedimentary rocks.

a. 1509 Istanbul earthquake
b. Fault breccia
c. Breccia
d. Ventifacts

7. A _____ is a pyroclastic material. They are extrusive igneous rocks, and are similar to pumice, which has so many cavities and is such low-density that it can float on water.
   a. Cinder
   b. Supervolcano
   c. Volcanic pipes
   d. Volcanic gases

8. A _____ or scoria cone is a steep conical hill of volcanic fragments that accumulate around and downwind from a volcanic vent. The rock fragments, often called cinders or scoria, are glassy and contain numerous gas bubbles 'frozen' into place as magma exploded into the air and then cooled quickly. _____s range in size from tens to hundreds of meters tall.
   a. Cinder cone
   b. 1703 Genroku earthquake
   c. 1509 Istanbul earthquake
   d. 1700 Cascadia earthquake

9. A _____ or dyke in geology is a type of sheet intrusion referring to any geologic body that cuts discordantly across

   - planar wall rock structures, such as bedding or foliation
   - massive rock formations, like igneous/magmatic intrusions and salt diapirs.

They can therefore be either intrusive or sedimentary in origin.

An intrusive _____ is an igneous body with a very high aspect ratio, which means that its thickness is usually much smaller than the other two dimensions. Thickness can vary from sub-centimeter scale to many meters and the lateral dimensions can extend over many kilometers. A _____ is an intrusion into an opening cross-cutting fissure, shouldering aside other pre-existing layers or bodies of rock; this implies that a _____ is always younger than the rocks that contain it.

   a. Gradualism
   b. Type locality
   c. Dike
   d. Detritus

10. A _____ is a mountain rising from the ocean seafloor that does not reach to the water's surface (sea level), and thus is not an island. These are typically formed from extinct volcanoes, that rise abruptly and are usually found rising from a seafloor of 1,000-4,000 meters depth. They are defined by oceanographers as independent features that rise to at least 1,000 meters above the seafloor.
    a. 1703 Genroku earthquake
    b. 1700 Cascadia earthquake
    c. 1509 Istanbul earthquake
    d. Seamount

11. A _____ is generally a large area of exposed Precambrian crystalline igneous and high-grade metamorphic rocks that form tectonically stable areas. In all cases, the age of these rocks is greater than 570 million years and sometimes dates back 2 to 3.5 billion years. They have been little affected by tectonic events following the end of the Precambrian Era, and are relatively flat regions where mountain building, faulting, and other tectonic processes are greatly diminished compared with the activity that occurs at the margins of the _____s and the boundaries between tectonic plates.

a. 1703 Genroku earthquake
b. 1700 Cascadia earthquake
c. 1509 Istanbul earthquake
d. Shield

12. A _____ is a large volcano with shallow-sloping sides.

They are formed by lava flows of low viscosity - lava that flows easily. Consequently, a volcanic mountain having a broad profile is built up over time by flow after flow of relatively fluid basaltic lava issuing from vents or fissures on the surface of the volcano

a. 1509 Istanbul earthquake
b. 1703 Genroku earthquake
c. Shield volcano
d. 1700 Cascadia earthquake

13. A _____ is a mass of molten rock (tephra) larger than 65 mm (2.5 inches) in diameter, formed when a volcano ejects viscous fragments of lava during an eruption. They cool into solid fragments before they reach the ground. Lava bombs can be thrown many kilometres from an erupting vent, and often acquire aerodynamic shapes during their flight.

a. 1703 Genroku earthquake
b. Volcanic bomb
c. 1509 Istanbul earthquake
d. 1700 Cascadia earthquake

14. A _____ is an opening in a planet's surface or crust, which allows hot, molten rock, ash, and gases to escape from below the surface. Volcanic activity involving the extrusion of rock tends to form mountains or features like mountains over a period of time.

a. 1700 Cascadia earthquake
b. 1509 Istanbul earthquake
c. 1703 Genroku earthquake
d. Volcano

15. The _____ is the epoch from 1.8 million to 11550 years BP covering the world's recent period of repeated glaciations. The _____ epoch follows the Pliocene epoch and is followed by the Holocene epoch. The _____ is the third epoch of the Neogene period or 6th epoch of the Cenozoic Era. The end of the _____ corresponds with the retreat of the last continental glacier. It also corresponds with the end of the Paleolithic age used in archaeology.

a. Tyrrhenian
b. Sicilian Stage
c. Late Pleistocene
d. Pleistocene

16. _____, also known as the Pleistocene glaciation, the current ice age or simply the ice age, refers to the period of the last few million years in which permanent ice sheets were established in Antarctica and perhaps Greenland, and fluctuating ice sheets have occurred elsewhere The major effects of the ice age were erosion and deposition of material over large parts of the continents, modification of river systems, creation of millions of lakes, changes in sea level, development of pluvial lakes far from the ice margins, isostatic adjustment of the crust, and abnormal winds. It affected oceans, flooding, and biological communities.

a. Snowball Earth
b. Rock glaciers
c. Wolstonian Stage
d. Quaternary glaciation

Chapter 37. Lassen Volcanic National Park

1. The _____ Era, is the most recent of the three classic geological eras and covers the period from 65.5 million years ago to the present. It is marked by the Cretaceous-Tertiary extinction event at the end of the Cretaceous that saw the demise of the last non-avian dinosaurs and the end of the Mesozoic Era. The _____ era is ongoing.
   a. 1703 Genroku earthquake
   b. Cenozoic
   c. 1700 Cascadia earthquake
   d. 1509 Istanbul earthquake

2. _____ is molten rock expelled by a volcano during eruption. When first expelled from a volcanic vent, it is a liquid at temperatures from 700 >°C to 1,200 >°C (1,300 >°F to 2,200 >°F.) Although _____ is quite viscous, with about 100,000 times the viscosity of water, it can flow great distances before cooling and solidifying, because of both its thixotropic and shear thinning properties.
   a. Pyroclastic flow
   b. Cinder
   c. Volcanic ash
   d. Lava

3. A _____ is an opening in a planet's surface or crust, which allows hot, molten rock, ash, and gases to escape from below the surface. Volcanic activity involving the extrusion of rock tends to form mountains or features like mountains over a period of time.
   a. 1703 Genroku earthquake
   b. 1700 Cascadia earthquake
   c. 1509 Istanbul earthquake
   d. Volcano

4. A _____ occurs when rising magma makes contact with ground or surface water. The extreme temperature of the magma) causes near-instantaneous evaporation to steam resulting in an explosion of steam, water, ash, rock, and volcanic bombs. At Mount St. Helens hundreds of steam explosions preceded a 1980 plinian eruption of the volcano.
   a. Limnic eruption
   b. Phreatomagmatic eruptions
   c. Plinian eruptions
   d. Phreatic eruption

5. _____ is molten rock that is found beneath the surface of the Earth, and may also exist on other terrestrial planets. Besides molten rock, _____ may also contain suspended crystals and gas bubbles. _____ often collects in a _____ chamber inside a volcano. _____ is capable of intrusion into adjacent rocks, extrusion onto the surface as lava, and explosive ejection as tephra to form pyroclastic rock.
   a. Magma
   b. Sedimentary rock
   c. Large igneous provinces
   d. Groundmass

6. _____ circulation in its most general sense is the circulation of hot water; 'hydros' in the Greek meaning water and 'thermos' meaning heat. _____ circulation occurs most often in the vicinity of sources of heat within the Earth's crust. This generally occurs near volcanic activity, but can occur in the deep crust related to the intrusion of granite, or as the result of orogeny or metamorphism.
   a. Headward erosion
   b. Seafloor spreading
   c. Hydrothermal
   d. Transgression

7. _____ is the youngest group of lava domes in Lassen Volcanic National Park, California, having been formed as five dacite domes 1,100-1,000 years ago. The cluster of domes are located north of Lassen Peak.

From the base of the crags and extending toward the northwest corner of the park is Chaos Jumbles, a cold rock avalanche which undermined _____' northwest slope 300 years ago.

a. 1509 Istanbul earthquake
b. Chaos Jumbles
c. 1700 Cascadia earthquake
d. Chaos Crags

8. A _____ is generally a large area of exposed Precambrian crystalline igneous and high-grade metamorphic rocks that form tectonically stable areas. In all cases, the age of these rocks is greater than 570 million years and sometimes dates back 2 to 3.5 billion years. They have been little affected by tectonic events following the end of the Precambrian Era, and are relatively flat regions where mountain building, faulting, and other tectonic processes are greatly diminished compared with the activity that occurs at the margins of the _____s and the boundaries between tectonic plates.
a. 1700 Cascadia earthquake
b. 1703 Genroku earthquake
c. 1509 Istanbul earthquake
d. Shield

9. A _____ is a large volcano with shallow-sloping sides.

They are formed by lava flows of low viscosity - lava that flows easily. Consequently, a volcanic mountain having a broad profile is built up over time by flow after flow of relatively fluid basaltic lava issuing from vents or fissures on the surface of the volcano

a. 1700 Cascadia earthquake
b. 1509 Istanbul earthquake
c. 1703 Genroku earthquake
d. Shield volcano

10. A _____ is a pyroclastic material. They are extrusive igneous rocks, and are similar to pumice, which has so many cavities and is such low-density that it can float on water.
a. Cinder
b. Volcanic gases
c. Volcanic pipes
d. Supervolcano

11. A _____ or scoria cone is a steep conical hill of volcanic fragments that accumulate around and downwind from a volcanic vent. The rock fragments, often called cinders or scoria, are glassy and contain numerous gas bubbles 'frozen' into place as magma exploded into the air and then cooled quickly. _____s range in size from tens to hundreds of meters tall.
a. 1703 Genroku earthquake
b. Cinder cone
c. 1509 Istanbul earthquake
d. 1700 Cascadia earthquake

12. The _____ is the epoch from 1.8 million to 11550 years BP covering the world's recent period of repeated glaciations. The _____ epoch follows the Pliocene epoch and is followed by the Holocene epoch. The _____ is the third epoch of the Neogene period or 6th epoch of the Cenozoic Era. The end of the _____ corresponds with the retreat of the last continental glacier. It also corresponds with the end of the Paleolithic age used in archaeology.
a. Pleistocene
b. Tyrrhenian
c. Late Pleistocene
d. Sicilian Stage

13. _____, also known as the Pleistocene glaciation, the current ice age or simply the ice age, refers to the period of the last few million years in which permanent ice sheets were established in Antarctica and perhaps Greenland, and fluctuating ice sheets have occurred elsewhere The major effects of the ice age were erosion and deposition of material over large parts of the continents, modification of river systems, creation of millions of lakes, changes in sea level, development of pluvial lakes far from the ice margins, isostatic adjustment of the crust, and abnormal winds. It affected oceans, flooding, and biological communities.

a. Wolstonian Stage
b. Quaternary glaciation
c. Snowball Earth
d. Rock glaciers

14. _____ is the second most abundant mineral in the Earth's continental crust. It is made up of a framework of silicon-oxygen tetrahedra SiO_4, with each silicon shared between two oxygens to give the overall formula SiO_2. _____ has a hardness of 7 on the Mohs scale and a density of 2.65 g/cmÂ³.

a. Shocked quartz
b. 1509 Istanbul earthquake
c. Quartz
d. 1700 Cascadia earthquake

15. _____ is a common extrusive volcanic rock. It is usually grey to black and fine-grained due to rapid cooling of lava at the surface of a planet. It may be porphyritic containing larger crystals in a fine matrix, or vesicular, or frothy scoria.

a. Basalt
b. 1509 Istanbul earthquake
c. 1700 Cascadia earthquake
d. 1703 Genroku earthquake

16. _____ usually refers to the thick foundation of ancient, and oldest metamorphic and igneous rock that forms the crust of continents, often in the form of granite. _____ is contrasted to overlying sedimentary rocks which are laid down on top of the _____s after the continent was formed, such as sandstone and limestone. The sedimentary rocks which may be deposited on top of the basement usually form a relatively thin veneer, but can be more than 3 miles thick.

a. Polystrate
b. Basement rock
c. Key bed
d. Bed

1. The _____ , usually abbreviated K for its German translation Kreide, is a geologic period and system from circa >145.5 >± 4 to >65.5 >± 0.3 million years ago . In the geologic timescale, the _____ follows on the Jurassic period and is followed by the Paleogene period. It is the youngest period of the Mesozoic era, and at 80 million years long, the longest period of the Phanerozoic eon. The end of the _____ defines the boundary between the Mesozoic and Cenozoic eras.
   a. Campanian
   b. Valanginian
   c. Hauterivian
   d. Cretaceous

2. The _____ is a a term for a geologic period 65 million to 1.8 million years ago. The _____ covered the time span between the superseded Secondary period and an out-of-date definition of the Quaternary period. The period began with the demise of the non-avian dinosaurs in the Cretaceous-_____ extinction event, at start of the Cenozoic era, spanning to beginning of the most recent Ice Age, at the end of the Pliocene epoch.
   a. Loihi Seamount
   b. Logarithmic Spiral Beach
   c. Historical geology
   d. Tertiary

3. A _____ is a mountain rising from the ocean seafloor that does not reach to the water's surface (sea level), and thus is not an island. These are typically formed from extinct volcanoes, that rise abruptly and are usually found rising from a seafloor of 1,000-4,000 meters depth. They are defined by oceanographers as independent features that rise to at least 1,000 meters above the seafloor.
   a. 1509 Istanbul earthquake
   b. 1703 Genroku earthquake
   c. 1700 Cascadia earthquake
   d. Seamount

4. The _____ Era is one of three geologic eras of the Phanerozoic eon. The division of time into eras dates back to Giovanni Arduino, in the 18th century, although his original name for the era now called the '_____' was 'Secondary' (making the modern era the 'Tertiary'.)

   The _____ was a time of tectonic, climatic and evolutionary activity. The continents gradually shifted from a state of connectedness into their present configuration; the drifting provided for speciation and other important evolutionary developments.

   a. 1700 Cascadia earthquake
   b. 1703 Genroku earthquake
   c. 1509 Istanbul earthquake
   d. Mesozoic

5. A _____ is an opening in Earth's crust, often in the neighborhood of volcanoes, which emits steam and gases such as carbon dioxide, sulfur dioxide, hydrochloric acid, and hydrogen sulfide.

   They may occur along tiny cracks or long fissures, in chaotic clusters or fields, and on the surfaces of lava flows and thick deposits of pyroclastic flows. A _____ field is an area of thermal springs and gas vents where magma or hot igneous rocks at shallow depth are releasing gases or interacting with groundwater.

   a. 1509 Istanbul earthquake
   b. 1703 Genroku earthquake
   c. 1700 Cascadia earthquake
   d. Fumarole

6. _____ is a size classification term for tephra, which is material that falls out of the air during a volcanic eruption. They are in some senses similar to ooids or pisoids in calcareous sediments.

   By definition _____ range in size from 2 mm to 64 mm in diameter. A pyroclastic particle greater than 64 mm in diameter is correctly known as a volcanic bomb when molten, or a volcanic block when solid.

a. Supervolcano
b. Volcanic ash
c. Wadati-Benioff zone
d. Lapilli

7. _____, meaning 'new eruption', is a volcano located on the Alaska Peninsula in Katmai National Park and Preserve, about 290 miles (470 km) southwest of Anchorage. Formed in 1912 during one of the largest volcanic eruptions of the 20th century, _____ released 30 times the volume of magma as the 1980 eruption of Mount St. Helens. Map showing volcanoes of Alaska.

One of the largest eruptions of the 20th century occurred in 1912, from June 6 to June 8, to form _____.

a. 1509 Istanbul earthquake
b. 1703 Genroku earthquake
c. Novarupta
d. 1700 Cascadia earthquake

8. A _____ is a mass of molten rock (tephra) larger than 65 mm (2.5 inches) in diameter, formed when a volcano ejects viscous fragments of lava during an eruption. They cool into solid fragments before they reach the ground. Lava bombs can be thrown many kilometres from an erupting vent, and often acquire aerodynamic shapes during their flight.

a. 1700 Cascadia earthquake
b. 1703 Genroku earthquake
c. 1509 Istanbul earthquake
d. Volcanic bomb

9. A _____ is a pyroclastic material. They are extrusive igneous rocks, and are similar to pumice, which has so many cavities and is such low-density that it can float on water.

a. Cinder
b. Supervolcano
c. Volcanic gases
d. Volcanic pipes

10. A _____ or scoria cone is a steep conical hill of volcanic fragments that accumulate around and downwind from a volcanic vent. The rock fragments, often called cinders or scoria, are glassy and contain numerous gas bubbles 'frozen' into place as magma exploded into the air and then cooled quickly. _____s range in size from tens to hundreds of meters tall.

a. 1700 Cascadia earthquake
b. 1509 Istanbul earthquake
c. 1703 Genroku earthquake
d. Cinder cone

11. The _____ Period is the geologic time period after the Neogene Period, spanning 1.805 +/- 0.005 million years ago to the present. The _____ includes two geologic epochs: the Pleistocene and the Holocene Epoch.

There is an ongoing debate of the status of _____ -- a recent proposal from International Commission on Stratigraphy (ICS) was to make _____ a subperiod under Neogene, but that was retracted after criticism from International Union for _____ Research (INQUA), so instead ICS and INQUA agreed to erect _____ as an Era, above Neogene, and to place the base for _____ at 2.588 >± 3.005, the base for Gelasian Stage.

a. Geomorphology
b. Tributary
c. Yilgarn Craton
d. Quaternary

12. A _____ is an opening in a planet's surface or crust, which allows hot, molten rock, ash, and gases to escape from below the surface. Volcanic activity involving the extrusion of rock tends to form mountains or features like mountains over a period of time.
   a. 1703 Genroku earthquake
   b. 1700 Cascadia earthquake
   c. 1509 Istanbul earthquake
   d. Volcano

13. The _____ is the earliest of three geologic eras of the Phanerozoic eon. The _____ spanned from roughly 542 to 251 million years ago (ICS, 2004), and is subdivided into six geologic periods; from oldest to youngest they are: the Cambrian, Ordovician, Silurian, Devonian, Carboniferous, and Permian.

The _____ covers the time from the first appearance of abundant, soft-shelled fossils to the time when the continents were beginning to be dominated by large, relatively sophisticated reptiles and modern plants. The lower (oldest) boundary was classically set at the first appearance of creatures known as trilobites and archeocyathids.

   a. 1509 Istanbul earthquake
   b. Paleozoic
   c. 1703 Genroku earthquake
   d. 1700 Cascadia earthquake

14. The _____ Era, is the most recent of the three classic geological eras and covers the period from 65.5 million years ago to the present. It is marked by the Cretaceous-Tertiary extinction event at the end of the Cretaceous that saw the demise of the last non-avian dinosaurs and the end of the Mesozoic Era. The _____ era is ongoing.
   a. 1700 Cascadia earthquake
   b. 1703 Genroku earthquake
   c. 1509 Istanbul earthquake
   d. Cenozoic

15. _____, also known as the Pleistocene glaciation, the current ice age or simply the ice age, refers to the period of the last few million years in which permanent ice sheets were established in Antarctica and perhaps Greenland, and fluctuating ice sheets have occurred elsewhere The major effects of the ice age were erosion and deposition of material over large parts of the continents, modification of river systems, creation of millions of lakes, changes in sea level, development of pluvial lakes far from the ice margins, isostatic adjustment of the crust, and abnormal winds. It affected oceans, flooding, and biological communities.
   a. Wolstonian Stage
   b. Snowball Earth
   c. Quaternary glaciation
   d. Rock glaciers

Chapter 39. Lake Clark National Park and Preserve

1. A _____ is a type of mudflow or landslide composed of pyroclastic material and water that flows down from a volcano, typically along a river valley. The term '_____' originated in the Javanese language of Indonesia. They can be best described as volcanic mudflows. They may not necessarily be caused by volcanic activity, but at the very least do originate from some type of volcanism.
    a. 1509 Istanbul earthquake
    b. 1700 Cascadia earthquake
    c. 1703 Genroku earthquake
    d. Lahar

2. A _____ is a geological phenomenon which includes a wide range of ground movement, such as rock falls, deep failure of slopes and shallow debris flows, which can occur in offshore, coastal and onshore environments. Although the action of gravity is the primary driving force for a _____ to occur, there are other contributing factors affecting the original slope stability. Typically, pre-conditional factors build up specific sub-surface conditions that make the area/slope prone to failure, whereas the actual _____ often requires a trigger before being released.
    a. 1700 Cascadia earthquake
    b. Landslide
    c. Mass wasting
    d. 1509 Istanbul earthquake

3. A _____ is a large, slow-moving mass of ice, formed from compacted layers of snow, that slowly deforms and flows in response to gravity and high pressure.

    _____ ice is the largest reservoir of fresh water on Earth, and second only to oceans as the largest reservoir of total water.

    a. Keeling Curve
    b. Deforestation
    c. Little Ice Age
    d. Glacier

4. _____ is the geomorphic process by which soil, regolith, and rock move downslope under the force of gravity. Types of _____ include creep, slides, flows, topples, and falls, each with its own characteristic features, and taking place over timescales from seconds to years. _____ occurs on both terrestrial and submarine slopes, and has been observed on Earth, Mars, and Venus.
    a. Mass wasting
    b. 1509 Istanbul earthquake
    c. 1700 Cascadia earthquake
    d. Soil liquefaction

5. The _____ Period is the geologic time period after the Neogene Period, spanning 1.805 +/- 0.005 million years ago to the present. The _____ includes two geologic epochs: the Pleistocene and the Holocene Epoch.

    There is an ongoing debate of the status of _____ -- a recent proposal from International Commission on Stratigraphy (ICS) was to make _____ a subperiod under Neogene, but that was retracted after criticism from International Union for _____ Research (INQUA), so instead ICS and INQUA agreed to erect _____ as an Era, above Neogene, and to place the base for _____ at 2.588 >± 3.005, the base for Gelasian Stage.

    a. Tributary
    b. Quaternary
    c. Yilgarn Craton
    d. Geomorphology

6. In geology, _____ is a type of mass wasting where waterlogged sediment slowly moves downslope over impermeable material. It can occur in any climate where the ground is saturated by water, though it is most often found in periglacial environments where the ground is permanently frozen, under which conditions the process is often called gelifluction. During warm seasonal periods the surface layer melts and slides over the frozen underlayer, slowly moving downslope due to frost heave that occurs normal to the slope.
   a. Solifluction
   b. Sturzstrom
   c. Rockfall
   d. Geohazard

7. The _____, usually abbreviated K for its German translation Kreide, is a geologic period and system from circa >145.5 >± 4 to >65.5 >± 0.3 million years ago . In the geologic timescale, the _____ follows on the Jurassic period and is followed by the Paleogene period. It is the youngest period of the Mesozoic era, and at 80 million years long, the longest period of the Phanerozoic eon. The end of the _____ defines the boundary between the Mesozoic and Cenozoic eras.
   a. Hauterivian
   b. Valanginian
   c. Campanian
   d. Cretaceous

8. The _____ Era is one of three geologic eras of the Phanerozoic eon. The division of time into eras dates back to Giovanni Arduino, in the 18th century, although his original name for the era now called the '_____' was 'Secondary' (making the modern era the 'Tertiary'.)

The _____ was a time of tectonic, climatic and evolutionary activity. The continents gradually shifted from a state of connectedness into their present configuration; the drifting provided for speciation and other important evolutionary developments.
   a. 1509 Istanbul earthquake
   b. 1703 Genroku earthquake
   c. 1700 Cascadia earthquake
   d. Mesozoic

9. The _____ is a a term for a geologic period 65 million to 1.8 million years ago. The _____ covered the time span between the superseded Secondary period and an out-of-date definition of the Quaternary period. The period began with the demise of the non-avian dinosaurs in the Cretaceous-_____ extinction event, at start of the Cenozoic era, spanning to beginning of the most recent Ice Age, at the end of the Pliocene epoch.
   a. Historical geology
   b. Logarithmic Spiral Beach
   c. Tertiary
   d. Loihi Seamount

10. The _____ is a geological epoch which began approximately 11≈700 years ago (10≈000 ^{14}C years ago). According to traditional geological thinking, the _____ continues to the present. The _____ is part of the Neogene and Quaternary periods.
    a. Neoglaciation
    b. 1509 Istanbul earthquake
    c. 1700 Cascadia earthquake
    d. Holocene

11. The _____ is the epoch from 1.8 million to 11550 years BP covering the world's recent period of repeated glaciations. The _____ epoch follows the Pliocene epoch and is followed by the Holocene epoch. The _____ is the third epoch of the Neogene period or 6th epoch of the Cenozoic Era. The end of the _____ corresponds with the retreat of the last continental glacier. It also corresponds with the end of the Paleolithic age used in archaeology.
    a. Tyrrhenian
    b. Late Pleistocene
    c. Sicilian Stage
    d. Pleistocene

12. _____, also known as the Pleistocene glaciation, the current ice age or simply the ice age, refers to the period of the last few million years in which permanent ice sheets were established in Antarctica and perhaps Greenland, and fluctuating ice sheets have occurred elsewhere The major effects of the ice age were erosion and deposition of material over large parts of the continents, modification of river systems, creation of millions of lakes, changes in sea level, development of pluvial lakes far from the ice margins, isostatic adjustment of the crust, and abnormal winds. It affected oceans, flooding, and biological communities.

   a. Snowball Earth
   c. Wolstonian Stage
   b. Quaternary glaciation
   d. Rock glaciers

Chapter 40. Hawaii Volcanoes National Park

1. An _____ is a chain or cluster of islands that are formed tectonically. They are usually found in the open sea; less commonly, a large land mass may neighbour them.
    a. AL 129-1
    b. AASHTO Soil Classification System
    c. Archipelago
    d. AL 333

2. A _____ is an opening in a planet's surface or crust, which allows hot, molten rock, ash, and gases to escape from below the surface. Volcanic activity involving the extrusion of rock tends to form mountains or features like mountains over a period of time.
    a. 1700 Cascadia earthquake
    b. Volcano
    c. 1703 Genroku earthquake
    d. 1509 Istanbul earthquake

3. A _____ is a mountain rising from the ocean seafloor that does not reach to the water's surface (sea level), and thus is not an island. These are typically formed from extinct volcanoes, that rise abruptly and are usually found rising from a seafloor of 1,000-4,000 meters depth. They are defined by oceanographers as independent features that rise to at least 1,000 meters above the seafloor.
    a. 1700 Cascadia earthquake
    b. 1703 Genroku earthquake
    c. 1509 Istanbul earthquake
    d. Seamount

4. The _____ is the epoch from 1.8 million to 11550 years BP covering the world's recent period of repeated glaciations. The _____ epoch follows the Pliocene epoch and is followed by the Holocene epoch. The _____ is the third epoch of the Neogene period or 6th epoch of the Cenozoic Era. The end of the _____ corresponds with the retreat of the last continental glacier. It also corresponds with the end of the Paleolithic age used in archaeology.
    a. Tyrrhenian
    b. Late Pleistocene
    c. Pleistocene
    d. Sicilian Stage

5. A _____ is generally a large area of exposed Precambrian crystalline igneous and high-grade metamorphic rocks that form tectonically stable areas. In all cases, the age of these rocks is greater than 570 million years and sometimes dates back 2 to 3.5 billion years. They have been little affected by tectonic events following the end of the Precambrian Era, and are relatively flat regions where mountain building, faulting, and other tectonic processes are greatly diminished compared with the activity that occurs at the margins of the _____s and the boundaries between tectonic plates.
    a. 1700 Cascadia earthquake
    b. 1703 Genroku earthquake
    c. 1509 Istanbul earthquake
    d. Shield

6. A _____ is a large volcano with shallow-sloping sides.

They are formed by lava flows of low viscosity - lava that flows easily. Consequently, a volcanic mountain having a broad profile is built up over time by flow after flow of relatively fluid basaltic lava issuing from vents or fissures on the surface of the volcano

    a. 1509 Istanbul earthquake
    b. Shield volcano
    c. 1700 Cascadia earthquake
    d. 1703 Genroku earthquake

7. _____ is the largest volcano on earth in terms of area covered and one of five volcanoes that form the Island of Hawaii in the U.S. state of Hawai>Ê»i in the Pacific Ocean. It is an active shield volcano, with a volume estimated at approximately 18,000 cubic miles (75,000 kmÂ³), although its peak is about 120 feet (37 m) lower than that of its neighbor, Mauna Kea. The Hawaiian name '_____' means 'Long Mountain'.

a. Mauna Loa
b. 1700 Cascadia earthquake
c. 1509 Istanbul earthquake
d. 1703 Genroku earthquake

8. _____ is a common extrusive volcanic rock. It is usually grey to black and fine-grained due to rapid cooling of lava at the surface of a planet. It may be porphyritic containing larger crystals in a fine matrix, or vesicular, or frothy scoria.
   a. 1700 Cascadia earthquake
   b. 1509 Istanbul earthquake
   c. 1703 Genroku earthquake
   d. Basalt

9. _____ is molten rock expelled by a volcano during eruption. When first expelled from a volcanic vent, it is a liquid at temperatures from 700 >°C to 1,200 >°C (1,300 >°F to 2,200 >°F.) Although _____ is quite viscous, with about 100,000 times the viscosity of water, it can flow great distances before cooling and solidifying, because of both its thixotropic and shear thinning properties.
   a. Cinder
   b. Pyroclastic flow
   c. Lava
   d. Volcanic ash

10. _____ is a naturally occurring glass formed as an extrusive igneous rock. It is produced when felsic lava extruded from a volcano cools without crystal growth. _____ is commonly found within the margins of rhyolitic lava flows known as _____ flows, where the chemical composition (high silica content) induces a high viscosity and polymerization degree of the lava.
    a. AL 129-1
    b. AL 333
    c. AASHTO Soil Classification System
    d. Obsidian

11. _____ is an igneous rock of volcanic origin.

They are usually fine-grained or aphanitic to glassy in texture. They often contain clasts of other rocks and phenocrysts.

   a. Large igneous provinces
   b. Vesicular texture
   c. Petrology
   d. Volcanic rock

12. _____ is a textural term for macrovesicular volcanic rock. It is commonly, but not exclusively, basaltic or andesitic in composition. _____ is light as a result of numerous macroscopic ellipsoidal vesicles, but most _____ has a specific gravity greater than 1, and sinks in water.
    a. Charnockite
    b. Coldwell Complex
    c. Lopolith
    d. Scoria

13. _____ are clastic rocks composed solely or primarily of volcanic materials. Where the volcanic material has been transported and reworked through mechanical action, such as by wind or water, these rocks are termed volcaniclastic. Commonly associated with explosive volcanic activity - such as Plinian or krakatoan eruption styles, or phreatomagmatic eruptions - pyroclastic deposits are commonly formed from airborne ash, lapilli and bombs or blocks ejected from the volcano itself, mixed in with shattered country rock.
    a. Great Dyke
    b. Lopolith
    c. Welded tuff
    d. Pyroclastic rocks

14. In geology, a _____ is a place where the Earth's crust and lithosphere are being pulled apart and is an example of extensional tectonics.

Typical _____ features are a central linear downdropped fault segment, called a graben, with parallel normal faulting and _____-flank uplifts on either side forming a _____ valley, where the _____ remains above sea level. The axis of the _____ area commonly contains volcanic rocks and active volcanism is a part of many, but not all active _____ systems.

a. Rift
b. 1700 Cascadia earthquake
c. 1509 Istanbul earthquake
d. 1703 Genroku earthquake

15. In geology, a _____ or _____ line is a planar fracture in rock in which the rock on one side of the fracture has moved with respect to the rock on the other side. Large _____s within the Earth's crust are the result of differential or shear motion and active _____ zones are the causal locations of most earthquakes. Earthquakes are caused by energy release during rapid slippage along a _____.
a. Cleavage
b. Compaction
c. Drainage system
d. Fault

16. A _____ is a geological phenomenon which includes a wide range of ground movement, such as rock falls, deep failure of slopes and shallow debris flows, which can occur in offshore, coastal and onshore environments. Although the action of gravity is the primary driving force for a _____ to occur, there are other contributing factors affecting the original slope stability. Typically, pre-conditional factors build up specific sub-surface conditions that make the area/slope prone to failure, whereas the actual _____ often requires a trigger before being released.
a. 1509 Istanbul earthquake
b. Mass wasting
c. 1700 Cascadia earthquake
d. Landslide

17. _____ are pillow-shaped structures sometimes seen in lavas and are attributed to the congealment of lava under water, or subaqeous extrusion. A pillow structure in certain extrusive igneous rock is characterized by discontinuous pillow-shaped masses, commonly up to 1 metre in diameter. _____ commonly occur at Constructive plate boundaries, forming part of a mid-ocean ridge.
a. Pillow lava
b. Fabric
c. Duricrust
d. Patterned ground

18. The term _____ refers to the elevation (on the ground) or altitude (in the air) of any object, relative to the average sea level datum. _____ is used extensively in radio (both in broadcasting and other telecommunications uses) by engineers to determine the coverage area a station will be able to reach. It is also used in aviation, where all heights are recorded and reported with respect to _____ , and in the atmospheric sciences.
a. AL 129-1
b. AASHTO Soil Classification System
c. AL 333
d. Above mean sea level

19. A _____ is an opening in Earth's crust, often in the neighborhood of volcanoes, which emits steam and gases such as carbon dioxide, sulfur dioxide, hydrochloric acid, and hydrogen sulfide.

They may occur along tiny cracks or long fissures, in chaotic clusters or fields, and on the surfaces of lava flows and thick deposits of pyroclastic flows. A _____ field is an area of thermal springs and gas vents where magma or hot igneous rocks at shallow depth are releasing gases or interacting with groundwater.

a. 1703 Genroku earthquake
c. 1700 Cascadia earthquake
b. 1509 Istanbul earthquake
d. Fumarole

20. A _____ is a vector field which surrounds magnets and electric currents, and is detected by the force it exerts on moving electric charges and on magnetic materials. When placed in a _____, magnetic dipoles tend to align their axes parallel to the _____. Magnetic fields also have their own energy with an energy density proportional to the square of the field intensity.
   a. Magnetic field
   c. 1703 Genroku earthquake
   b. 1509 Istanbul earthquake
   d. 1700 Cascadia earthquake

21. In chronostratigraphy, a _____ is a succession of rock strata laid down in an single age on the geologic timescale, which usually represents millions of years of deposition. A given _____ of rock and the corresponding age of time will by convention have the same name, and the same boundaries.
   a. Paleomagnetism
   c. Relative dating
   b. Lichenometry
   d. Stage

Chapter 41. Haleakala National Park

1. The _____ is a geological epoch which began approximately 11‰700 years ago (10‰000 ^{14}C years ago). According to traditional geological thinking, the _____ continues to the present. The _____ is part of the Neogene and Quaternary periods.
    a. 1700 Cascadia earthquake
    b. 1509 Istanbul earthquake
    c. Holocene
    d. Neoglaciation

2. The _____ is the epoch from 1.8 million to 11550 years BP covering the world's recent period of repeated glaciations. The _____ epoch follows the Pliocene epoch and is followed by the Holocene epoch. The _____ is the third epoch of the Neogene period or 6th epoch of the Cenozoic Era. The end of the _____ corresponds with the retreat of the last continental glacier. It also corresponds with the end of the Paleolithic age used in archaeology.
    a. Tyrrhenian
    b. Pleistocene
    c. Late Pleistocene
    d. Sicilian Stage

3. _____, also known as the Pleistocene glaciation, the current ice age or simply the ice age, refers to the period of the last few million years in which permanent ice sheets were established in Antarctica and perhaps Greenland, and fluctuating ice sheets have occurred elsewhere The major effects of the ice age were erosion and deposition of material over large parts of the continents, modification of river systems, creation of millions of lakes, changes in sea level, development of pluvial lakes far from the ice margins, isostatic adjustment of the crust, and abnormal winds. It affected oceans, flooding, and biological communities.
    a. Rock glaciers
    b. Snowball Earth
    c. Wolstonian Stage
    d. Quaternary glaciation

4. _____ is the removal of solids (sediment, soil, rock and other particles) in the natural environment. It usually occurs due to transport by wind, water, or ice; by down-slope creep of soil and other material under the force of gravity; or by living organisms, such as burrowing animals, in the case of bioerosion.

    _____ is distinguished from weathering, which is the process of chemical or physical breakdown of the minerals in the rocks, although the two processes may occur concurrently.

    a. AL 129-1
    b. AASHTO Soil Classification System
    c. AL 333
    d. Erosion

5. _____ is the decomposition of Earth rocks, soils and their minerals through direct contact with the planet's atmosphere. _____ occurs in situ, or 'with no movement', and thus should not be confused with erosion, which involves the movement of rocks and minerals by agents such as water, ice, wind and gravity.

    Two important classifications of _____ processes exist -- physical and chemical _____.

    a. Physical weathering
    b. Weathering
    c. 1509 Istanbul earthquake
    d. 1700 Cascadia earthquake

Chapter 42. The National Park of American Samoa

1. A _____ is a landform, often referred to as a drowned river valley. _____s are almost always estuaries. _____s form where sea levels rise relative to the land either as a result of eustatic sea level change (where the global sea levels rise), or isostatic sea level change (where the land sinks.)
   a. 1700 Cascadia earthquake
   b. Tombolo
   c. 1509 Istanbul earthquake
   d. Ria

2. A _____ is a mountain rising from the ocean seafloor that does not reach to the water's surface (sea level), and thus is not an island. These are typically formed from extinct volcanoes, that rise abruptly and are usually found rising from a seafloor of 1,000-4,000 meters depth. They are defined by oceanographers as independent features that rise to at least 1,000 meters above the seafloor.
   a. 1509 Istanbul earthquake
   b. 1703 Genroku earthquake
   c. 1700 Cascadia earthquake
   d. Seamount

3. _____ is a naturally occurring glass formed as an extrusive igneous rock. It is produced when felsic lava extruded from a volcano cools without crystal growth. _____ is commonly found within the margins of rhyolitic lava flows known as _____ flows, where the chemical composition (high silica content) induces a high viscosity and polymerization degree of the lava.
   a. Obsidian
   b. AL 333
   c. AL 129-1
   d. AASHTO Soil Classification System

4. A _____ is generally a large area of exposed Precambrian crystalline igneous and high-grade metamorphic rocks that form tectonically stable areas. In all cases, the age of these rocks is greater than 570 million years and sometimes dates back 2 to 3.5 billion years. They have been little affected by tectonic events following the end of the Precambrian Era, and are relatively flat regions where mountain building, faulting, and other tectonic processes are greatly diminished compared with the activity that occurs at the margins of the _____s and the boundaries between tectonic plates.
   a. 1509 Istanbul earthquake
   b. Shield
   c. 1703 Genroku earthquake
   d. 1700 Cascadia earthquake

5. A _____ is a large volcano with shallow-sloping sides.

They are formed by lava flows of low viscosity - lava that flows easily. Consequently, a volcanic mountain having a broad profile is built up over time by flow after flow of relatively fluid basaltic lava issuing from vents or fissures on the surface of the volcano

   a. 1509 Istanbul earthquake
   b. 1703 Genroku earthquake
   c. 1700 Cascadia earthquake
   d. Shield volcano

6. A _____ is an opening in a planet's surface or crust, which allows hot, molten rock, ash, and gases to escape from below the surface. Volcanic activity involving the extrusion of rock tends to form mountains or features like mountains over a period of time.
   a. 1703 Genroku earthquake
   b. Volcano
   c. 1509 Istanbul earthquake
   d. 1700 Cascadia earthquake

7. A _____ is a pyroclastic material. They are extrusive igneous rocks, and are similar to pumice, which has so many cavities and is such low-density that it can float on water.

a. Volcanic gases
b. Cinder
c. Volcanic pipes
d. Supervolcano

8. A _____ or scoria cone is a steep conical hill of volcanic fragments that accumulate around and downwind from a volcanic vent. The rock fragments, often called cinders or scoria, are glassy and contain numerous gas bubbles 'frozen' into place as magma exploded into the air and then cooled quickly. _____s range in size from tens to hundreds of meters tall.

a. 1700 Cascadia earthquake
b. 1703 Genroku earthquake
c. Cinder cone
d. 1509 Istanbul earthquake

9. In chronostratigraphy, a _____ is a succession of rock strata laid down in an single age on the geologic timescale, which usually represents millions of years of deposition. A given _____ of rock and the corresponding age of time will by convention have the same name, and the same boundaries.

a. Paleomagnetism
b. Stage
c. Relative dating
d. Lichenometry

10. _____ is a type of rock consisting of consolidated volcanic ash ejected from vents during a volcanic eruption. _____ is sometimes called tufa, particularly when used as construction material, although tufa also refers to a quite different rock.

The products of a volcanic eruption are volcanic gases, lava, steam, and tephra. Magma is blown apart when it interacts violently with volcanic gases and steam. Solid material produced and thrown into the air by such volcanic eruptions is called tephra, regardless of composition or fragment size. If the resulting pieces of ejecta are small enough, the material is called volcanic ash, defined as such particles less than 2 mm in diameter, sand-sized or smaller.

a. Tuff
b. Phanerite
c. Lopolith
d. Pyroclastic rocks

11. The _____ is located in the Pacific Ocean and is 10,882 meters (35,702 ft) deep at its deepest point, known as the Horizon Deep.

The trench lies at the northern end of the Kermadec-Tonga Subduction Zone, an active subduction zone where the Pacific Plate is being subducted below the Tonga Plate and the Indo-Australian Plate. The _____ extends north-northeast from the Kermadec Islands north of the North Island of New Zealand.

a. 1703 Genroku earthquake
b. 1509 Istanbul earthquake
c. 1700 Cascadia earthquake
d. Tonga Trench

12. _____ is the removal of solids (sediment, soil, rock and other particles) in the natural environment. It usually occurs due to transport by wind, water, or ice; by down-slope creep of soil and other material under the force of gravity; or by living organisms, such as burrowing animals, in the case of bioerosion.

_____ is distinguished from weathering, which is the process of chemical or physical breakdown of the minerals in the rocks, although the two processes may occur concurrently.

a. Erosion
b. AASHTO Soil Classification System
c. AL 333
d. AL 129-1

13. The _____ is the epoch from 1.8 million to 11550 years BP covering the world's recent period of repeated glaciations. The _____ epoch follows the Pliocene epoch and is followed by the Holocene epoch. The _____ is the third epoch of the Neogene period or 6th epoch of the Cenozoic Era. The end of the _____ corresponds with the retreat of the last continental glacier. It also corresponds with the end of the Paleolithic age used in archaeology.
    a. Tyrrhenian
    b. Sicilian Stage
    c. Late Pleistocene
    d. Pleistocene

14. The _____ is a geological epoch which began approximately 11‰700 years ago (10‰000 ^{14}C years ago). According to traditional geological thinking, the _____ continues to the present. The _____ is part of the Neogene and Quaternary periods.
    a. 1509 Istanbul earthquake
    b. 1700 Cascadia earthquake
    c. Neoglaciation
    d. Holocene

15. _____ is soil or sediments deposited by a river or other running water. _____ is typically made up of a variety of materials, including fine particles of silt and clay and larger particles of sand and gravel.

Flowing water associated with glaciers may also deposit _____, but deposits directly from ice are not _____ .

    a. AASHTO Soil Classification System
    b. AL 129-1
    c. AL 333
    d. Alluvium

16. _____ is a term given to an accumulation of broken rock fragments at the base of crags, mountain cliffs, or valley shoulders. Landforms associated with these materials are sometimes called _____ slopes or talus piles. These deposits typically have a concave upwards form, while the maximum inclination of such deposits corresponds to the angle of repose of the mean debris size.
    a. 1703 Genroku earthquake
    b. 1509 Istanbul earthquake
    c. 1700 Cascadia earthquake
    d. Scree

174 *Chapter 43. Yellowstone National Park*

1. The _____ , usually abbreviated K for its German translation Kreide, is a geologic period and system from circa >145.5 >± 4 to >65.5 >± 0.3 million years ago . In the geologic timescale, the _____ follows on the Jurassic period and is followed by the Paleogene period. It is the youngest period of the Mesozoic era, and at 80 million years long, the longest period of the Phanerozoic eon. The end of the _____ defines the boundary between the Mesozoic and Cenozoic eras.
    a. Cretaceous
    b. Valanginian
    c. Campanian
    d. Hauterivian

2. The _____ is a geological epoch which began approximately 11‰700 years ago (10‰000 ^{14}C years ago). According to traditional geological thinking, the _____ continues to the present. The _____ is part of the Neogene and Quaternary periods.
    a. 1509 Istanbul earthquake
    b. 1700 Cascadia earthquake
    c. Neoglaciation
    d. Holocene

3. The _____ is an informal name for the supereon comprising the eons of the geologic timescale that came before the current Phanerozoic eon. It spans from the formation of Earth around 4500 Mya (million years ago) to the evolution of abundant macroscopic hard-shelled animals, which marked the beginning of the Cambrian, the first period of the first era of the Phanerozoic eon, some 542 Mya. It is named after the Roman name for Wales - Cambria - where rocks from this age were first studied.
    a. 1509 Istanbul earthquake
    b. 1703 Genroku earthquake
    c. 1700 Cascadia earthquake
    d. Precambrian

4. A _____ is a mountain rising from the ocean seafloor that does not reach to the water's surface (sea level), and thus is not an island. These are typically formed from extinct volcanoes, that rise abruptly and are usually found rising from a seafloor of 1,000-4,000 meters depth. They are defined by oceanographers as independent features that rise to at least 1,000 meters above the seafloor.
    a. 1509 Istanbul earthquake
    b. 1700 Cascadia earthquake
    c. 1703 Genroku earthquake
    d. Seamount

5. The _____ is the volcanic caldera in Yellowstone National Park in the United States. The caldera is located in the northwest corner of Wyoming, in which the vast majority of the park is contained. The major features of the caldera measure about 55 kilometers (34 mi) by 72 kilometers (45 mi) as determined by geological field work conducted by Bob Christiansen of the United States Geological Survey in the 1960s and 1970s.
    a. 1703 Genroku earthquake
    b. 1509 Istanbul earthquake
    c. Yellowstone caldera
    d. 1700 Cascadia earthquake

6. A _____ is a cauldron-like volcanic feature usually formed by the collapse of land following a volcanic eruption such as the one at Yellowstone National Park. They are sometimes confused with volcanic craters.
    a. 1509 Istanbul earthquake
    b. 1700 Cascadia earthquake
    c. 1703 Genroku earthquake
    d. Caldera

7. In geology and earth science, a _____ is an area of highland, usually consisting of relatively flat terrain. A highly eroded _____ is called a dissected _____. A volcanic _____ is a _____ produced by volcanic activity.
    a. 1703 Genroku earthquake
    b. Plateau
    c. 1509 Istanbul earthquake
    d. 1700 Cascadia earthquake

8. The _____ , is a term in physics and materials science and refers to a characteristic property of a ferromagnetic or piezoelectric material.

The _____ of a ferromagnetic material is the temperature above which it loses its characteristic ferromagnetic ability (768>°C or 1414 >°F for iron.) At temperatures below the _____ the magnetic moments are partially aligned within magnetic domains in ferromagnetic materials.

 a. 1700 Cascadia earthquake   b. 1509 Istanbul earthquake
 c. Curie point   d. 1703 Genroku earthquake

9. An _____ is the result of a sudden release of energy in the Earth's crust that creates seismic waves. They are recorded with a seismometer or the related and mostly obsolete Richter magnitude, with a magnitude 3 or lower _____ being mostly imperceptible and magnitude 7 causing serious damage over large areas.
 a. AASHTO Soil Classification System   b. AL 333
 c. AL 129-1   d. Earthquake

10. The _____ or epicentre is the point on the Earth's surface that is directly above the hypocenter or focus, the point where an earthquake or underground explosion originates.

The _____ is usually the location of greatest damage. However, in some cases the _____ is above the start of a much larger event.

 a. AL 333   b. AL 129-1
 c. AASHTO Soil Classification System   d. Epicenter

11. In geology, _____ refers to heat sources within the planet. _____ is technically an adjective (e.g., _____ energy) but in U.S. English the word has attained frequent use as a noun .

The planet's internal heat was originally generated during its accretion, due to gravitational binding energy, and since then additional heat has continued to be generated by decay heat from the radioactive decay of elements.

 a. Cleavage   b. Grade
 c. Geothermal   d. Tarn

12. The _____ is the rate of increase in temperature per unit depth in the Earth. It varies with location and is typically measured by determining the bottom open-hole temperature after borehole drilling. To achieve accuracy the drilling fluid needs time to reach the ambient temperature.
 a. Geothermal desalination   b. Geothermal power
 c. Hot Dry Rock Geothermal Energy   d. Geothermal gradient

13. The _____ Era is one of three geologic eras of the Phanerozoic eon. The division of time into eras dates back to Giovanni Arduino, in the 18th century, although his original name for the era now called the '_____' was 'Secondary' (making the modern era the 'Tertiary'.)

The _____ was a time of tectonic, climatic and evolutionary activity. The continents gradually shifted from a state of connectedness into their present configuration; the drifting provided for speciation and other important evolutionary developments.

a. 1703 Genroku earthquake
b. Mesozoic
c. 1509 Istanbul earthquake
d. 1700 Cascadia earthquake

14. _____ are type of elastic wave, also called seismic waves, that can travel through gases, elastic solids and liquids, including the Earth. _____ can be produced by earthquakes and recorded by seismometers.
   a. P-waves
   b. 1509 Istanbul earthquake
   c. 1700 Cascadia earthquake
   d. 1703 Genroku earthquake

15. _____ are waves that travel through the Earth or other elastic body, for example as the result of an earthquake, explosion, or some other process that imparts forces to the body. _____ are also continually excited on Earth by the incessant pounding of ocean waves (referred to as the microseism) and the wind. _____ are studied by seismologists, and measured by a seismograph, which records the output of a seismometer, or geophone.
   a. Rayleigh waves
   b. Strong ground motion
   c. Maximum magnitude
   d. Seismic waves

16. The _____ of any physical feature such as a hill, stream, roof, railroad, or road refers to the amount of inclination of that surface where zero indicates level (with respect to gravity) and larger numbers indicate higher degrees of 'tilt'. Often slope is calculated as a ratio of 'rise over run' in which run is the horizontal distance and rise is the vertical distance.

There are several systems for expressing slope:

1. as an angle of inclination from the horizontal of a right triangle. (This is the angle >α opposite the 'rise' side of the triangle.)
2. as a percentage (also known as the _____), the formula for which is > which could also be expressed as the tangent of the angle of inclination times 100. In the U.S., the _____ is the most commonly used unit for communicating slopes in transportation, surveying, construction, and civil engineering.
3. as a per mille figure, the formula for which is > which could also be expressed as the tangent of the angle of inclination times 1000. This is commonly used in Europe to denote the incline of a railway.
4. as a ratio of one part rise per so many parts run. For example, a slope that has a rise of 5 feet for every 100 feet of run would have a slope ratio of 1 in 20.

Any one of these expressions may be used interchangeably to express the characteristics of a slope. _____ is usually expressed as a percentage, but this may easily be converted to the angle >α from horizontal since that carries the same information.

   a. Heavy metal
   b. Grade
   c. Diamond Head
   d. Compaction

17. _____ is the transition of thermal energy or simply heat from a hotter object to a cooler object When an object or fluid is at a different temperature than its surroundings or another object, transfer of thermal energy or heat exchange, occurs in such a way that the body and the surroundings reach thermal equilibrium. _____ always occurs from a higher-temperature object to a cooler temperature one as described by the second law of thermodynamics or the Clausius statement.

a. 1509 Istanbul earthquake
b. 1700 Cascadia earthquake
c. 1703 Genroku earthquake
d. Heat transfer

18. _____ are events where a local area experiences sequences of many earthquakes striking in a relatively short period of time. The length of time used to define the swarm itself varies, but the United States Geological Survey points out that an event may be on the order of days, weeks, or months. They are differentiated from earthquakes succeeded by a series of aftershocks by the observation that no single earthquake in the sequence is obviously the main shock.
a. AASHTO Soil Classification System
b. AL 333
c. AL 129-1
d. Earthquake swarms

19. _____ describes the large scale motions of Earth's lithosphere. The theory encompasses the older concepts of continental drift, developed during the first decades of the 20th century by Alfred Wegener, and seafloor spreading, understood during the 1960s.

The outermost part of the Earth's interior is made up of two layers: the lithosphere and the asthenosphere.

a. Continental crust
b. Nappe
c. Mantle convection
d. Plate tectonics

20. The _____ is a a term for a geologic period 65 million to 1.8 million years ago. The _____ covered the time span between the superseded Secondary period and an out-of-date definition of the Quaternary period. The period began with the demise of the non-avian dinosaurs in the Cretaceous-_____ extinction event, at start of the Cenozoic era, spanning to beginning of the most recent Ice Age, at the end of the Pliocene epoch.
a. Logarithmic Spiral Beach
b. Historical geology
c. Tertiary
d. Loihi Seamount

21. _____ is the number of occurrences of a repeating event per unit time. It is also referred to as temporal _____. The period is the duration of one cycle in a repeating event, so the period is the reciprocal of the _____.
a. 1700 Cascadia earthquake
b. 1703 Genroku earthquake
c. 1509 Istanbul earthquake
d. Frequency

22. _____s is a field of study within geology concerned generally with the structures within the lithosphere of the Earth and particularly with the forces and movements that have operated in a region to create these structures.

_____s is concerned with the orogenies and _____ development of cratons and _____ terranes as well as the earthquake and volcanic belts which directly affect much of the global population. _____ studies are also important for understanding erosion patterns in geomorphology and as guides for the economic geologist searching for petroleum and metallic ores.

a. Rivera Plate
b. Tectonic
c. Fault trace
d. Cocos Plate

23. _____ is a field of study within geology concerned generally with the structures within the lithosphere of the Earth and particularly with the forces and movements that have operated in a region to create these structures.

_____ is concerned with the orogenies and tectonic development of cratons and tectonic terranes as well as the earthquake and volcanic belts which directly affect much of the global population. Tectonic studies are also important for understanding erosion patterns in geomorphology and as guides for the economic geologist searching for petroleum and metallic ores.

a. Tectonics
b. Rivera Plate
c. Cocos Plate
d. Fault trace

24. _____ is a common extrusive volcanic rock. It is usually grey to black and fine-grained due to rapid cooling of lava at the surface of a planet. It may be porphyritic containing larger crystals in a fine matrix, or vesicular, or frothy scoria.

a. 1700 Cascadia earthquake
b. Basalt
c. 1509 Istanbul earthquake
d. 1703 Genroku earthquake

25. The _____ epoch (55.8 >± 0.2 - 33.9 >± 0.1 Ma) is a major division of the geologic timescale and the second epoch of the Palaeogene period in the Cenozoic era. The _____ spans the time from the end of the Paleocene epoch to the beginning of the Oligocene epoch. The start of the _____ is marked by the emergence of the first modern mammals.

a. AASHTO Soil Classification System
b. AL 333
c. Eocene
d. AL 129-1

26. _____ is an igneous, volcanic (extrusive) rock, of felsic (silicon-rich) composition. It may have any texture from aphanitic to porphyritic. The mineral assemblage is usually quartz, alkali feldspar and plagioclase. Biotite and hornblende are common accessory minerals.

_____ can be considered as the extrusive equivalent to the plutonic granite rock, and consequently, outcroppings of it often bear a resemblance to granite. Due to their high content of silica and low iron and magnesium contents, _____ melts are highly polymerized and form highly viscous lavas.

a. 1700 Cascadia earthquake
b. 1703 Genroku earthquake
c. 1509 Istanbul earthquake
d. Rhyolite

27. In geology, a _____ is a location on the Earth's surface that has experienced active volcanism for a long period of time.

J. Tuzo Wilson came up with the idea in 1963 that volcanic chains like the Hawaiian Islands result from the slow movement of a tectonic plate across a 'fixed' _____ deep beneath the surface of the planet.

a. 1700 Cascadia earthquake
b. Hotspot
c. 1703 Genroku earthquake
d. 1509 Istanbul earthquake

28. A _____ is an opening in Earth's crust, often in the neighborhood of volcanoes, which emits steam and gases such as carbon dioxide, sulfur dioxide, hydrochloric acid, and hydrogen sulfide.

They may occur along tiny cracks or long fissures, in chaotic clusters or fields, and on the surfaces of lava flows and thick deposits of pyroclastic flows. A _____ field is an area of thermal springs and gas vents where magma or hot igneous rocks at shallow depth are releasing gases or interacting with groundwater.

   a. 1509 Istanbul earthquake
   b. 1703 Genroku earthquake
   c. 1700 Cascadia earthquake
   d. Fumarole

29. _____ is a liquid or semi-liquid mixture of water and some combination of soil, silt, and clay. Ancient _____ deposits harden over geological time to form sedimentary rock such as siltstone or solid, mudrock lutites. When geological deposits of _____ are formed in estuaries the resultant layers are termed bay _____s.
   a. Mud
   b. Continental slope
   c. Thermal pollution
   d. Surface runoff

30. A _____, mud pool or paint pot is a sort of hot spring or fumarole consisting of a pool of usually bubbling mud. The mud is generally of white to greyish color, but is sometimes stained with reddish or pink spots from iron compounds. When the slurry is particularly colorful, the feature is then called a paint pot.
   a. 1700 Cascadia earthquake
   b. 1509 Istanbul earthquake
   c. 1703 Genroku earthquake
   d. Mudpot

31. A _____ column (or _____) is a column of rising air in the lower altitudes of the Earth's atmosphere. They are created by the uneven heating of the Earth's surface from solar radiation, and an example of convection. The Sun warms the ground, which in turn warms the air directly above it.
   a. 1700 Cascadia earthquake
   b. 1509 Istanbul earthquake
   c. 1703 Genroku earthquake
   d. Thermal

32. _____ is a sedimentary rock. It is a natural chemical precipitate of carbonate minerals; typically aragonite, but often recrystallized to, or primarily, calcite.

_____ forms as calcium carbonate is deposited from the water of mineral springs or rivulets that are saturated with dissolved calcium bicarbonate. The spring water from which the calcium carbonate precipitates can be hot, warm or cold. The rate of deposition increases with the temperature of the water, or alternatively, when biotic material accelerates the process of precipitation.

   a. 1700 Cascadia earthquake
   b. 1703 Genroku earthquake
   c. 1509 Istanbul earthquake
   d. Travertine

33. The _____ Era, is the most recent of the three classic geological eras and covers the period from 65.5 million years ago to the present. It is marked by the Cretaceous-Tertiary extinction event at the end of the Cretaceous that saw the demise of the last non-avian dinosaurs and the end of the Mesozoic Era. The _____ era is ongoing.
   a. Cenozoic
   b. 1700 Cascadia earthquake
   c. 1703 Genroku earthquake
   d. 1509 Istanbul earthquake

34. _____ is molten rock expelled by a volcano during eruption. When first expelled from a volcanic vent, it is a liquid at temperatures from 700 >°C to 1,200 >°C (1,300 >°F to 2,200 >°F.) Although _____ is quite viscous, with about 100,000 times the viscosity of water, it can flow great distances before cooling and solidifying, because of both its thixotropic and shear thinning properties.
   a. Volcanic ash
   b. Pyroclastic flow
   c. Cinder
   d. Lava

35. _____ is a naturally occurring glass formed as an extrusive igneous rock. It is produced when felsic lava extruded from a volcano cools without crystal growth. _____ is commonly found within the margins of rhyolitic lava flows known as _____ flows, where the chemical composition (high silica content) induces a high viscosity and polymerization degree of the lava.
   a. Obsidian
   b. AASHTO Soil Classification System
   c. AL 333
   d. AL 129-1

36. The _____ is the earliest of three geologic eras of the Phanerozoic eon. The _____ spanned from roughly 542 to 251 million years ago (ICS, 2004), and is subdivided into six geologic periods; from oldest to youngest they are: the Cambrian, Ordovician, Silurian, Devonian, Carboniferous, and Permian.

The _____ covers the time from the first appearance of abundant, soft-shelled fossils to the time when the continents were beginning to be dominated by large, relatively sophisticated reptiles and modern plants. The lower (oldest) boundary was classically set at the first appearance of creatures known as trilobites and archeocyathids.

   a. 1700 Cascadia earthquake
   b. 1703 Genroku earthquake
   c. 1509 Istanbul earthquake
   d. Paleozoic

37. The _____ is the epoch from 1.8 million to 11550 years BP covering the world's recent period of repeated glaciations. The _____ epoch follows the Pliocene epoch and is followed by the Holocene epoch. The _____ is the third epoch of the Neogene period or 6th epoch of the Cenozoic Era. The end of the _____ corresponds with the retreat of the last continental glacier. It also corresponds with the end of the Paleolithic age used in archaeology.
   a. Late Pleistocene
   b. Tyrrhenian
   c. Pleistocene
   d. Sicilian Stage

38. In chronostratigraphy, a _____ is a succession of rock strata laid down in an single age on the geologic timescale, which usually represents millions of years of deposition. A given _____ of rock and the corresponding age of time will by convention have the same name, and the same boundaries.
   a. Paleomagnetism
   b. Lichenometry
   c. Relative dating
   d. Stage

39. _____, is the process of coastal sediments returning to the visible portion of a beach or foreshore following a submersion event. A sustainable beach or foreshore often goes through a cycle of submersion during rough weather then _____ during calmer periods. If a coastline is not in a healthy sustainable condition, then erosion can be more serious and _____ does not fully restore the original volume of the visible beach or foreshore leading to permanent beach or foreshore loss.

a. AL 333   b. Accretion
c. AASHTO Soil Classification System   d. AL 129-1

Chapter 44. Grand Teton National Park

1. _____ is one of the three main rock types (the others being igneous and metamorphic rock.) _____ is formed by deposition and consolidation of mineral and organic material and from precipitation of minerals from solution. The processes that form _____ occur at the surface of the Earth and within bodies of water.
   a. Felsic
   b. Serpentinite
   c. Large igneous provinces
   d. Sedimentary rock

2. The _____ Era, is the most recent of the three classic geological eras and covers the period from 65.5 million years ago to the present. It is marked by the Cretaceous-Tertiary extinction event at the end of the Cretaceous that saw the demise of the last non-avian dinosaurs and the end of the Mesozoic Era. The _____ era is ongoing.
   a. Cenozoic
   b. 1509 Istanbul earthquake
   c. 1703 Genroku earthquake
   d. 1700 Cascadia earthquake

3. The _____ Era is one of three geologic eras of the Phanerozoic eon. The division of time into eras dates back to Giovanni Arduino, in the 18th century, although his original name for the era now called the '_____' was 'Secondary' (making the modern era the 'Tertiary'.)

   The _____ was a time of tectonic, climatic and evolutionary activity. The continents gradually shifted from a state of connectedness into their present configuration; the drifting provided for speciation and other important evolutionary developments.

   a. 1700 Cascadia earthquake
   b. 1703 Genroku earthquake
   c. Mesozoic
   d. 1509 Istanbul earthquake

4. _____ is any particulate matter that can be transported by fluid flow, and which eventually is deposited.

   They are most often transported by water (fluvial processes) transported by wind (aeolian processes) and glaciers. Beach sands and river channel deposits are examples of fluvial transport and deposition, though _____ also often settles out of slow-moving or standing water in lakes and oceans.

   a. Sediment
   b. Salt glacier
   c. Fech fech
   d. Brickearth

5. The _____ is a geological epoch which began approximately 11‰700 years ago (10‰000 ^{14}C years ago). According to traditional geological thinking, the _____ continues to the present. The _____ is part of the Neogene and Quaternary periods.
   a. Neoglaciation
   b. Holocene
   c. 1700 Cascadia earthquake
   d. 1509 Istanbul earthquake

6. The _____ is an informal name for the supereon comprising the eons of the geologic timescale that came before the current Phanerozoic eon. It spans from the formation of Earth around 4500 Mya (million years ago) to the evolution of abundant macroscopic hard-shelled animals, which marked the beginning of the Cambrian, the first period of the first era of the Phanerozoic eon, some 542 Mya. It is named after the Roman name for Wales - Cambria - where rocks from this age were first studied.
   a. Precambrian
   b. 1703 Genroku earthquake
   c. 1700 Cascadia earthquake
   d. 1509 Istanbul earthquake

7. The _____ is a a term for a geologic period 65 million to 1.8 million years ago. The _____ covered the time span between the superseded Secondary period and an out-of-date definition of the Quaternary period. The period began with the demise of the non-avian dinosaurs in the Cretaceous-_____ extinction event, at start of the Cenozoic era, spanning to beginning of the most recent Ice Age, at the end of the Pliocene epoch.
 a. Tertiary   b. Historical geology
 c. Logarithmic Spiral Beach   d. Loihi Seamount

8. _____ is the geomorphic process by which soil, regolith, and rock move downslope under the force of gravity. Types of _____ include creep, slides, flows, topples, and falls, each with its own characteristic features, and taking place over timescales from seconds to years. _____ occurs on both terrestrial and submarine slopes, and has been observed on Earth, Mars, and Venus.
 a. 1700 Cascadia earthquake   b. 1509 Istanbul earthquake
 c. Soil liquefaction   d. Mass wasting

9. _____ is the decomposition of Earth rocks, soils and their minerals through direct contact with the planet's atmosphere. _____ occurs in situ, or 'with no movement', and thus should not be confused with erosion, which involves the movement of rocks and minerals by agents such as water, ice, wind and gravity.

Two important classifications of _____ processes exist -- physical and chemical _____ .

 a. 1700 Cascadia earthquake   b. 1509 Istanbul earthquake
 c. Physical weathering   d. Weathering

10. In geology, a _____ or _____ line is a planar fracture in rock in which the rock on one side of the fracture has moved with respect to the rock on the other side. Large _____s within the Earth's crust are the result of differential or shear motion and active _____ zones are the causal locations of most earthquakes. Earthquakes are caused by energy release during rapid slippage along a _____.
 a. Drainage system   b. Compaction
 c. Cleavage   d. Fault

11. A _____ is a geological phenomenon which includes a wide range of ground movement, such as rock falls, deep failure of slopes and shallow debris flows, which can occur in offshore, coastal and onshore environments. Although the action of gravity is the primary driving force for a _____ to occur, there are other contributing factors affecting the original slope stability. Typically, pre-conditional factors build up specific sub-surface conditions that make the area/slope prone to failure, whereas the actual _____ often requires a trigger before being released.
 a. 1700 Cascadia earthquake   b. 1509 Istanbul earthquake
 c. Mass wasting   d. Landslide

12. The _____ , usually abbreviated K for its German translation Kreide, is a geologic period and system from circa >145.5 >± 4 to >65.5 >± 0.3 million years ago . In the geologic timescale, the _____ follows on the Jurassic period and is followed by the Paleogene period. It is the youngest period of the Mesozoic era, and at 80 million years long, the longest period of the Phanerozoic eon. The end of the _____ defines the boundary between the Mesozoic and Cenozoic eras.
 a. Campanian   b. Hauterivian
 c. Valanginian   d. Cretaceous

13. The _____ is the earliest of three geologic eras of the Phanerozoic eon. The _____ spanned from roughly 542 to 251 million years ago (ICS, 2004), and is subdivided into six geologic periods; from oldest to youngest they are: the Cambrian, Ordovician, Silurian, Devonian, Carboniferous, and Permian.

The _____ covers the time from the first appearance of abundant, soft-shelled fossils to the time when the continents were beginning to be dominated by large, relatively sophisticated reptiles and modern plants. The lower (oldest) boundary was classically set at the first appearance of creatures known as trilobites and archeocyathids.

- a. 1509 Istanbul earthquake
- b. Paleozoic
- c. 1703 Genroku earthquake
- d. 1700 Cascadia earthquake

14. The _____ is the epoch from 1.8 million to 11550 years BP covering the world's recent period of repeated glaciations. The _____ epoch follows the Pliocene epoch and is followed by the Holocene epoch. The _____ is the third epoch of the Neogene period or 6th epoch of the Cenozoic Era. The end of the _____ corresponds with the retreat of the last continental glacier. It also corresponds with the end of the Paleolithic age used in archaeology.
- a. Sicilian Stage
- b. Late Pleistocene
- c. Tyrrhenian
- d. Pleistocene

15. _____, also known as the Pleistocene glaciation, the current ice age or simply the ice age, refers to the period of the last few million years in which permanent ice sheets were established in Antarctica and perhaps Greenland, and fluctuating ice sheets have occurred elsewhere The major effects of the ice age were erosion and deposition of material over large parts of the continents, modification of river systems, creation of millions of lakes, changes in sea level, development of pluvial lakes far from the ice margins, isostatic adjustment of the crust, and abnormal winds. It affected oceans, flooding, and biological communities.
- a. Rock glaciers
- b. Quaternary glaciation
- c. Snowball Earth
- d. Wolstonian Stage

Chapter 45. Great Basin National Park

1. The _____ is the first geological period of the Phanerozoic eon, lasting from 542 ± 0.3 million years ago to 488.3 ± 1.7 million years ago (ICS, 2004); it is succeeded by the Ordovician. Its subdivisions, and indeed its base, are somewhat in flux. The period was established by Adam Sedgwick, who named it after Cambria, the classical name for Wales, where Britain's _____ rocks are best exposed.
    a. 1703 Genroku earthquake
    b. Cambrian
    c. 1509 Istanbul earthquake
    d. 1700 Cascadia earthquake

2. _____ is the natural or artificial removal of surface and sub-surface water from an area. Many agricultural soils need _____ to improve production or to manage water supplies.

    The earliest archaeological record of an advanced system of _____ comes from the Indus Valley Civilization from around 3100 BC in what is now Pakistan and North India.

    a. 1509 Istanbul earthquake
    b. 1700 Cascadia earthquake
    c. 1703 Genroku earthquake
    d. Drainage

3. A _____, is the line separating neighbouring drainage basins (catchments.) In hilly country, the divide lies along topographical peaks and ridges, but in flat country (especially where the ground is marshy) the divide may be invisible - just a more or less notional line on the ground on either side of which falling raindrops will start a journey to different rivers, and even to different sides of a region or continent.
    a. 1703 Genroku earthquake
    b. 1509 Istanbul earthquake
    c. 1700 Cascadia earthquake
    d. Drainage divide

4. In geology and climatology, a _____ was an extended period of abundant rainfall lasting many thousands of years. The term is especially applied to such periods during the Pleistocene Epoch. A minor, short _____ may be termed a 'subpluvial'.
    a. Mesosphere
    b. 1509 Istanbul earthquake
    c. Polar front
    d. Pluvial

5. A _____ is a lake that experiences significant increase in depth and extent as a result of increased precipitation and reduced evaporation. Such lakes are likely to be endorheic.

    They represent changes in the hydrological cycle -- wet cycles generate large lakes, whereas dry cycles cause the lakes to dry up leaving large flat plains.

    a. 1703 Genroku earthquake
    b. Pluvial lake
    c. 1509 Istanbul earthquake
    d. 1700 Cascadia earthquake

6. The _____ is a a term for a geologic period 65 million to 1.8 million years ago. The _____ covered the time span between the superseded Secondary period and an out-of-date definition of the Quaternary period. The period began with the demise of the non-avian dinosaurs in the Cretaceous-_____ extinction event, at start of the Cenozoic era, spanning to beginning of the most recent Ice Age, at the end of the Pliocene epoch.
    a. Logarithmic Spiral Beach
    b. Historical geology
    c. Loihi Seamount
    d. Tertiary

7. The _____ Period is the geologic time period after the Neogene Period, spanning 1.805 +/- 0.005 million years ago to the present. The _____ includes two geologic epochs: the Pleistocene and the Holocene Epoch.

There is an ongoing debate of the status of _____ -- a recent proposal from International Commission on Stratigraphy (ICS) was to make _____ a subperiod under Neogene, but that was retracted after criticism from International Union for _____ Research (INQUA), so instead ICS and INQUA agreed to erect _____ as an Era, above Neogene, and to place the base for _____ at 2.588 >± 3.005, the base for Gelasian Stage.

a. Tributary
b. Geomorphology
c. Yilgarn Craton
d. Quaternary

8. _____ landforms (mountains, hills, ridges, etc.) are created when large areas of bedrock are widely broken up by faults creating large vertical displacements of continental crust.

Vertical motion of the resulting blocks, sometimes accompanied by tilting, can then lead to high escarpments. These mountains are formed by the earth's crust being stretched and extended by tensional forces. Fault block mountains commonly accompany rifting, another indicator of tensional tectonic forces.

a. Rejuvenated
b. Differential weathering
c. Coastal erosion
d. Fault-block

9. An _____ is a type of rock that contains minerals such as gemstones and metals that can be extracted through mining and refined for use. Samples of _____ in the form of exceptionally beautiful crystals, exotic layering visible when sectioned or polished or metallic presentations such as large nuggets or crystalline formations of metals such as gold or copper may command a value far beyond their value as mere _____ or raw metal for subsequent reduction to utilitarian purposes.

The grade or concentration of an _____ mineral, or metal, as well as its form of occurrence, will directly affect the costs associated with mining the _____.

a. Ore genesis
b. AASHTO Soil Classification System
c. Iron ores
d. Ore

10. _____ are distinctive geomorphological landforms of blocky detritus which may extend outward and downslope from talus cones or from glaciers or the terminal moraines of glaciers. Their growth and formation is subject to some debate, with three main theories in prominence:

- They originated from cirque glaciers and contain a glacial ice core or interstitial ice between the rocks which causes the formation to move downslope;

- A permafrost origin, which implies that the features are related to permafrost action rather than glacial action;

- A mass wasting or landslide origin which does not require the presence of ice and suggests a sudden catastrophic origin with little subsequent movement.

_____ may move or creep at a very slow rate in part dependent on the amount of ice present.

a. Pre-Pastonian Stage
b. Pastonian Stage
c. Pressure melting point
d. Rock glaciers

11. A _____ is a large, slow-moving mass of ice, formed from compacted layers of snow, that slowly deforms and flows in response to gravity and high pressure.

_____ ice is the largest reservoir of fresh water on Earth, and second only to oceans as the largest reservoir of total water.

a. Little Ice Age
b. Deforestation
c. Keeling Curve
d. Glacier

12. A _____ is a speleothem found in limestone caves that changes its axis from the vertical at one or more stages during its growth. They have a curving or angular form that looks as if they were grown in zero gravity. They are most likely the result of capillary forces acting on tiny water droplets, a force often strong enough at this scale to defy gravity.
   a. 1703 Genroku earthquake
   b. 1700 Cascadia earthquake
   c. 1509 Istanbul earthquake
   d. Helictite

13. The _____ Era is one of three geologic eras of the Phanerozoic eon. The division of time into eras dates back to Giovanni Arduino, in the 18th century, although his original name for the era now called the '_____' was 'Secondary' (making the modern era the 'Tertiary'.)

The _____ was a time of tectonic, climatic and evolutionary activity. The continents gradually shifted from a state of connectedness into their present configuration; the drifting provided for speciation and other important evolutionary developments.

a. Mesozoic
b. 1509 Istanbul earthquake
c. 1703 Genroku earthquake
d. 1700 Cascadia earthquake

14. The _____ is a geologic subperiod and stratigraphic subsystem of the Carboniferous Period. It is the later subperiod of the Carboniferous, lasting from roughly 318.1>± 1.3 to 299>± 0.8 Ma (million years ago.) As with most other geochronologic units, the rock beds that define the _____ are well identified, but the exact date of the start and end are uncertain by a few million years.
   a. Dinantian
   b. Mississippian
   c. Pennsylvanian
   d. Calciferous sandstone

15. The _____ is the earliest of three geologic eras of the Phanerozoic eon. The _____ spanned from roughly 542 to 251 million years ago (ICS, 2004), and is subdivided into six geologic periods; from oldest to youngest they are: the Cambrian, Ordovician, Silurian, Devonian, Carboniferous, and Permian.

The _____ covers the time from the first appearance of abundant, soft-shelled fossils to the time when the continents were beginning to be dominated by large, relatively sophisticated reptiles and modern plants. The lower (oldest) boundary was classically set at the first appearance of creatures known as trilobites and archeocyathids.

a. 1703 Genroku earthquake
b. 1509 Istanbul earthquake
c. Paleozoic
d. 1700 Cascadia earthquake

Chapter 46. Saguaro National Park

1. _____ is a fine-grained, compact rock produced by dynamic crystallization of the constituent minerals resulting in a reduction of the grain size of the rock. It is classified as a metamorphic rock. _____ can have many different mineralogical compositions; it is a classification based on the textural appearance of the rock.
    a. Geothermobarometry
    b. Foliation
    c. Mylonite
    d. Granulites

2. In geology, a _____ or _____ line is a planar fracture in rock in which the rock on one side of the fracture has moved with respect to the rock on the other side. Large _____s within the Earth's crust are the result of differential or shear motion and active _____ zones are the causal locations of most earthquakes. Earthquakes are caused by energy release during rapid slippage along a _____.
    a. Cleavage
    b. Compaction
    c. Drainage system
    d. Fault

3. _____ is a detrital sedimentary rock, specifically a type of sandstone containing at least 25% feldspar., Arkosic sand is sand that is similarly rich in feldspar, and thus the potential precursor of _____. The other mineral components may vary, but quartz is commonly dominant, and some mica is often present. Apart from the mineral content, rock fragments may also be a significant component.
    a. AASHTO Soil Classification System
    b. AL 129-1
    c. AL 333
    d. Arkose

4. _____ is an igneous, volcanic (extrusive) rock, of felsic (silicon-rich) composition. It may have any texture from aphanitic to porphyritic. The mineral assemblage is usually quartz, alkali feldspar and plagioclase. Biotite and hornblende are common accessory minerals.

    _____ can be considered as the extrusive equivalent to the plutonic granite rock, and consequently, outcroppings of it often bear a resemblance to granite. Due to their high content of silica and low iron and magnesium contents, _____ melts are highly polymerized and form highly viscous lavas.

    a. 1509 Istanbul earthquake
    b. Rhyolite
    c. 1700 Cascadia earthquake
    d. 1703 Genroku earthquake

5. _____ forms a group of medium-grade metamorphic rocks, chiefly notable for the preponderance of lamellar minerals such as micas, chlorite, talc, hornblende, graphite, and others. Quartz often occurs in drawn-out grains to such an extent that a particular form called quartz _____ is produced. By definition, _____ contains more than 50% platy and elongated minerals, often finely interleaved with quartz and feldspar.
    a. Hornfels
    b. Porphyroblast
    c. Schist
    d. Talc carbonate

6. The _____ is a geologic period and system, the second of six of the Paleozoic era, and covers the time between 488.3>±1.7 to 443.7>±1.5 million years ago (ICS, 2004.) It follows the Cambrian period and is followed by the Silurian period. The _____ was defined by Charles Lapworth in 1879, to resolve a dispute between followers of Adam Sedgwick and Roderick Murchison, who were placing the same rock beds in northern Wales into the Cambrian and Silurian periods respectively.
    a. AL 333
    b. AASHTO Soil Classification System
    c. AL 129-1
    d. Ordovician

7. The _____ is a geologic subperiod and stratigraphic subsystem of the Carboniferous Period. It is the later subperiod of the Carboniferous, lasting from roughly 318.1>± 1.3 to 299>± 0.8 Ma (million years ago.) As with most other geochronologic units, the rock beds that define the _____ are well identified, but the exact date of the start and end are uncertain by a few million years.
   a. Calciferous sandstone
   b. Dinantian
   c. Mississippian
   d. Pennsylvanian

8. The _____ is an informal name for the supereon comprising the eons of the geologic timescale that came before the current Phanerozoic eon. It spans from the formation of Earth around 4500 Mya (million years ago) to the evolution of abundant macroscopic hard-shelled animals, which marked the beginning of the Cambrian, the first period of the first era of the Phanerozoic eon, some 542 Mya. It is named after the Roman name for Wales - Cambria - where rocks from this age were first studied.
   a. 1703 Genroku earthquake
   b. Precambrian
   c. 1700 Cascadia earthquake
   d. 1509 Istanbul earthquake

9. The _____ is a geological eon representing a period before the first abundant complex life on Earth. The _____ extended from 2500 Ma to 542.0 >± 1.0 Ma (million years ago), and is the most recent part of the old, informally named 'e;Precambrian'e; time.

The Proterozoic consists of 3 geologic eras, from oldest to youngest:

- Paleoproterozoic
- Mesoproterozoic
- Neoproterozoic

The well-identified events were:

- The transition to an oxygenated atmosphere during the Mesoproterozoic.
- Several glaciations, including the hypothesized Snowball Earth during the Cryogenian period in the late Neoproterozoic.
- The Ediacaran Period (635 to 542 Ma) which is characterized by the evolution of abundant soft-bodied multicellular organisms.

The geoloic record of the Proterozoic is much better than that for the preceding Archean. In contrast to the deep-water deposits of the Archean, the Proterozoic features many strata that were laid down in extensive shallow epicontinental seas; furthermore, many of these rocks are less metamorphosed than Archean-age ones, and plenty are unaltered.

   a. 1700 Cascadia earthquake
   b. Proterozoic Eon
   c. 1509 Istanbul earthquake
   d. 1703 Genroku earthquake

10. _____ is a hard metamorphic rock which was originally sandstone. Sandstone is converted into _____ through heating and pressure usually related to tectonic compression within orogenic belts. Pure _____ is usually white to grey, though _____s often occur in various shades of pink and red due to varying amounts of iron oxide .

a. Quartzite
b. Talc carbonate
c. Hornfels
d. Slate

11. The _____ , usually abbreviated K for its German translation Kreide, is a geologic period and system from circa >145.5 >± 4 to >65.5 >± 0.3 million years ago . In the geologic timescale, the _____ follows on the Jurassic period and is followed by the Paleogene period. It is the youngest period of the Mesozoic era, and at 80 million years long, the longest period of the Phanerozoic eon. The end of the _____ defines the boundary between the Mesozoic and Cenozoic eras.

a. Cretaceous
b. Hauterivian
c. Valanginian
d. Campanian

12. The _____ Era is one of three geologic eras of the Phanerozoic eon. The division of time into eras dates back to Giovanni Arduino, in the 18th century, although his original name for the era now called the '_____' was 'Secondary' (making the modern era the 'Tertiary'.)

The _____ was a time of tectonic, climatic and evolutionary activity. The continents gradually shifted from a state of connectedness into their present configuration; the drifting provided for speciation and other important evolutionary developments.

a. 1703 Genroku earthquake
b. 1509 Istanbul earthquake
c. Mesozoic
d. 1700 Cascadia earthquake

13. _____ is the rise of land masses that were depressed by the huge weight of ice sheets during the last glacial period, through a process known as isostatic depression. It affects northern Europe (especially Scotland, Fennoscandia and northern Denmark), Siberia, Canada, and the Great Lakes of Canada and the United States.

During the last glacial period, much of northern Europe, Asia, North America, Greenland and Antarctica were covered by ice sheets. The ice was as thick as three kilometres during the last glacial maximum about 20,000 years ago. The enormous weight of this ice caused the surface of the crust to deform and downwarp under the ice load, forcing the fluid mantle material to flow away from the loaded area. At the end of the ice age when the glaciers retreated, the removal of the weight from the depressed land led to uplift or rebound of the land and the return flow of mantle material back under the deglaciated area.

a. Rock glaciers
b. Post-glacial rebound
c. Quaternary glaciation
d. Bergschrund

14. _____, meaning 'new eruption', is a volcano located on the Alaska Peninsula in Katmai National Park and Preserve, about 290 miles (470 km) southwest of Anchorage. Formed in 1912 during one of the largest volcanic eruptions of the 20th century, _____ released 30 times the volume of magma as the 1980 eruption of Mount St. Helens. Map showing volcanoes of Alaska.

One of the largest eruptions of the 20th century occurred in 1912, from June 6 to June 8, to form _____.

a. 1509 Istanbul earthquake
b. Novarupta
c. 1700 Cascadia earthquake
d. 1703 Genroku earthquake

15. The _____ is a continental transform fault that runs a length of roughly 800 miles (1,300 km) through California in the United States. The fault's motion is right-lateral strike-slip (horizontal motion.) It forms the tectonic boundary between the Pacific Plate and the North American Plate.
   a. 1700 Cascadia earthquake
   b. 1703 Genroku earthquake
   c. 1509 Istanbul earthquake
   d. San Andreas fault

16. _____ is a type of rock consisting of consolidated volcanic ash ejected from vents during a volcanic eruption. _____ is sometimes called tufa, particularly when used as construction material, although tufa also refers to a quite different rock.

The products of a volcanic eruption are volcanic gases, lava, steam, and tephra. Magma is blown apart when it interacts violently with volcanic gases and steam. Solid material produced and thrown into the air by such volcanic eruptions is called tephra, regardless of composition or fragment size. If the resulting pieces of ejecta are small enough, the material is called volcanic ash, defined as such particles less than 2 mm in diameter, sand-sized or smaller.

   a. Tuff
   b. Phanerite
   c. Lopolith
   d. Pyroclastic rocks

17. A _____ is an opening in a planet's surface or crust, which allows hot, molten rock, ash, and gases to escape from below the surface. Volcanic activity involving the extrusion of rock tends to form mountains or features like mountains over a period of time.
   a. 1509 Istanbul earthquake
   b. Volcano
   c. 1703 Genroku earthquake
   d. 1700 Cascadia earthquake

18. _____ is a common extrusive volcanic rock. It is usually grey to black and fine-grained due to rapid cooling of lava at the surface of a planet. It may be porphyritic containing larger crystals in a fine matrix, or vesicular, or frothy scoria.
   a. 1703 Genroku earthquake
   b. 1509 Istanbul earthquake
   c. 1700 Cascadia earthquake
   d. Basalt

19. A _____ is a mountain rising from the ocean seafloor that does not reach to the water's surface (sea level), and thus is not an island. These are typically formed from extinct volcanoes, that rise abruptly and are usually found rising from a seafloor of 1,000-4,000 meters depth. They are defined by oceanographers as independent features that rise to at least 1,000 meters above the seafloor.
   a. 1509 Istanbul earthquake
   b. Seamount
   c. 1703 Genroku earthquake
   d. 1700 Cascadia earthquake

20. _____ is molten rock expelled by a volcano during eruption. When first expelled from a volcanic vent, it is a liquid at temperatures from 700 >°C to 1,200 >°C (1,300 >°F to 2,200 >°F.) Although _____ is quite viscous, with about 100,000 times the viscosity of water, it can flow great distances before cooling and solidifying, because of both its thixotropic and shear thinning properties.
   a. Volcanic ash
   b. Cinder
   c. Pyroclastic flow
   d. Lava

21. The _____ is the earliest of three geologic eras of the Phanerozoic eon. The _____ spanned from roughly 542 to 251 million years ago (ICS, 2004), and is subdivided into six geologic periods; from oldest to youngest they are: the Cambrian, Ordovician, Silurian, Devonian, Carboniferous, and Permian.

The _____ covers the time from the first appearance of abundant, soft-shelled fossils to the time when the continents were beginning to be dominated by large, relatively sophisticated reptiles and modern plants. The lower (oldest) boundary was classically set at the first appearance of creatures known as trilobites and archeocyathids.

   a. 1703 Genroku earthquake
   c. 1509 Istanbul earthquake
   b. Paleozoic
   d. 1700 Cascadia earthquake

22. A _____ or dyke in geology is a type of sheet intrusion referring to any geologic body that cuts discordantly across

   • planar wall rock structures, such as bedding or foliation
   • massive rock formations, like igneous/magmatic intrusions and salt diapirs.

They can therefore be either intrusive or sedimentary in origin.

An intrusive _____ is an igneous body with a very high aspect ratio, which means that its thickness is usually much smaller than the other two dimensions. Thickness can vary from sub-centimeter scale to many meters and the lateral dimensions can extend over many kilometers. A _____ is an intrusion into an opening cross-cutting fissure, shouldering aside other pre-existing layers or bodies of rock; this implies that a _____ is always younger than the rocks that contain it.

   a. Detritus
   c. Gradualism
   b. Dike
   d. Type locality

23. _____ is a common and widely distributed type of rock formed by high-grade regional metamorphic processes from pre-existing formations that were originally either igneous or sedimentary rocks. Gneissic rocks are usually medium to coarse foliated and largely recrystallized but do not carry large quantities of micas, chlorite or other platy minerals. _____es that are metamorphosed igneous rocks or their equivalent are termed granite _____es, diorite _____es, etc.
   a. 1703 Genroku earthquake
   c. 1509 Istanbul earthquake
   b. 1700 Cascadia earthquake
   d. Gneiss

24. _____ is the result of the transformation of an existing rock type, the protolith, in a process called metamorphism, which means 'change in form'. The protolith is subjected to heat and pressure (temperatures greater than 150 to 200 >°C and pressures of 1500 bars) causing profound physical and/or chemical change. The protolith may be sedimentary rock, igneous rock or another older _____.
   a. Serpentinite
   c. Pluton
   b. Laccolith
   d. Metamorphic rock

25. _____ are exposures of deep crust exhumed in association with largely amagmatic extension. They form, and are exhumed, through relatively fast transport of middle and lower continental crust to the Earth's surface. During this process, high-grade metamorphic rocks (eclogite-, granulite- to amphibolite- facies) are exposed below low-angle detachment faults (mylonite shear zones) that show ductile deformation on the lower side (footwall) with amphibolite- to greenschist-facies syndeformational metamorphism, and ductile-brittle to brittle deformation on the upper-side (hanging-wall.)
   a. 1509 Istanbul earthquake
   b. Metamorphic core complexes
   c. 1703 Genroku earthquake
   d. 1700 Cascadia earthquake

26. The _____ is a a term for a geologic period 65 million to 1.8 million years ago. The _____ covered the time span between the superseded Secondary period and an out-of-date definition of the Quaternary period. The period began with the demise of the non-avian dinosaurs in the Cretaceous-_____ extinction event, at start of the Cenozoic era, spanning to beginning of the most recent Ice Age, at the end of the Pliocene epoch.
   a. Tertiary
   b. Loihi Seamount
   c. Logarithmic Spiral Beach
   d. Historical geology

Chapter 47. Joshua Tree National Park by D.D. Trent

1. A _____ in geology is an intrusive igneous rock body that crystallized from a magma slowly cooling below the surface of the Earth. _____s include batholiths, dikes, sills, laccoliths, lopoliths, and other igneous bodies. In practice, '_____' usually refers to a distinctive mass of igneous rock, typically kilometers in dimension, without a tabular shape like those of dikes and sills.
   a. Tephra
   b. Pluton
   c. Petrology
   d. Matrix

2. The _____ , usually abbreviated K for its German translation Kreide, is a geologic period and system from circa >145.5 >± 4 to >65.5 >± 0.3 million years ago . In the geologic timescale, the _____ follows on the Jurassic period and is followed by the Paleogene period. It is the youngest period of the Mesozoic era, and at 80 million years long, the longest period of the Phanerozoic eon. The end of the _____ defines the boundary between the Mesozoic and Cenozoic eras.
   a. Hauterivian
   b. Campanian
   c. Valanginian
   d. Cretaceous

3. The _____ is a geological eon representing a period before the first abundant complex life on Earth. The _____ extended from 2500 Ma to 542.0 >± 1.0 Ma (million years ago), and is the most recent part of the old, informally named 'e;Precambrian'e; time.

The Proterozoic consists of 3 geologic eras, from oldest to youngest:

- Paleoproterozoic
- Mesoproterozoic
- Neoproterozoic

The well-identified events were:

- The transition to an oxygenated atmosphere during the Mesoproterozoic.
- Several glaciations, including the hypothesized Snowball Earth during the Cryogenian period in the late Neoproterozoic.
- The Ediacaran Period (635 to 542 Ma) which is characterized by the evolution of abundant soft-bodied multicellular organisms.

The geoloic record of the Proterozoic is much better than that for the preceding Archean. In contrast to the deep-water deposits of the Archean, the Proterozoic features many strata that were laid down in extensive shallow epicontinental seas; furthermore, many of these rocks are less metamorphosed than Archean-age ones, and plenty are unaltered.

   a. 1509 Istanbul earthquake
   b. 1700 Cascadia earthquake
   c. 1703 Genroku earthquake
   d. Proterozoic Eon

4. The _____ is a geologic period and system that extends from about 251 to 199 Mya (million years ago.) As the first period of the Mesozoic Era, the _____ follows the Permian and is followed by the Jurassic. Both the start and end of the _____ are marked by major extinction events.
   a. 1700 Cascadia earthquake
   b. Rhaetian
   c. 1509 Istanbul earthquake
   d. Triassic

5. _____ is the result of the transformation of an existing rock type, the protolith, in a process called metamorphism, which means 'change in form'. The protolith is subjected to heat and pressure (temperatures greater than 150 to 200 >°C and pressures of 1500 bars) causing profound physical and/or chemical change. The protolith may be sedimentary rock, igneous rock or another older _____.
   a. Laccolith
   b. Serpentinite
   c. Pluton
   d. Metamorphic rock

6. _____ is one of the three main rock types (the others being sedimentary and metamorphic rock.) _____ is formed by magma (molten rock) being cooled and becoming solid . They may form with or without crystallization, either below the surface as intrusive (plutonic) rocks or on the surface as extrusive (volcanic) rocks. They make up approximately 95% of the upper part of the Earth's crust, but their great abundance is hidden on the Earth's surface by a relatively thin but widespread layer of sedimentary and metamorphic rocks.
   a. Ignimbrite
   b. Igneous rock
   c. Extrusive
   d. Igneous differentiation

7. A _____ is a large emplacement of igneous intrusive rock that forms from cooled magma deep in the Earth's crust. they are almost always made mostly of felsic or intermediate rock-types, such as granite, quartz monzonite, or diorite

Although they may appear uniform, _____s are in fact structures with complex histories and compositions.

   a. Welded tuff
   b. Litchfieldite
   c. Country rock
   d. Batholith

8. _____ is the second most abundant mineral in the Earth's continental crust . It is made up of a framework of silicon-oxygen tetrahedra SiO_4, with each silicon shared between two oxygens to give the overall formula SiO_2. _____ has a hardness of 7 on the Mohs scale and a density of 2.65 g/cm³.
   a. 1700 Cascadia earthquake
   b. 1509 Istanbul earthquake
   c. Shocked quartz
   d. Quartz

9. In geology, a _____ or _____ line is a planar fracture in rock in which the rock on one side of the fracture has moved with respect to the rock on the other side. Large _____s within the Earth's crust are the result of differential or shear motion and active _____ zones are the causal locations of most earthquakes. Earthquakes are caused by energy release during rapid slippage along a _____.
   a. Drainage system
   b. Cleavage
   c. Compaction
   d. Fault

10. _____ is the study of the three-dimensional distribution of rock units with respect to their deformational histories. The primary goal of _____ is to use measurements of present-day rock geometries to uncover information about the history of deformation (strain) in the rocks, and ultimately, to understand the stress field that resulted in the observed strain and geometries. This understanding of the dynamics of the stress field can be linked to important events in the regional geologic past; a common goal is to understand the structural evolution of a particular area with respect to regionally widespread patterns of rock deformation (e.g., mountain building, rifting) due to plate tectonics.
    a. Structural geology
    b. Petermann Orogeny
    c. Monocline
    d. Strike and dip

Chapter 47. Joshua Tree National Park by D.D. Trent

11. In geology the term _____ refers to a fracture in rock where there has been no lateral movement in the plane of the fracture (up, down or sideways) of one side relative to the other. This makes it different from a fault which is defined as a fracture in rock where one side slides laterally past to the other. _____s normally have a regular spacing related to either the mechanical properties of the individual rock or the thickness of the layer involved.
   a. Joint
   b. 1509 Istanbul earthquake
   c. 1703 Genroku earthquake
   d. 1700 Cascadia earthquake

12. The _____ is a continental transform fault that runs a length of roughly 800 miles (1,300 km) through California in the United States. The fault's motion is right-lateral strike-slip (horizontal motion.) It forms the tectonic boundary between the Pacific Plate and the North American Plate.
   a. 1700 Cascadia earthquake
   b. 1509 Istanbul earthquake
   c. 1703 Genroku earthquake
   d. San Andreas fault

13. A _____ is a mountain rising from the ocean seafloor that does not reach to the water's surface (sea level), and thus is not an island. These are typically formed from extinct volcanoes, that rise abruptly and are usually found rising from a seafloor of 1,000-4,000 meters depth. They are defined by oceanographers as independent features that rise to at least 1,000 meters above the seafloor.
   a. 1509 Istanbul earthquake
   b. Seamount
   c. 1703 Genroku earthquake
   d. 1700 Cascadia earthquake

14. _____ is a clay mineral with the chemical composition $Al_2Si_2O_5(OH)_4$. It is a layered silicate mineral, with one tetrahedral sheet linked through oxygen atoms to one octahedral sheet of alumina octahedra. Rocks that are rich in _____ are known as china clay or kaolin. _____ clay occurs in abundance in soils that have formed from the chemical weathering of rocks in hot, moist climates - for example in tropical rainforest areas
   a. 1509 Istanbul earthquake
   b. Kaolinite
   c. Glauconite
   d. Clay minerals

15. _____ is the decomposition of Earth rocks, soils and their minerals through direct contact with the planet's atmosphere. _____ occurs in situ, or 'with no movement', and thus should not be confused with erosion, which involves the movement of rocks and minerals by agents such as water, ice, wind and gravity.

   Two important classifications of _____ processes exist -- physical and chemical _____.

   a. Weathering
   b. 1700 Cascadia earthquake
   c. Physical weathering
   d. 1509 Istanbul earthquake

16. _____ is the layer of soil under the topsoil on the surface of the ground. The _____ may include substances such as clay and has only been partially broken down by air, sunlight, water etc., to produce true soil. Below the _____ is the substratum, which can be residual bedrock, sediments, or aeolian deposits, largely unaffected by soil-forming factors active in the _____.
   a. 1703 Genroku earthquake
   b. 1700 Cascadia earthquake
   c. 1509 Istanbul earthquake
   d. Subsoil

17. An _____ is a fan-shaped deposit formed where a fast flowing stream flattens, slows, and spreads typically at the exit of a canyon onto a flatter plain. A convergence of neighboring fans into a single apron of deposits against a slope is called a bajada, or compound _____.

a. AL 333
b. Alluvial fan
c. AASHTO Soil Classification System
d. AL 129-1

18. A _____ is a gently inclined erosional surface carved into bedrock. It is thinly covered with Fluvial gravel that has developed at the foot of mountains. It develops when running water erodes most of the mass of the mountain. It is typically a concave surface gently sloping away from mountainous desert areas.
   a. Stream Load
   b. Patterned ground
   c. Gradualism
   d. Pediment

19. A _____ is a dry or ephemeral lakebed, generally extending to the shore, or remnant of, an endorheic lake. Such flats consist of fine-grained sediments infused with alkali salts. _____s are also known as alkali flats, sabkhas, dry lakes or mud flats.
   a. 1509 Istanbul earthquake
   b. 1700 Cascadia earthquake
   c. 1703 Genroku earthquake
   d. Playa

20. _____ is the removal of solids (sediment, soil, rock and other particles) in the natural environment. It usually occurs due to transport by wind, water, or ice; by down-slope creep of soil and other material under the force of gravity; or by living organisms, such as burrowing animals, in the case of bioerosion.

   _____ is distinguished from weathering, which is the process of chemical or physical breakdown of the minerals in the rocks, although the two processes may occur concurrently.

   a. AASHTO Soil Classification System
   b. AL 333
   c. Erosion
   d. AL 129-1

21. _____ are the preserved remains or traces of animals, plants, and other organisms from the remote past. The totality of _____, both discovered and undiscovered, and their placement in fossiliferous rock formations and sedimentary layers (strata) is known as the fossil record. The study of _____ across geological time, how they were formed, and the evolutionary relationships between taxa (phylogeny) are some of the most important functions of the science of paleontology.
   a. 1509 Istanbul earthquake
   b. Fossils
   c. 1703 Genroku earthquake
   d. 1700 Cascadia earthquake

22. In the earth sciences and geology sub-fields, a _____ or physical feature comprises a geomorphological unit, and is largely defined by its surface form and location in the landscape, as part of the terrain, and as such, is typically an element of topography. _____ elements also include seascape and oceanic waterbody interface features such as bays, peninsulas, seas and so forth, including sub-surface terrain features such as submersed mountain ranges, volcanoes, and the great ocean basins under the thin skin of water, for the whole earth is the province and domain of geology. This panorama in Great Smoky Mountains National Park has the readily identifiable physical features of a rolling plain, actually part of a broad valley, distant foothills, and a backdrop of the old much weathered Appalachian mountain range.

_____s are categorised by characteristic physical attributes such as elevation, slope, orientation, stratification, rock exposure, and soil type.

a. 1700 Cascadia earthquake
c. 1509 Istanbul earthquake
b. Polar deserts
d. Landform

23. A _____ or inselberg is an isolated rock hill, knob, ridge, or small mountain that rises abruptly from a gently sloping or virtually level surrounding plain. The term '_____' is usually used in the United States, whereas 'inselberg' is the more common international term. In southern and southern-central Africa, a similar formation of granite is known as a kopje (in fact a Dutch word) from the Afrikaans word: koppie.

_____ is an originally Native American term for an isolated hill or a lone mountain that has risen above the surrounding area, typically by surviving erosion.

a. 1509 Istanbul earthquake
c. Monadnock
b. Rogen moraine
d. Sandur

24. The _____ of any physical feature such as a hill, stream, roof, railroad, or road refers to the amount of inclination of that surface where zero indicates level (with respect to gravity) and larger numbers indicate higher degrees of 'tilt'. Often slope is calculated as a ratio of 'rise over run' in which run is the horizontal distance and rise is the vertical distance.

There are several systems for expressing slope:

1. as an angle of inclination from the horizontal of a right triangle. (This is the angle >α opposite the 'rise' side of the triangle.)
2. as a percentage (also known as the _____), the formula for which is [x]> which could also be expressed as the tangent of the angle of inclination times 100. In the U.S., the _____ is the most commonly used unit for communicating slopes in transportation, surveying, construction, and civil engineering.
3. as a per mille figure, the formula for which is [x]> which could also be expressed as the tangent of the angle of inclination times 1000. This is commonly used in Europe to denote the incline of a railway.
4. as a ratio of one part rise per so many parts run. For example, a slope that has a rise of 5 feet for every 100 feet of run would have a slope ratio of 1 in 20.

Any one of these expressions may be used interchangeably to express the characteristics of a slope. _____ is usually expressed as a percentage, but this may easily be converted to the angle >α from horizontal since that carries the same information.

a. Heavy metal
c. Diamond Head
b. Compaction
d. Grade

25. _____ is a dark coating found on exposed rock surfaces in arid environments.

_____ forms only on physically stable rock surfaces that are no longer subject to frequent precipitation, fracturing or wind abrasion. The varnish is primarily composed of particles of clay along with iron and manganese oxides. There is also a host of trace elements and almost always some organic matter. The color of the varnish varies from shades of brown to black.

a. 1700 Cascadia earthquake
b. Desert varnish
c. 1703 Genroku earthquake
d. 1509 Istanbul earthquake

1. The fault surface of _____ is usually near vertical and the footwall moves either left or right or laterally with very little vertical motion. _____ with left-lateral motion are also known as sinistral faults. Those with right-lateral motion are also known as dextral faults.
   a. Pahoehoe lava
   b. Star dunes
   c. Strike-slip faults
   d. Suspended load

2. In geology, a _____ or _____ line is a planar fracture in rock in which the rock on one side of the fracture has moved with respect to the rock on the other side. Large _____s within the Earth's crust are the result of differential or shear motion and active _____ zones are the causal locations of most earthquakes. Earthquakes are caused by energy release during rapid slippage along a _____.
   a. Compaction
   b. Drainage system
   c. Cleavage
   d. Fault

3. _____ landforms (mountains, hills, ridges, etc.) are created when large areas of bedrock are widely broken up by faults creating large vertical displacements of continental crust.

Vertical motion of the resulting blocks, sometimes accompanied by tilting, can then lead to high escarpments. These mountains are formed by the earth's crust being stretched and extended by tensional forces. Fault block mountains commonly accompany rifting, another indicator of tensional tectonic forces.

   a. Differential weathering
   b. Rejuvenated
   c. Coastal erosion
   d. Fault-block

4. The _____ is a geological eon representing a period before the first abundant complex life on Earth. The _____ extended from 2500 Ma to 542.0 >± 1.0 Ma (million years ago), and is the most recent part of the old, informally named 'e;Precambrian'e; time.

The Proterozoic consists of 3 geologic eras, from oldest to youngest:

- Paleoproterozoic
- Mesoproterozoic
- Neoproterozoic

The well-identified events were:

- The transition to an oxygenated atmosphere during the Mesoproterozoic.
- Several glaciations, including the hypothesized Snowball Earth during the Cryogenian period in the late Neoproterozoic.
- The Ediacaran Period (635 to 542 Ma) which is characterized by the evolution of abundant soft-bodied multicellular organisms.

The geoloic record of the Proterozoic is much better than that for the preceding Archean. In contrast to the deep-water deposits of the Archean, the Proterozoic features many strata that were laid down in extensive shallow epicontinental seas; furthermore, many of these rocks are less metamorphosed than Archean-age ones, and plenty are unaltered.

a. 1700 Cascadia earthquake
b. Proterozoic Eon
c. 1509 Istanbul earthquake
d. 1703 Genroku earthquake

5. A _____ is the topographic expression of faulting attributed to the displacement of the land surface by movement along the fault. It can be caused by differential erosion along an old inactive geologic fault (a sort of old rupture) with hard and weak rock, or by a movement on an active fault. In many cases, bluffs form from the upthrown block and can be very steep.
a. Subsequent streams
b. Fault scarp
c. Toreva block
d. Consequent streams

6. A _____ is a dry or ephemeral lakebed, generally extending to the shore, or remnant of, an endorheic lake. Such flats consist of fine-grained sediments infused with alkali salts. _____s are also known as alkali flats, sabkhas, dry lakes or mud flats.
a. 1700 Cascadia earthquake
b. 1703 Genroku earthquake
c. 1509 Istanbul earthquake
d. Playa

7. Natural _____ are flat expanses of ground covered with salt and other minerals, usually shining white under the sun. They are found in deserts, and should not be confused with salt evaporation ponds.
a. Differential weathering
b. Coastal erosion
c. Bradyseism
d. Salt pans

8. The _____ is a a term for a geologic period 65 million to 1.8 million years ago. The _____ covered the time span between the superseded Secondary period and an out-of-date definition of the Quaternary period. The period began with the demise of the non-avian dinosaurs in the Cretaceous-_____ extinction event, at start of the Cenozoic era, spanning to beginning of the most recent Ice Age, at the end of the Pliocene epoch.
a. Historical geology
b. Logarithmic Spiral Beach
c. Loihi Seamount
d. Tertiary

9. _____ is one of the three main rock types (the others being sedimentary and metamorphic rock.) _____ is formed by magma (molten rock) being cooled and becoming solid . They may form with or without crystallization, either below the surface as intrusive (plutonic) rocks or on the surface as extrusive (volcanic) rocks. They make up approximately 95% of the upper part of the Earth's crust, but their great abundance is hidden on the Earth's surface by a relatively thin but widespread layer of sedimentary and metamorphic rocks.
a. Ignimbrite
b. Extrusive
c. Igneous rock
d. Igneous differentiation

10. A _____ in geology is a fragment of crustal material formed on one tectonic plate and accreted -- 'sutured' -- to crust lying on another plate. The crustal block or fragment preserves its own distinctive geologic history, which is different from that of the surrounding areas (hence the term 'exotic' _____). The suture zone between a _____ and the crust it attaches to is usually identifiable as a fault.
a. 1509 Istanbul earthquake
b. Terrane
c. 1703 Genroku earthquake
d. 1700 Cascadia earthquake

11. The _____ is the earliest of three geologic eras of the Phanerozoic eon. The _____ spanned from roughly 542 to 251 million years ago (ICS, 2004), and is subdivided into six geologic periods; from oldest to youngest they are: the Cambrian, Ordovician, Silurian, Devonian, Carboniferous, and Permian.

The _____ covers the time from the first appearance of abundant, soft-shelled fossils to the time when the continents were beginning to be dominated by large, relatively sophisticated reptiles and modern plants. The lower (oldest) boundary was classically set at the first appearance of creatures known as trilobites and archeocyathids.

a. Paleozoic
b. 1509 Istanbul earthquake
c. 1703 Genroku earthquake
d. 1700 Cascadia earthquake

12. _____ is the name of a sedimentary carbonate rock and a mineral, both composed of calcium magnesium carbonate $CaMg_2$ found in crystals.

_____ rock (also dolostone) is composed predominantly of the mineral _____. Limestone that is partially replaced by _____ is referred to as dolomitic limestone, or in old U.S. geologic literature as magnesian limestone.

a. Superficial deposits
b. Pelagic sediments
c. Dolostone
d. Dolomite

13. The _____ Era is one of three geologic eras of the Phanerozoic eon. The division of time into eras dates back to Giovanni Arduino, in the 18th century, although his original name for the era now called the '_____' was 'Secondary' (making the modern era the 'Tertiary'.)

The _____ was a time of tectonic, climatic and evolutionary activity. The continents gradually shifted from a state of connectedness into their present configuration; the drifting provided for speciation and other important evolutionary developments.

a. 1700 Cascadia earthquake
b. 1703 Genroku earthquake
c. 1509 Istanbul earthquake
d. Mesozoic

14. _____ is a hard metamorphic rock which was originally sandstone. Sandstone is converted into _____ through heating and pressure usually related to tectonic compression within orogenic belts. Pure _____ is usually white to grey, though _____s often occur in various shades of pink and red due to varying amounts of iron oxide .
a. Hornfels
b. Slate
c. Talc carbonate
d. Quartzite

15. The _____ is the zone of the ocean floor that separates the thin oceanic crust from thick continental crust. _____s constitute about 28% of the oceanic area.

The transition from continental to oceanic crust commonly occurs within the outer part of the margin, called continental rise.

a. 1509 Istanbul earthquake
b. Swash
c. Cuspate forelands
d. Continental margin

16. A _____ in geology is an intrusive igneous rock body that crystallized from a magma slowly cooling below the surface of the Earth. _____s include batholiths, dikes, sills, laccoliths, lopoliths, and other igneous bodies. In practice, '_____' usually refers to a distinctive mass of igneous rock, typically kilometers in dimension, without a tabular shape like those of dikes and sills.
   a. Matrix
   b. Tephra
   c. Petrology
   d. Pluton

1. The _____ is the epoch from 1.8 million to 11550 years BP covering the world's recent period of repeated glaciations. The _____ epoch follows the Pliocene epoch and is followed by the Holocene epoch. The _____ is the third epoch of the Neogene period or 6th epoch of the Cenozoic Era. The end of the _____ corresponds with the retreat of the last continental glacier. It also corresponds with the end of the Paleolithic age used in archaeology.
   a. Sicilian Stage
   b. Pleistocene
   c. Late Pleistocene
   d. Tyrrhenian

2. An _____ is a rapid flow of snow down a slope, from either natural triggers or human activity. Typically occurring in mountainous terrain, an _____ can mix air and water with the descending snow. Powerful _____s have the capability to entrain ice, rocks, trees, and other material on the slope; however _____s are always initiated in snow, are primarily composed of flowing snow, and are distinct from mudslides, rock slides, rock _____s, and serac collapses from an icefall.
   a. Avalanche
   b. AL 333
   c. AASHTO Soil Classification System
   d. AL 129-1

3. A _____ is a large emplacement of igneous intrusive rock that forms from cooled magma deep in the Earth's crust. they are almost always made mostly of felsic or intermediate rock-types, such as granite, quartz monzonite, or diorite

   Although they may appear uniform, _____s are in fact structures with complex histories and compositions.
   a. Litchfieldite
   b. Batholith
   c. Country rock
   d. Welded tuff

4. Two important classifications of weathering processes exist -- physical and _____. Mechanical or physical weathering involves the breakdown of rocks and soils through direct contact with atmospheric conditions, such as heat, water, ice and pressure. The second classification, _____, involves the direct effect of atmospheric chemicals or biologically produced chemicals (also known as biological weathering) in the breakdown of rocks, soils and minerals.
   a. Chemical weathering
   b. 1700 Cascadia earthquake
   c. Physical weathering
   d. 1509 Istanbul earthquake

5. _____ is the decomposition of Earth rocks, soils and their minerals through direct contact with the planet's atmosphere. _____ occurs in situ, or 'with no movement', and thus should not be confused with erosion, which involves the movement of rocks and minerals by agents such as water, ice, wind and gravity.

   Two important classifications of _____ processes exist -- physical and chemical _____.
   a. 1509 Istanbul earthquake
   b. 1700 Cascadia earthquake
   c. Weathering
   d. Physical weathering

6. _____ is a common and widely occurring type of intrusive, felsic, igneous rock. _____ has a medium to coarse texture, occasionally with some individual crystals larger than the groundmass forming a rock known as porphyry. _____s can be pink to dark gray or even black, depending on their chemistry and mineralogy.
   a. 1703 Genroku earthquake
   b. 1509 Istanbul earthquake
   c. 1700 Cascadia earthquake
   d. Granite

7. _____ is the natural or artificial removal of surface and sub-surface water from an area. Many agricultural soils need _____ to improve production or to manage water supplies.

The earliest archaeological record of an advanced system of _____ comes from the Indus Valley Civilization from around 3100 BC in what is now Pakistan and North India.

   a. 1703 Genroku earthquake
   b. 1700 Cascadia earthquake
   c. 1509 Istanbul earthquake
   d. Drainage

8. A _____, is the line separating neighbouring drainage basins (catchments.) In hilly country, the divide lies along topographical peaks and ridges, but in flat country (especially where the ground is marshy) the divide may be invisible - just a more or less notional line on the ground on either side of which falling raindrops will start a journey to different rivers, and even to different sides of a region or continent.
   a. 1703 Genroku earthquake
   b. 1700 Cascadia earthquake
   c. Drainage divide
   d. 1509 Istanbul earthquake

9. A _____ is a large, slow-moving mass of ice, formed from compacted layers of snow, that slowly deforms and flows in response to gravity and high pressure.

_____ ice is the largest reservoir of fresh water on Earth, and second only to oceans as the largest reservoir of total water.

   a. Little Ice Age
   b. Glacier
   c. Keeling Curve
   d. Deforestation

10. In stratigraphy, _____ is the native consolidated rock underlying the surface of a terrestrial planet, usually the Earth. Above the _____ is usually an area of broken and weathered unconsolidated rock in the basal subsoil. The top of the _____ is known as rockhead and identifying this, via excavations, drilling or geophysical methods, is an important task in most civil engineering projects.
   a. Biozones
   b. Sequence stratigraphy
   c. Polystrate
   d. Bedrock

11. _____ is an intrusive igneous rock similar to granite, but contains more plagioclase than potassium feldspar. It usually contains abundant biotite mica and hornblende, giving it a darker appearance than true granite. Mica may be present in well-formed hexagonal crystals, and hornblende may appear as needle-like crystals.
   a. Granodiorite
   b. 1509 Istanbul earthquake
   c. 1700 Cascadia earthquake
   d. 1703 Genroku earthquake

12. In geology, an _____ is a body of igneous rock that has crystallized from molten magma below the surface of the Earth. Bodies of magma that solidify underground before they reach the surface of the earth are called plutons the Roman god of the underworld. Correspondingly, rocks of this kind are also referred to as igneous plutonic rocks or igneous intrusive rocks.
   a. AL 333
   b. AL 129-1
   c. Intrusion
   d. AASHTO Soil Classification System

13. The _____ Era is one of three geologic eras of the Phanerozoic eon. The division of time into eras dates back to Giovanni Arduino, in the 18th century, although his original name for the era now called the '_____' was 'Secondary' (making the modern era the 'Tertiary'.)

The _____ was a time of tectonic, climatic and evolutionary activity. The continents gradually shifted from a state of connectedness into their present configuration; the drifting provided for speciation and other important evolutionary developments.

a. 1509 Istanbul earthquake
b. 1703 Genroku earthquake
c. Mesozoic
d. 1700 Cascadia earthquake

14. The _____ is the earliest of three geologic eras of the Phanerozoic eon. The _____ spanned from roughly 542 to 251 million years ago (ICS, 2004), and is subdivided into six geologic periods; from oldest to youngest they are: the Cambrian, Ordovician, Silurian, Devonian, Carboniferous, and Permian.

The _____ covers the time from the first appearance of abundant, soft-shelled fossils to the time when the continents were beginning to be dominated by large, relatively sophisticated reptiles and modern plants. The lower (oldest) boundary was classically set at the first appearance of creatures known as trilobites and archeocyathids.

a. Paleozoic
b. 1700 Cascadia earthquake
c. 1703 Genroku earthquake
d. 1509 Istanbul earthquake

15. _____ is a carbonate mineral, one of the two common, naturally occurring polymorphs of calcium carbonate, $CaCO_3$. The other polymorph is the mineral calcite. _____'s crystal lattice differs from that of calcite, resulting in a different crystal shape, an orthorhombic system with acicular crystals.

a. Aragonite
b. AASHTO Soil Classification System
c. AL 129-1
d. Apatite

16. The _____ Era, is the most recent of the three classic geological eras and covers the period from 65.5 million years ago to the present. It is marked by the Cretaceous-Tertiary extinction event at the end of the Cretaceous that saw the demise of the last non-avian dinosaurs and the end of the Mesozoic Era. The _____ era is ongoing.

a. 1700 Cascadia earthquake
b. 1703 Genroku earthquake
c. 1509 Istanbul earthquake
d. Cenozoic

17. The _____ , usually abbreviated K for its German translation Kreide, is a geologic period and system from circa >145.5 >± 4 to >65.5 >± 0.3 million years ago . In the geologic timescale, the _____ follows on the Jurassic period and is followed by the Paleogene period. It is the youngest period of the Mesozoic era, and at 80 million years long, the longest period of the Phanerozoic eon. The end of the _____ defines the boundary between the Mesozoic and Cenozoic eras.

a. Campanian
b. Hauterivian
c. Valanginian
d. Cretaceous

18. _____ refers to natural mountain building, and may be studied as a tectonic structural event, (b) as a geographical event, and (c) a chronological event. Orogenic events (a) cause distinctive structural phenomena and related tectonic activity, (b) affect certain regions of rocks and crust, and (c) happen within a specific period of time.

a. Orogenesis
b. Orogeny
c. Antler orogeny
d. Alice Springs Orogeny

19. The _____ is a geological epoch which began approximately 11‰700 years ago (10‰000 ^{14}C years ago). According to traditional geological thinking, the _____ continues to the present. The _____ is part of the Neogene and Quaternary periods.
  a. Neoglaciation
  b. 1509 Istanbul earthquake
  c. 1700 Cascadia earthquake
  d. Holocene

20. _____, also known as the Pleistocene glaciation, the current ice age or simply the ice age, refers to the period of the last few million years in which permanent ice sheets were established in Antarctica and perhaps Greenland, and fluctuating ice sheets have occurred elsewhere The major effects of the ice age were erosion and deposition of material over large parts of the continents, modification of river systems, creation of millions of lakes, changes in sea level, development of pluvial lakes far from the ice margins, isostatic adjustment of the crust, and abnormal winds. It affected oceans, flooding, and biological communities.
  a. Snowball Earth
  b. Rock glaciers
  c. Wolstonian Stage
  d. Quaternary glaciation

21. The general term '_____' or, more precisely, 'glacial age' denotes a geological period of long-term reduction in the temperature of the Earth's surface and atmosphere, resulting in an expansion of continental ice sheets, polar ice sheets and alpine glaciers. Within a long-term _____, individual pulses of extra cold climate are termed 'glaciations'. Glaciologically, _____ implies the presence of extensive ice sheets in the northern and southern hemispheres; by this definition we are still in an _____.
  a. AL 129-1
  b. AL 333
  c. AASHTO Soil Classification System
  d. Ice Age

22. The _____ was a period of cooling occurring after a warmer North Atlantic era known as the Medieval Warm Period. While not a true ice age, the term was introduced into scientific literature by Fran>çois E. Matthes in 1939. Climatologists and historians working with local records no longer expect to agree on either the start or end dates of this period, which varied according to local conditions.
  a. Deforestation
  b. Pacific Decadal Oscillation
  c. Glacier
  d. Little Ice Age

1. A _____ is a mountain rising from the ocean seafloor that does not reach to the water's surface (sea level), and thus is not an island. These are typically formed from extinct volcanoes, that rise abruptly and are usually found rising from a seafloor of 1,000-4,000 meters depth. They are defined by oceanographers as independent features that rise to at least 1,000 meters above the seafloor.
   a. 1509 Istanbul earthquake
   b. 1700 Cascadia earthquake
   c. 1703 Genroku earthquake
   d. Seamount

2. The _____ , usually abbreviated K for its German translation Kreide, is a geologic period and system from circa >145.5 >± 4 to >65.5 >± 0.3 million years ago . In the geologic timescale, the _____ follows on the Jurassic period and is followed by the Paleogene period. It is the youngest period of the Mesozoic era, and at 80 million years long, the longest period of the Phanerozoic eon. The end of the _____ defines the boundary between the Mesozoic and Cenozoic eras.
   a. Hauterivian
   b. Cretaceous
   c. Campanian
   d. Valanginian

3. The _____ is the epoch from 1.8 million to 11550 years BP covering the world's recent period of repeated glaciations. The _____ epoch follows the Pliocene epoch and is followed by the Holocene epoch. The _____ is the third epoch of the Neogene period or 6th epoch of the Cenozoic Era. The end of the _____ corresponds with the retreat of the last continental glacier. It also corresponds with the end of the Paleolithic age used in archaeology.
   a. Late Pleistocene
   b. Sicilian Stage
   c. Tyrrhenian
   d. Pleistocene

4. The _____ is a a term for a geologic period 65 million to 1.8 million years ago. The _____ covered the time span between the superseded Secondary period and an out-of-date definition of the Quaternary period. The period began with the demise of the non-avian dinosaurs in the Cretaceous-_____ extinction event, at start of the Cenozoic era, spanning to beginning of the most recent Ice Age, at the end of the Pliocene epoch.
   a. Tertiary
   b. Historical geology
   c. Loihi Seamount
   d. Logarithmic Spiral Beach

5. _____ is a sedimentary rock, a hardened deposit of calcium carbonate. This calcium carbonate cements together other materials, including gravel, sand, clay, and silt. It is found in aridisol and mollisol soil orders.
   a. 1509 Istanbul earthquake
   b. 1703 Genroku earthquake
   c. 1700 Cascadia earthquake
   d. Caliche

6. The _____ Era is one of three geologic eras of the Phanerozoic eon. The division of time into eras dates back to Giovanni Arduino, in the 18th century, although his original name for the era now called the '_____' was 'Secondary' (making the modern era the 'Tertiary'.)

The _____ was a time of tectonic, climatic and evolutionary activity. The continents gradually shifted from a state of connectedness into their present configuration; the drifting provided for speciation and other important evolutionary developments.

   a. 1703 Genroku earthquake
   b. 1700 Cascadia earthquake
   c. 1509 Istanbul earthquake
   d. Mesozoic

7. A _____ in geology is an intrusive igneous rock body that crystallized from a magma slowly cooling below the surface of the Earth. _____s include batholiths, dikes, sills, laccoliths, lopoliths, and other igneous bodies. In practice, '_____' usually refers to a distinctive mass of igneous rock, typically kilometers in dimension, without a tabular shape like those of dikes and sills.

   a. Tephra
   b. Pluton
   c. Matrix
   d. Petrology

8. A _____ is a large emplacement of igneous intrusive rock that forms from cooled magma deep in the Earth's crust. they are almost always made mostly of felsic or intermediate rock-types, such as granite, quartz monzonite, or diorite

Although they may appear uniform, _____s are in fact structures with complex histories and compositions.

   a. Litchfieldite
   b. Country rock
   c. Batholith
   d. Welded tuff

9. _____ geological formations have their origins in turbidity current deposits, which are deposits from a form of underwater avalanche that are responsible for distributing vast amounts of clastic sediment into the deep ocean.

They were first properly described by Bouma (1962), who studied deepwater sediments and recognized particular fining up intervals within deep water, fine grained shales, which were anomalous because they started at pebble conglomerates and terminated in shales.

This was anomalous because within the deep ocean it had historically been assumed that there was no mechanism by which tractional flow could carry and deposit coarse-grained sediments into the abyssal depths.

   a. 1509 Istanbul earthquake
   b. 1700 Cascadia earthquake
   c. 1703 Genroku earthquake
   d. Turbidite

1. The _____ Period is the geologic time period after the Neogene Period, spanning 1.805 +/- 0.005 million years ago to the present. The _____ includes two geologic epochs: the Pleistocene and the Holocene Epoch.

There is an ongoing debate of the status of _____ -- a recent proposal from International Commission on Stratigraphy (ICS) was to make _____ a subperiod under Neogene, but that was retracted after criticism from International Union for _____ Research (INQUA), so instead ICS and INQUA agreed to erect _____ as an Era, above Neogene, and to place the base for _____ at 2.588 >± 3.005, the base for Gelasian Stage.

a. Geomorphology
b. Quaternary
c. Yilgarn Craton
d. Tributary

2. A _____ is an extent of land where water from rain or snow melt drains downhill into a body of water, such as a river, lake, reservoir, estuary, wetland, sea or ocean. The _____ includes both the streams and rivers that convey the water as well as the land surfaces from which water drains into those channels, and is separated from adjacent basins by a drainage divide.

The _____ acts like a funnel, collecting all the water within the area covered by the basin and channelling it into a waterway.

a. 1703 Genroku earthquake
b. 1509 Istanbul earthquake
c. Drainage basin
d. 1700 Cascadia earthquake

3. The _____ , usually abbreviated K for its German translation Kreide, is a geologic period and system from circa >145.5 >± 4 to >65.5 >± 0.3 million years ago . In the geologic timescale, the _____ follows on the Jurassic period and is followed by the Paleogene period. It is the youngest period of the Mesozoic era, and at 80 million years long, the longest period of the Phanerozoic eon. The end of the _____ defines the boundary between the Mesozoic and Cenozoic eras.

a. Valanginian
b. Hauterivian
c. Campanian
d. Cretaceous

4. In geology, a _____ is a large scale breccia, a mappable body of rock characterized by a lack of continuous bedding and the inclusion of fragments of rock of all sizes, contained in a fine-grained deformed matrix. The _____ typically consists of a jumble of large blocks of varied lithologies of altered oceanic crustal material and blocks of continental slope sediments in a sheared mudstone matrix. Some larger blocks of rock may be as much as 1 km across.

a. Stratification
b. Melange
c. Leaching
d. Diamond Head

5. A _____ is a geological phenomenon which includes a wide range of ground movement, such as rock falls, deep failure of slopes and shallow debris flows, which can occur in offshore, coastal and onshore environments. Although the action of gravity is the primary driving force for a _____ to occur, there are other contributing factors affecting the original slope stability. Typically, pre-conditional factors build up specific sub-surface conditions that make the area/slope prone to failure, whereas the actual _____ often requires a trigger before being released.

a. Landslide
b. 1509 Istanbul earthquake
c. Mass wasting
d. 1700 Cascadia earthquake

Chapter 52. Hot Springs National Park

1. In nuclear physics, a _____ is a nuclide produced by radioactive decay. Radioactive decay often involves a sequence of steps For example, U-238 decays to Th-234 which decays to Pa-234 which decays, and so on, to Pb-206:

>

In this example:

- Th-234, Pa-234,…,Pb-206 are the _____s of U-238.
- Th-234 is the daughter of the parent U-238.
- Pa-234 is the granddaughter of U-238.

Note that Th-234, Pa-234,…,Pb-206 might also be referred to as the daughter products of U-238.

_____s are extremely important in understanding radioactive decay and the management of radioactive waste.

    a. Decay product
    c. Mass deficiency
    b. Positron emission
    d. Mass excess

2. The _____ is a geologic period and system, the second of six of the Paleozoic era, and covers the time between 488.3>±1.7 to 443.7>±1.5 million years ago (ICS, 2004.) It follows the Cambrian period and is followed by the Silurian period. The _____ was defined by Charles Lapworth in 1879, to resolve a dispute between followers of Adam Sedgwick and Roderick Murchison, who were placing the same rock beds in northern Wales into the Cambrian and Silurian periods respectively.
    a. AL 129-1
    c. AASHTO Soil Classification System
    b. AL 333
    d. Ordovician

3. The _____ is the epoch from 1.8 million to 11550 years BP covering the world's recent period of repeated glaciations. The _____ epoch follows the Pliocene epoch and is followed by the Holocene epoch. The _____ is the third epoch of the Neogene period or 6th epoch of the Cenozoic Era. The end of the _____ corresponds with the retreat of the last continental glacier. It also corresponds with the end of the Paleolithic age used in archaeology.
    a. Late Pleistocene
    c. Tyrrhenian
    b. Sicilian Stage
    d. Pleistocene

4. The _____ Era is one of three geologic eras of the Phanerozoic eon. The division of time into eras dates back to Giovanni Arduino, in the 18th century, although his original name for the era now called the '_____' was 'Secondary' (making the modern era the 'Tertiary'.)

The _____ was a time of tectonic, climatic and evolutionary activity. The continents gradually shifted from a state of connectedness into their present configuration; the drifting provided for speciation and other important evolutionary developments.

    a. 1703 Genroku earthquake
    c. 1509 Istanbul earthquake
    b. 1700 Cascadia earthquake
    d. Mesozoic

5. In geology, _____ refers to heat sources within the planet. _____ is technically an adjective (e.g., _____ energy) but in U.S. English the word has attained frequent use as a noun.

The planet's internal heat was originally generated during its accretion, due to gravitational binding energy, and since then additional heat has continued to be generated by decay heat from the radioactive decay of elements.

a. Geothermal
b. Cleavage
c. Tarn
d. Grade

6. The _____ is a geologic subperiod and stratigraphic subsystem of the Carboniferous Period. It is the earliest/lowermost of two divisions of the Carboniferous, lasting from roughly 359 to 318 Ma (million years ago.) As with most other geochronologic units, the rock beds that define the _____ are well identified, but the exact start and end dates are uncertain by a few million years.

a. Pennsylvanian
b. Calciferous sandstone
c. Dinantian
d. Mississippian

7. _____ is the second most abundant mineral in the Earth's continental crust. It is made up of a framework of silicon-oxygen tetrahedra SiO_4, with each silicon shared between two oxygens to give the overall formula SiO_2. _____ has a hardness of 7 on the Mohs scale and a density of 2.65 g/cm³.

a. 1700 Cascadia earthquake
b. Quartz
c. Shocked quartz
d. 1509 Istanbul earthquake

8. The _____ , usually abbreviated K for its German translation Kreide, is a geologic period and system from circa >145.5 >± 4 to >65.5 >± 0.3 million years ago. In the geologic timescale, the _____ follows on the Jurassic period and is followed by the Paleogene period. It is the youngest period of the Mesozoic era, and at 80 million years long, the longest period of the Phanerozoic eon. The end of the _____ defines the boundary between the Mesozoic and Cenozoic eras.

a. Valanginian
b. Hauterivian
c. Campanian
d. Cretaceous

9. The _____ is a geologic subperiod and stratigraphic subsystem of the Carboniferous Period. It is the later subperiod of the Carboniferous, lasting from roughly 318.1>± 1.3 to 299>± 0.8 Ma (million years ago.) As with most other geochronologic units, the rock beds that define the _____ are well identified, but the exact date of the start and end are uncertain by a few million years.

a. Pennsylvanian
b. Dinantian
c. Calciferous sandstone
d. Mississippian

10. _____ refers to natural mountain building, and may be studied as a tectonic structural event, (b) as a geographical event, and (c) a chronological event. Orogenic events (a) cause distinctive structural phenomena and related tectonic activity, (b) affect certain regions of rocks and crust, and (c) happen within a specific period of time.

a. Antler orogeny
b. Alice Springs Orogeny
c. Orogenesis
d. Orogeny

Chapter 53. Big Bend National Park

1. The _____ is the earliest of three geologic eras of the Phanerozoic eon. The _____ spanned from roughly 542 to 251 million years ago (ICS, 2004), and is subdivided into six geologic periods; from oldest to youngest they are: the Cambrian, Ordovician, Silurian, Devonian, Carboniferous, and Permian.

The _____ covers the time from the first appearance of abundant, soft-shelled fossils to the time when the continents were beginning to be dominated by large, relatively sophisticated reptiles and modern plants. The lower (oldest) boundary was classically set at the first appearance of creatures known as trilobites and archeocyathids.

   a. 1700 Cascadia earthquake   b. 1703 Genroku earthquake
   c. 1509 Istanbul earthquake   d. Paleozoic

2. The _____ is a a term for a geologic period 65 million to 1.8 million years ago. The _____ covered the time span between the superseded Secondary period and an out-of-date definition of the Quaternary period. The period began with the demise of the non-avian dinosaurs in the Cretaceous-_____ extinction event, at start of the Cenozoic era, spanning to beginning of the most recent Ice Age, at the end of the Pliocene epoch.

   a. Loihi Seamount   b. Logarithmic Spiral Beach
   c. Historical geology   d. Tertiary

3. _____ is the term used in geology for the increase in land elevation due to the deposition of sediment. _____ occurs in areas in which the supply of sediment is greater than the amount of material that the system is able to transport. The mass balance between sediment being transported and sediment in the bed is described by the Exner equation.

   a. Erosion prediction   b. Orientation Tensor
   c. Ostwald ripening   d. Aggradation

4. The _____ is the epoch from 1.8 million to 11550 years BP covering the world's recent period of repeated glaciations. The _____ epoch follows the Pliocene epoch and is followed by the Holocene epoch. The _____ is the third epoch of the Neogene period or 6th epoch of the Cenozoic Era. The end of the _____ corresponds with the retreat of the last continental glacier. It also corresponds with the end of the Paleolithic age used in archaeology.

   a. Tyrrhenian   b. Sicilian Stage
   c. Pleistocene   d. Late Pleistocene

5. _____ are the preserved remains or traces of animals, plants, and other organisms from the remote past. The totality of _____, both discovered and undiscovered, and their placement in fossiliferous rock formations and sedimentary layers (strata) is known as the fossil record. The study of _____ across geological time, how they were formed, and the evolutionary relationships between taxa (phylogeny) are some of the most important functions of the science of paleontology.

   a. 1700 Cascadia earthquake   b. 1509 Istanbul earthquake
   c. 1703 Genroku earthquake   d. Fossils

6. _____ refers to natural mountain building, and may be studied as a tectonic structural event, (b) as a geographical event, and (c) a chronological event. Orogenic events (a) cause distinctive structural phenomena and related tectonic activity, (b) affect certain regions of rocks and crust, and (c) happen within a specific period of time.

   a. Orogeny   b. Orogenesis
   c. Antler orogeny   d. Alice Springs Orogeny

7. The _____ , usually abbreviated K for its German translation Kreide, is a geologic period and system from circa >145.5 >± 4 to >65.5 >± 0.3 million years ago . In the geologic timescale, the _____ follows on the Jurassic period and is followed by the Paleogene period. It is the youngest period of the Mesozoic era, and at 80 million years long, the longest period of the Phanerozoic eon. The end of the _____ defines the boundary between the Mesozoic and Cenozoic eras.
   a. Campanian
   b. Hauterivian
   c. Valanginian
   d. Cretaceous

8. The _____ epoch (55.8 >± 0.2 - 33.9 >± 0.1 Ma) is a major division of the geologic timescale and the second epoch of the Palaeogene period in the Cenozoic era. The _____ spans the time from the end of the Paleocene epoch to the beginning of the Oligocene epoch. The start of the _____ is marked by the emergence of the first modern mammals.
   a. AASHTO Soil Classification System
   b. AL 129-1
   c. AL 333
   d. Eocene

9. The _____ or Palaeocene, 'early dawn of the recent' is a geologic epoch that lasted from 65.5 >± 0.3 Ma to 55.8 >± 0.2 Ma (million years ago.) It is the first epoch of the Palaeogene Period in the modern Cenozoic era. As with most other older geologic periods, the strata that define the epoch's beginning and end are well identified but the exact date of the end is uncertain.
   a. Paleocene
   b. 1700 Cascadia earthquake
   c. 1703 Genroku earthquake
   d. 1509 Istanbul earthquake

10. The _____ is a geological epoch which began approximately 11‰700 years ago (10‰000 ^{14}C years ago). According to traditional geological thinking, the _____ continues to the present. The _____ is part of the Neogene and Quaternary periods.
    a. 1700 Cascadia earthquake
    b. 1509 Istanbul earthquake
    c. Holocene
    d. Neoglaciation

Chapter 54. Shenandoah National Park

1. The _____ is the first geological period of the Phanerozoic eon, lasting from 542 ± 0.3 million years ago to 488.3 ± 1.7 million years ago (ICS, 2004); it is succeeded by the Ordovician. Its subdivisions, and indeed its base, are somewhat in flux. The period was established by Adam Sedgwick, who named it after Cambria, the classical name for Wales, where Britain's _____ rocks are best exposed.
   a. 1509 Istanbul earthquake
   b. 1700 Cascadia earthquake
   c. 1703 Genroku earthquake
   d. Cambrian

2. The _____ is the earliest of three geologic eras of the Phanerozoic eon. The _____ spanned from roughly 542 to 251 million years ago (ICS, 2004), and is subdivided into six geologic periods; from oldest to youngest they are: the Cambrian, Ordovician, Silurian, Devonian, Carboniferous, and Permian.

   The _____ covers the time from the first appearance of abundant, soft-shelled fossils to the time when the continents were beginning to be dominated by large, relatively sophisticated reptiles and modern plants. The lower (oldest) boundary was classically set at the first appearance of creatures known as trilobites and archeocyathids.

   a. Paleozoic
   b. 1509 Istanbul earthquake
   c. 1703 Genroku earthquake
   d. 1700 Cascadia earthquake

3. _____ is the naturally occurring, unconsolidated or loose covering on the Earth's surface. _____ is composed of particles of broken rock that have been altered by chemical, biological and environmental processes including weathering and erosion. _____ is different from its parent rock(s) source(s), altered by interactions between the lithosphere, hydrosphere, atmosphere, and the biosphere.
   a. Slump
   b. 1509 Istanbul earthquake
   c. Topsoil
   d. Soil

4. The _____ Era is one of three geologic eras of the Phanerozoic eon. The division of time into eras dates back to Giovanni Arduino, in the 18th century, although his original name for the era now called the '_____' was 'Secondary' (making the modern era the 'Tertiary'.)

   The _____ was a time of tectonic, climatic and evolutionary activity. The continents gradually shifted from a state of connectedness into their present configuration; the drifting provided for speciation and other important evolutionary developments.

   a. 1509 Istanbul earthquake
   b. Mesozoic
   c. 1703 Genroku earthquake
   d. 1700 Cascadia earthquake

5. The _____ is a geological eon representing a period before the first abundant complex life on Earth. The _____ extended from 2500 Ma to 542.0 >± 1.0 Ma (million years ago), and is the most recent part of the old, informally named 'e;Precambrian'e; time.

   The Proterozoic consists of 3 geologic eras, from oldest to youngest:

   - Paleoproterozoic
   - Mesoproterozoic
   - Neoproterozoic

The well-identified events were:

- The transition to an oxygenated atmosphere during the Mesoproterozoic.
- Several glaciations, including the hypothesized Snowball Earth during the Cryogenian period in the late Neoproterozoic.
- The Ediacaran Period (635 to 542 Ma) which is characterized by the evolution of abundant soft-bodied multicellular organisms.

The geoloic record of the Proterozoic is much better than that for the preceding Archean. In contrast to the deep-water deposits of the Archean, the Proterozoic features many strata that were laid down in extensive shallow epicontinental seas; furthermore, many of these rocks are less metamorphosed than Archean-age ones, and plenty are unaltered.

a. 1700 Cascadia earthquake
b. 1509 Istanbul earthquake
c. 1703 Genroku earthquake
d. Proterozoic Eon

6. In stratigraphy, _____ is the native consolidated rock underlying the surface of a terrestrial planet, usually the Earth. Above the _____ is usually an area of broken and weathered unconsolidated rock in the basal subsoil. The top of the _____ is known as rockhead and identifying this, via excavations, drilling or geophysical methods, is an important task in most civil engineering projects.
   a. Polystrate
   b. Sequence stratigraphy
   c. Biozones
   d. Bedrock

7. The _____ Era, is the most recent of the three classic geological eras and covers the period from 65.5 million years ago to the present. It is marked by the Cretaceous-Tertiary extinction event at the end of the Cretaceous that saw the demise of the last non-avian dinosaurs and the end of the Mesozoic Era. The _____ era is ongoing.
   a. 1509 Istanbul earthquake
   b. 1703 Genroku earthquake
   c. Cenozoic
   d. 1700 Cascadia earthquake

8. The _____ was an ocean that existed in the Neoproterozoic and Paleozoic eras of the geologic timescale (between 600 and 400 million years ago.) The _____ was situated in the southern hemisphere, between the paleocontinents of Laurentia, Baltica and Avalonia. The ocean disappeared with the Caledonian, Taconic and Acadian orogenies, when these three continents joined to form one big landmass called Laurussia.
   a. Iapetus ocean
   b. AASHTO Soil Classification System
   c. AL 333
   d. AL 129-1

9. The _____ is an informal name for the supereon comprising the eons of the geologic timescale that came before the current Phanerozoic eon. It spans from the formation of Earth around 4500 Mya (million years ago) to the evolution of abundant macroscopic hard-shelled animals, which marked the beginning of the Cambrian, the first period of the first era of the Phanerozoic eon, some 542 Mya. It is named after the Roman name for Wales - Cambria - where rocks from this age were first studied.
   a. Precambrian
   b. 1509 Istanbul earthquake
   c. 1703 Genroku earthquake
   d. 1700 Cascadia earthquake

10. _____ refers to natural mountain building, and may be studied as a tectonic structural event, (b) as a geographical event, and (c) a chronological event. Orogenic events (a) cause distinctive structural phenomena and related tectonic activity, (b) affect certain regions of rocks and crust, and (c) happen within a specific period of time.
   a. Alice Springs Orogeny   b. Orogeny
   c. Antler orogeny   d. Orogenesis

11. The _____ is a geologic period and system, the second of six of the Paleozoic era, and covers the time between 488.3>±1.7 to 443.7>±1.5 million years ago (ICS, 2004.) It follows the Cambrian period and is followed by the Silurian period. The _____ was defined by Charles Lapworth in 1879, to resolve a dispute between followers of Adam Sedgwick and Roderick Murchison, who were placing the same rock beds in northern Wales into the Cambrian and Silurian periods respectively.
   a. Ordovician   b. AL 333
   c. AASHTO Soil Classification System   d. AL 129-1

12. _____ was the supercontinent that is theorized to have existed during the Paleozoic and Mesozoic eras about 250 million years ago, before the component continents were separated into their current configuration.

The name was first used by the German originator of the continental drift theory, Alfred Wegener, in the 1920 edition of his book The Origin of Continents and Oceans , in which a postulated supercontinent _____ played a key role.

The single enormous ocean which surrounded Pangaea is known as Panthalassa.

   a. 1703 Genroku earthquake   b. Pangea
   c. 1509 Istanbul earthquake   d. 1700 Cascadia earthquake

13. In geology, a _____ is a landmass comprising more than one continental core, or craton. The assembly of cratons and accreted terranes that form Eurasia qualifies as a _____ today.

Most commonly, paleogeographers employ the term _____ to refer to a single landmass consisting of all the modern continents.

   a. 1700 Cascadia earthquake   b. 1509 Istanbul earthquake
   c. 1703 Genroku earthquake   d. Supercontinent

14. In geology the term _____ refers to a fracture in rock where there has been no lateral movement in the plane of the fracture (up, down or sideways) of one side relative to the other. This makes it different from a fault which is defined as a fracture in rock where one side slides laterally past to the other. _____s normally have a regular spacing related to either the mechanical properties of the individual rock or the thickness of the layer involved.
   a. 1700 Cascadia earthquake   b. Joint
   c. 1703 Genroku earthquake   d. 1509 Istanbul earthquake

15. _____, in structural geology and related disciplines, describes the tendency of a rock to break along preferred planes of weakness.

Rocks deformed under very low to low metamorphic grade often develop planes along which the rock can easily be split. Slates are an example of a rock with a penetrative _____ caused partly by the realignement of phyllosilicate minerals with increasing flattening strain.

    a. Lingula
    c. Diamond Head
    b. Geothermal
    d. Cleavage

16. _____, is a geomorphological phenomenon occurring when a stream or river drainage system or watershed is diverted from its own bed, and flows instead down the bed of a neighbouring stream. This can happen for several reasons, including:

- Tectonic earth movements, where the slope of the land changes, and the stream is tipped out of its former course.
- Natural damming, such as by a landslide or ice sheet.
- Erosion

    a. Meander
    c. Distributary
    b. 1509 Istanbul earthquake
    d. Stream capture

17. _____ is the removal of solids (sediment, soil, rock and other particles) in the natural environment. It usually occurs due to transport by wind, water, or ice; by down-slope creep of soil and other material under the force of gravity; or by living organisms, such as burrowing animals, in the case of bioerosion.

_____ is distinguished from weathering, which is the process of chemical or physical breakdown of the minerals in the rocks, although the two processes may occur concurrently.

    a. AL 333
    c. AASHTO Soil Classification System
    b. AL 129-1
    d. Erosion

18. The _____ is a middle Paleozoic mountain building event (orogeny), especially in the northern Appalachians, between New York and Newfoundland. The _____ most greatly affected the Northern Appalachian region (New England northeastward into the Gasp>é region of Canada.) The _____ should not be regarded as a single tectonic event, but rather as an orogenic era.
    a. Acadian orogeny
    c. Orogenesis
    b. Alice Springs Orogeny
    d. Alpine orogeny

19. The _____ is a geologic period and system of the Paleozoic era spanning from >416 to 359.2 million years ago (ICS, 2004.).

During the _____ Period, which occurred in the Paleozoic era, the first fish evolved legsand started to walk on land as tetrapods around 365 Ma.

    a. Devonian
    c. Gogo Formation
    b. Xitun Formation
    d. 1509 Istanbul earthquake

20. _____ crater is a crater on Mars's moon Deimos. It is about 3km in diameter. _____ crater is named after Jonathan _____, who predicted the existence of the moons of Mars.
   a. 1703 Genroku earthquake
   b. 1700 Cascadia earthquake
   c. 1509 Istanbul earthquake
   d. Swift

21. The _____ is the epoch from 1.8 million to 11550 years BP covering the world's recent period of repeated glaciations. The _____ epoch follows the Pliocene epoch and is followed by the Holocene epoch. The _____ is the third epoch of the Neogene period or 6th epoch of the Cenozoic Era. The end of the _____ corresponds with the retreat of the last continental glacier. It also corresponds with the end of the Paleolithic age used in archaeology.
   a. Sicilian Stage
   b. Pleistocene
   c. Tyrrhenian
   d. Late Pleistocene

Chapter 55. Great Smokey Mountains National Park

1. A _____ is a large, slow-moving mass of ice, formed from compacted layers of snow, that slowly deforms and flows in response to gravity and high pressure.

_____ ice is the largest reservoir of fresh water on Earth, and second only to oceans as the largest reservoir of total water.

   a. Keeling Curve
   b. Deforestation
   c. Glacier
   d. Little Ice Age

2. _____ is the geomorphic process by which soil, regolith, and rock move downslope under the force of gravity. Types of _____ include creep, slides, flows, topples, and falls, each with its own characteristic features, and taking place over timescales from seconds to years. _____ occurs on both terrestrial and submarine slopes, and has been observed on Earth, Mars, and Venus.
   a. 1509 Istanbul earthquake
   b. Mass wasting
   c. 1700 Cascadia earthquake
   d. Soil liquefaction

3. The _____ is a geological eon representing a period before the first abundant complex life on Earth. The _____ extended from 2500 Ma to 542.0 >± 1.0 Ma (million years ago), and is the most recent part of the old, informally named 'e;Precambrian'e; time.

The Proterozoic consists of 3 geologic eras, from oldest to youngest:

- Paleoproterozoic
- Mesoproterozoic
- Neoproterozoic

The well-identified events were:

- The transition to an oxygenated atmosphere during the Mesoproterozoic.
- Several glaciations, including the hypothesized Snowball Earth during the Cryogenian period in the late Neoproterozoic.
- The Ediacaran Period (635 to 542 Ma) which is characterized by the evolution of abundant soft-bodied multicellular organisms.

The geoloic record of the Proterozoic is much better than that for the preceding Archean. In contrast to the deep-water deposits of the Archean, the Proterozoic features many strata that were laid down in extensive shallow epicontinental seas; furthermore, many of these rocks are less metamorphosed than Archean-age ones, and plenty are unaltered.

   a. 1700 Cascadia earthquake
   b. 1509 Istanbul earthquake
   c. 1703 Genroku earthquake
   d. Proterozoic Eon

4. The _____ is a geologic period and system of the Paleozoic era spanning from >416 to 359.2 million years ago (ICS, 2004.).

During the _____ Period, which occurred in the Paleozoic era, the first fish evolved legsand started to walk on land as tetrapods around 365 Ma.

   a. Gogo Formation
   c. Xitun Formation
   b. 1509 Istanbul earthquake
   d. Devonian

5. The _____ is the earliest of three geologic eras of the Phanerozoic eon. The _____ spanned from roughly 542 to 251 million years ago (ICS, 2004), and is subdivided into six geologic periods; from oldest to youngest they are: the Cambrian, Ordovician, Silurian, Devonian, Carboniferous, and Permian.

The _____ covers the time from the first appearance of abundant, soft-shelled fossils to the time when the continents were beginning to be dominated by large, relatively sophisticated reptiles and modern plants. The lower (oldest) boundary was classically set at the first appearance of creatures known as trilobites and archeocyathids.

   a. 1703 Genroku earthquake
   c. Paleozoic
   b. 1509 Istanbul earthquake
   d. 1700 Cascadia earthquake

6. In geology, a _____ or _____ line is a planar fracture in rock in which the rock on one side of the fracture has moved with respect to the rock on the other side. Large _____s within the Earth's crust are the result of differential or shear motion and active _____ zones are the causal locations of most earthquakes. Earthquakes are caused by energy release during rapid slippage along a _____.
   a. Fault
   c. Drainage system
   b. Compaction
   d. Cleavage

7. The term _____ is used in geology when one or a stack of originally flat and planar surfaces, such as sedimentary strata, are bent or curved as a result of plastic (i.e. permanent) deformation. Synsedimentary _____s are those due to slumping of sedimentary material before it is lithified. _____s in rocks vary in size from microscopic crinkles to mountain-sized _____s.
   a. 1509 Istanbul earthquake
   c. 1703 Genroku earthquake
   b. 1700 Cascadia earthquake
   d. Fold

8. The _____ is a geologic period and system, the second of six of the Paleozoic era, and covers the time between 488.3>±1.7 to 443.7>±1.5 million years ago (ICS, 2004.) It follows the Cambrian period and is followed by the Silurian period. The _____ was defined by Charles Lapworth in 1879, to resolve a dispute between followers of Adam Sedgwick and Roderick Murchison, who were placing the same rock beds in northern Wales into the Cambrian and Silurian periods respectively.
   a. AASHTO Soil Classification System
   c. Ordovician
   b. AL 333
   d. AL 129-1

9. The _____ Era is one of three geologic eras of the Phanerozoic eon. The division of time into eras dates back to Giovanni Arduino, in the 18th century, although his original name for the era now called the '_____' was 'Secondary' (making the modern era the 'Tertiary'.)

The _____ was a time of tectonic, climatic and evolutionary activity. The continents gradually shifted from a state of connectedness into their present configuration; the drifting provided for speciation and other important evolutionary developments.

a. Mesozoic
c. 1509 Istanbul earthquake
b. 1700 Cascadia earthquake
d. 1703 Genroku earthquake

10. The _____ Era, is the most recent of the three classic geological eras and covers the period from 65.5 million years ago to the present. It is marked by the Cretaceous-Tertiary extinction event at the end of the Cretaceous that saw the demise of the last non-avian dinosaurs and the end of the Mesozoic Era. The _____ era is ongoing.

a. 1700 Cascadia earthquake
c. 1703 Genroku earthquake
b. 1509 Istanbul earthquake
d. Cenozoic

11. _____ is the removal of solids (sediment, soil, rock and other particles) in the natural environment. It usually occurs due to transport by wind, water, or ice; by down-slope creep of soil and other material under the force of gravity; or by living organisms, such as burrowing animals, in the case of bioerosion.

_____ is distinguished from weathering, which is the process of chemical or physical breakdown of the minerals in the rocks, although the two processes may occur concurrently.

a. AL 333
c. AASHTO Soil Classification System
b. Erosion
d. AL 129-1

Chapter 56. Black Canyon of the Gunnison National Park

1. The _____ is an informal name for the supereon comprising the eons of the geologic timescale that came before the current Phanerozoic eon. It spans from the formation of Earth around 4500 Mya (million years ago) to the evolution of abundant macroscopic hard-shelled animals, which marked the beginning of the Cambrian, the first period of the first era of the Phanerozoic eon, some 542 Mya. It is named after the Roman name for Wales - Cambria - where rocks from this age were first studied.
   a. 1700 Cascadia earthquake
   b. 1703 Genroku earthquake
   c. 1509 Istanbul earthquake
   d. Precambrian

2. _____ is the name given to a rock consisting mainly of hornblende amphibole, the use of the term being restricted, however, to metamorphic rocks. The modern terminology for a holocrystalline plutonic igneous rocks composed primarily of hornblende amphibole is a hornblendite, which are usually crystal cumulates. Rocks with >90% amphibole which have a feldspar groundmass may be a lamprophyre.
   a. Amphibolite
   b. AL 129-1
   c. AASHTO Soil Classification System
   d. AL 333

3. A _____ is a tributary valley with the floor at a higher relief than the main channel into which it flows. They are most commonly associated with U-shaped valleys when a tributary glacier flows into a glacier of larger volume. The main glacier erodes a deep U-shaped valley with nearly vertical sides while the tributary glacier, with a smaller volume of ice, makes a shallower U-shaped valley.
   a. 1703 Genroku earthquake
   b. 1509 Istanbul earthquake
   c. Hanging valley
   d. 1700 Cascadia earthquake

4. In geology the term _____ refers to a fracture in rock where there has been no lateral movement in the plane of the fracture (up, down or sideways) of one side relative to the other. This makes it different from a fault which is defined as a fracture in rock where one side slides laterally past to the other. _____s normally have a regular spacing related to either the mechanical properties of the individual rock or the thickness of the layer involved.
   a. Joint
   b. 1703 Genroku earthquake
   c. 1509 Istanbul earthquake
   d. 1700 Cascadia earthquake

5. A _____ is an elevated area of land with a flat top and sides that are usually steep cliffs. It takes its name from its characteristic table-top shape. It is a characteristic landform of arid environments, particularly the southwestern United States.

   _____s form usually in areas where horizontally layered rocks are uplifted by tectonic activity, but may form also in its absence.

   _____s are formed by weathering and erosion. Variations in the ability of different types of rock to resist weathering and erosion cause the weaker types of rocks to be eroded away, leaving the more resistant types of rocks topographically higher relative to their surroundings. This process is called differential erosion.

   a. 1509 Istanbul earthquake
   b. Palustrine
   c. Mesa
   d. Truncated spur

6. _____ forms a group of medium-grade metamorphic rocks, chiefly notable for the preponderance of lamellar minerals such as micas, chlorite, talc, hornblende, graphite, and others. Quartz often occurs in drawn-out grains to such an extent that a particular form called quartz _____ is produced. By definition, _____ contains more than 50% platy and elongated minerals, often finely interleaved with quartz and feldspar.

a. Hornfels
b. Talc carbonate
c. Porphyroblast
d. Schist

7. Study of geological _____ is related to the study of structural geology, rock microstructure or rock texture and fault mechanics.

_____ is the response of a rock to deformation usually by compressive stress and forms particular textures. _____ can be homogeneous or non-homogeneous, and may be pure _____ or simple _____.

a. Tectonites
b. Molasse basin
c. Shear
d. Syncline

8. A _____ is an opening in a planet's surface or crust, which allows hot, molten rock, ash, and gases to escape from below the surface. Volcanic activity involving the extrusion of rock tends to form mountains or features like mountains over a period of time.
a. 1509 Istanbul earthquake
b. 1700 Cascadia earthquake
c. 1703 Genroku earthquake
d. Volcano

9. _____ is the decomposition of Earth rocks, soils and their minerals through direct contact with the planet's atmosphere. _____ occurs in situ, or 'with no movement', and thus should not be confused with erosion, which involves the movement of rocks and minerals by agents such as water, ice, wind and gravity.

Two important classifications of _____ processes exist -- physical and chemical _____.

a. 1509 Istanbul earthquake
b. Physical weathering
c. 1700 Cascadia earthquake
d. Weathering

10. _____ is an intrusive igneous rock similar to granite, but contains more plagioclase than potassium feldspar. It usually contains abundant biotite mica and hornblende, giving it a darker appearance than true granite. Mica may be present in well-formed hexagonal crystals, and hornblende may appear as needle-like crystals.
a. Granodiorite
b. 1700 Cascadia earthquake
c. 1703 Genroku earthquake
d. 1509 Istanbul earthquake

11. In geology, _____ is sediment or sedimentary rock that shows evidence of having been subjected to metamorphism. _____ is a metamorphic rock formed from sedimentary rock. These rocks are older metamophic rocks of Archaean basement complex.
a. Keystone
b. Conglomerate
c. Concretion
d. Metasediment

12. _____ is the second most abundant mineral in the Earth's continental crust . It is made up of a framework of silicon-oxygen tetrahedra SiO_4, with each silicon shared between two oxygens to give the overall formula SiO_2. _____ has a hardness of 7 on the Mohs scale and a density of 2.65 g/cmÂ³.
a. 1509 Istanbul earthquake
b. Shocked quartz
c. 1700 Cascadia earthquake
d. Quartz

13. _____ is a hard metamorphic rock which was originally sandstone. Sandstone is converted into _____ through heating and pressure usually related to tectonic compression within orogenic belts. Pure _____ is usually white to grey, though _____s often occur in various shades of pink and red due to varying amounts of iron oxide .
   a. Slate
   b. Talc carbonate
   c. Hornfels
   d. Quartzite

14. _____ is a common phyllosilicate mineral within the mica group, with the approximate chemical formula $K(Mg, Fe)_3AlSi_3O_{10}(F, OH)_2$. More generally, it refers to the dark mica series, primarily a solid-solution series between the iron-endmember annite, and the magnesium-endmember phlogopite; more aluminous endmembers include siderophyllite.
   a. Magnesium
   b. Chromite
   c. 1509 Istanbul earthquake
   d. Biotite

15. A _____ or dyke in geology is a type of sheet intrusion referring to any geologic body that cuts discordantly across

- planar wall rock structures, such as bedding or foliation
- massive rock formations, like igneous/magmatic intrusions and salt diapirs.

They can therefore be either intrusive or sedimentary in origin.

An intrusive _____ is an igneous body with a very high aspect ratio, which means that its thickness is usually much smaller than the other two dimensions. Thickness can vary from sub-centimeter scale to many meters and the lateral dimensions can extend over many kilometers. A _____ is an intrusion into an opening cross-cutting fissure, shouldering aside other pre-existing layers or bodies of rock; this implies that a _____ is always younger than the rocks that contain it.

   a. Type locality
   b. Detritus
   c. Gradualism
   d. Dike

16. _____ is a very coarse-grained igneous rock that has a grain size of 20 mm or more; such rocks are referred to as pegmatitic.

Most _____ is composed of quartz, feldspar and mica; in essence a 'granite'. Rarer 'intermediate' and 'mafic' _____ containing amphibole, Ca-plagioclase feldspar, pyroxene and other minerals are known, found in recrystallised zones and apophyses associated with large layered intrusions.

   a. Pegmatite
   b. 1509 Istanbul earthquake
   c. 1700 Cascadia earthquake
   d. 1703 Genroku earthquake

17. _____ is a common and widely occurring type of intrusive, felsic, igneous rock. _____ has a medium to coarse texture, occasionally with some individual crystals larger than the groundmass forming a rock known as porphyry. _____s can be pink to dark gray or even black, depending on their chemistry and mineralogy.
   a. 1700 Cascadia earthquake
   b. 1703 Genroku earthquake
   c. 1509 Istanbul earthquake
   d. Granite

18. In geology, a _____ or _____ line is a planar fracture in rock in which the rock on one side of the fracture has moved with respect to the rock on the other side. Large _____s within the Earth's crust are the result of differential or shear motion and active _____ zones are the causal locations of most earthquakes. Earthquakes are caused by energy release during rapid slippage along a _____.
   a. Drainage system
   b. Cleavage
   c. Compaction
   d. Fault

19. _____ is a rock at the frontier between igneous and metamorphic rocks. They can also be known as diatexite.

   _____ forms under extreme temperature conditions during prograde metamorphism, where partial melting occurs in pre-existing rocks.

   a. Metamorphic zone
   b. Large igneous provinces
   c. Magma
   d. Migmatite

20. The term _____ is used in geology when one or a stack of originally flat and planar surfaces, such as sedimentary strata, are bent or curved as a result of plastic (i.e. permanent) deformation. Synsedimentary _____s are those due to slumping of sedimentary material before it is lithified. _____s in rocks vary in size from microscopic crinkles to mountain-sized _____s.
   a. 1509 Istanbul earthquake
   b. Fold
   c. 1700 Cascadia earthquake
   d. 1703 Genroku earthquake

21. _____ is the solid-state recrystallization of pre-existing rocks due to changes in physical and chemical conditions, primarily heat, pressure, and the introduction of chemically active fluids. Both mineralogical, chemical and crystallographic changes can occur during this process.

   Three types of _____ exist: dynamic, contact and regional.

   a. Gibraltar Arc
   b. Lake capture
   c. Pumice raft
   d. Metamorphism

22. The _____ is the first geological period of the Phanerozoic eon, lasting from 542 ± 0.3 million years ago to 488.3 ± 1.7 million years ago (ICS, 2004); it is succeeded by the Ordovician. Its subdivisions, and indeed its base, are somewhat in flux. The period was established by Adam Sedgwick, who named it after Cambria, the classical name for Wales, where Britain's _____ rocks are best exposed.
   a. 1509 Istanbul earthquake
   b. 1703 Genroku earthquake
   c. 1700 Cascadia earthquake
   d. Cambrian

23. The _____ is a geologic period and system, the second of six of the Paleozoic era, and covers the time between 488.3>±1.7 to 443.7>±1.5 million years ago (ICS, 2004.) It follows the Cambrian period and is followed by the Silurian period. The _____ was defined by Charles Lapworth in 1879, to resolve a dispute between followers of Adam Sedgwick and Roderick Murchison, who were placing the same rock beds in northern Wales into the Cambrian and Silurian periods respectively.
   a. AL 129-1
   b. AL 333
   c. AASHTO Soil Classification System
   d. Ordovician

Chapter 56. Black Canyon of the Gunnison National Park

24. The _____ is the earliest of three geologic eras of the Phanerozoic eon. The _____ spanned from roughly 542 to 251 million years ago (ICS, 2004), and is subdivided into six geologic periods; from oldest to youngest they are: the Cambrian, Ordovician, Silurian, Devonian, Carboniferous, and Permian.

The _____ covers the time from the first appearance of abundant, soft-shelled fossils to the time when the continents were beginning to be dominated by large, relatively sophisticated reptiles and modern plants. The lower (oldest) boundary was classically set at the first appearance of creatures known as trilobites and archeocyathids.

   a. 1509 Istanbul earthquake
   b. 1703 Genroku earthquake
   c. 1700 Cascadia earthquake
   d. Paleozoic

25. The _____ is a distinctive sequence of Late Jurassic sedimentary rock that is found in the western United States, which has been the most fertile source of dinosaur fossils in North America. It is composed of mudstone, sandstone, siltstone and limestone and is light grey, greenish gray, or red. Most of the fossils occur in the green siltstone beds and lower sandstones, relics of the rivers and floodplains of the Jurassic period.

   a. 1700 Cascadia earthquake
   b. 1509 Istanbul earthquake
   c. 1703 Genroku earthquake
   d. Morrison Formation

26. The _____ , usually abbreviated K for its German translation Kreide, is a geologic period and system from circa >145.5 >± 4 to >65.5 >± 0.3 million years ago . In the geologic timescale, the _____ follows on the Jurassic period and is followed by the Paleogene period. It is the youngest period of the Mesozoic era, and at 80 million years long, the longest period of the Phanerozoic eon. The end of the _____ defines the boundary between the Mesozoic and Cenozoic eras.

   a. Cretaceous
   b. Valanginian
   c. Campanian
   d. Hauterivian

27. _____ is a fine-grained sedimentary rock whose original constituents were clay minerals or muds. It is characterized by thin laminae breaking with an irregular curving fracture, often splintery and usually parallel to the often-indistinguishable bedding plane. This property is called fissility.

   a. Claystone
   b. Shale
   c. Concretion
   d. Jasperoid

28. _____ is a rock composed of angular fragments of minerals or rocks in a matrix (cementing material), that may be similar or different in composition to the fragments. A _____ may have a variety of different origins, as indicated by the named types including sedimentary _____ , tectonic _____ , igneous _____ , impact _____ and hydrothermal _____ .

Sedimentary _____ s are a type of clastic sedimentary rock which are composed of angular to subangular, randomly oriented clasts of other sedimentary rocks.

   a. Fault breccia
   b. Ventifacts
   c. Breccia
   d. 1509 Istanbul earthquake

29. The _____ is a a term for a geologic period 65 million to 1.8 million years ago. The _____ covered the time span between the superseded Secondary period and an out-of-date definition of the Quaternary period. The period began with the demise of the non-avian dinosaurs in the Cretaceous-_____ extinction event, at start of the Cenozoic era, spanning to beginning of the most recent Ice Age, at the end of the Pliocene epoch.

    a. Loihi Seamount
    b. Logarithmic Spiral Beach
    c. Historical geology
    d. Tertiary

30. _____ is a type of rock consisting of consolidated volcanic ash ejected from vents during a volcanic eruption. _____ is sometimes called tufa, particularly when used as construction material, although tufa also refers to a quite different rock.

The products of a volcanic eruption are volcanic gases, lava, steam, and tephra. Magma is blown apart when it interacts violently with volcanic gases and steam. Solid material produced and thrown into the air by such volcanic eruptions is called tephra, regardless of composition or fragment size. If the resulting pieces of ejecta are small enough, the material is called volcanic ash, defined as such particles less than 2 mm in diameter, sand-sized or smaller.

    a. Tuff
    b. Pyroclastic rocks
    c. Lopolith
    d. Phanerite

Chapter 1
1. a	2. b	3. d	4. a	5. b	6. d	7. b	8. d	9. d	10. a
11. d	12. b	13. d	14. d	15. d	16. d	17. d	18. d	19. a	20. a
21. d	22. d	23. d	24. d	25. b	26. c	27. a	28. d	29. d	30. d
31. d	32. c	33. a	34. b	35. d	36. d	37. c	38. c	39. c	40. b
41. c	42. c	43. b	44. b	45. b	46. d	47. d	48. d	49. d	50. a
51. a	52. b	53. c	54. d	55. c	56. b	57. a			

Chapter 2
1. b	2. d	3. b	4. d	5. b	6. d	7. a	8. d	9. a	10. b
11. d	12. b	13. b	14. b	15. d	16. d	17. c	18. b	19. d	20. d
21. a	22. d	23. a	24. c	25. b	26. a	27. b	28. d	29. a	

Chapter 3
1. a	2. a	3. d	4. a	5. c	6. c	7. d	8. d	9. b	10. d
11. b	12. d	13. d	14. d	15. d	16. d	17. d	18. b	19. a	20. b
21. b	22. d	23. a	24. c						

Chapter 4
1. b	2. c	3. d	4. a	5. b	6. d	7. d	8. a	9. a	10. d
11. d	12. b	13. b	14. d	15. b	16. d	17. d	18. c	19. d	20. d
21. b	22. d	23. d	24. d	25. a	26. d	27. d	28. d		

Chapter 5
1. c	2. a	3. a	4. d	5. b	6. b	7. a	8. c	9. b	10. c
11. a	12. b	13. b							

Chapter 6
1. a	2. d	3. d	4. c	5. c	6. c	7. b	8. d	9. c	10. d
11. b	12. c	13. d							

Chapter 7
1. c	2. b	3. d	4. c	5. d	6. b	7. c	8. d	9. d	10. c
11. d									

Chapter 8
1. a	2. c	3. a	4. d	5. d	6. a	7. a	8. d	9. d	10. d
11. d	12. b	13. b	14. c	15. d	16. d	17. b	18. d	19. a	20. d
21. b	22. c	23. c	24. d	25. b	26. d	27. d			

Chapter 9
1. d	2. d	3. c	4. d	5. a	6. a	7. c	8. d	9. d	10. b
11. a	12. a	13. c	14. d	15. c	16. c	17. d	18. c	19. d	20. d
21. d									

ANSWER KEY

Chapter 10
1. d 2. d 3. a 4. d 5. c 6. a 7. b 8. b

Chapter 11
1. d 2. d 3. c 4. d 5. d 6. d 7. c 8. d 9. d 10. d
11. d 12. b 13. d 14. b 15. d 16. b 17. d 18. d 19. c 20. a

Chapter 12
1. b 2. d 3. d 4. d 5. a 6. a 7. d 8. d 9. d 10. b
11. a 12. d 13. b 14. d 15. d 16. d 17. b 18. d 19. d

Chapter 13
1. b 2. d 3. a 4. d 5. d 6. b 7. a 8. c 9. b 10. c
11. d 12. d 13. d 14. b 15. d 16. a 17. d 18. d 19. c 20. d
21. c 22. b 23. d 24. a 25. b 26. d 27. d 28. a 29. b 30. d
31. b 32. d 33. b 34. d 35. a 36. d 37. b 38. d 39. b 40. d
41. c 42. d 43. d 44. c 45. d 46. c 47. c 48. a 49. a 50. a
51. c 52. a 53. d

Chapter 14
1. c 2. c 3. a 4. a 5. b 6. a 7. d 8. d 9. c 10. d
11. a 12. d 13. a 14. d 15. d 16. a 17. b 18. d 19. a 20. d
21. d 22. d 23. b 24. c 25. d

Chapter 15
1. a 2. b 3. c 4. c 5. a 6. d 7. a 8. d 9. b

Chapter 16
1. b 2. d 3. a 4. d 5. d 6. d 7. d 8. b 9. a 10. d
11. d 12. d 13. c 14. c 15. b 16. d

Chapter 17
1. a 2. d 3. d 4. a 5. b 6. b 7. c 8. a 9. d 10. d
11. d 12. b 13. b 14. c

Chapter 18
1. a 2. b 3. d 4. d 5. c 6. d 7. b 8. b 9. d 10. a
11. d 12. d 13. c

Chapter 19
1. d 2. d 3. a 4. c 5. d 6. b 7. d 8. d

Chapter 20
1. d 2. a 3. d 4. d 5. a 6. d

Chapter 21
    1. c   2. b   3. a   4. d   5. d   6. b   7. d   8. d   9. d

Chapter 22
    1. d   2. b   3. c   4. d   5. c   6. b   7. b   8. d   9. d   10. d
    11. b   12. d   13. a   14. d   15. d   16. b   17. d   18. b   19. c   20. b
    21. d   22. d   23. d   24. d   25. d

Chapter 23
    1. a   2. c   3. a   4. c   5. d   6. d   7. d   8. c   9. d   10. d
    11. d   12. a   13. d   14. a   15. d   16. d   17. d   18. a

Chapter 24
    1. d   2. d   3. d   4. d   5. c   6. d   7. b   8. d   9. c   10. c
    11. d   12. d   13. d   14. b   15. b   16. d   17. a   18. d   19. d   20. b
    21. a

Chapter 25
    1. d   2. b   3. a   4. b   5. d   6. a   7. a   8. d   9. d   10. d
    11. d   12. a   13. a   14. c   15. d   16. d   17. c   18. a   19. d   20. d
    21. d   22. d   23. a   24. a   25. b   26. c   27. b   28. d   29. d   30. d
    31. d   32. d   33. a   34. d   35. a   36. b   37. b   38. d   39. d   40. b
    41. b

Chapter 26
    1. d   2. d   3. a   4. b   5. d   6. c   7. c   8. d   9. d   10. d
    11. d   12. b   13. d   14. d   15. b   16. d   17. c   18. a   19. d   20. d
    21. a   22. d   23. b   24. d   25. b   26. d   27. a   28. d   29. d

Chapter 27
    1. d   2. d   3. b   4. c   5. d   6. a   7. d   8. d

Chapter 28
    1. a   2. d   3. c   4. a   5. d   6. d   7. c   8. a   9. c   10. c
    11. d   12. d   13. d   14. c   15. d   16. d   17. d   18. d   19. b   20. b
    21. b   22. c   23. d   24. d   25. a   26. d   27. b   28. d   29. d

Chapter 29
    1. d   2. c   3. b   4. d   5. c   6. b   7. d   8. d   9. d   10. b
    11. a   12. c   13. d   14. b   15. d   16. c   17. d   18. b   19. d   20. a
    21. d   22. a   23. d   24. a   25. c   26. d   27. b   28. b   29. d

ANSWER KEY

Chapter 30
1. c   2. d   3. d   4. a   5. d   6. b   7. b   8. a   9. d   10. a
11. d   12. d   13. d   14. c   15. c   16. a   17. d   18. b   19. d   20. c

Chapter 31
1. a   2. a   3. d   4. b   5. d   6. d   7. a   8. c   9. d   10. d
11. d   12. b   13. b   14. d   15. c   16. a   17. a   18. c   19. d

Chapter 32
1. a   2. c   3. c   4. c   5. b   6. b   7. c   8. d   9. c   10. b
11. a   12. d   13. b   14. d   15. d

Chapter 33
1. a   2. d   3. a   4. d   5. b   6. d   7. d   8. d   9. d   10. d
11. b

Chapter 34
1. d   2. d   3. d   4. d   5. d   6. a   7. b   8. d   9. a   10. d
11. d   12. b   13. b   14. c   15. b   16. c   17. d   18. b   19. c   20. b
21. d   22. d   23. a   24. b   25. d   26. c   27. d   28. d   29. d   30. a
31. b   32. d   33. d   34. d   35. d   36. d   37. a   38. a   39. d   40. c
41. a   42. d   43. d   44. d   45. a   46. b   47. d   48. d

Chapter 35
1. b   2. a   3. d   4. d   5. c   6. c   7. c   8. d   9. d   10. d
11. d   12. c   13. a   14. d   15. d   16. d   17. c   18. d   19. d   20. d
21. d   22. d   23. b

Chapter 36
1. d   2. b   3. c   4. d   5. d   6. c   7. a   8. a   9. c   10. d
11. d   12. c   13. b   14. d   15. d   16. d

Chapter 37
1. b   2. d   3. d   4. d   5. a   6. c   7. d   8. d   9. d   10. a
11. b   12. a   13. b   14. c   15. a   16. b

Chapter 38
1. d   2. d   3. d   4. d   5. d   6. d   7. c   8. d   9. a   10. d
11. d   12. d   13. b   14. d   15. c

Chapter 39
1. d   2. b   3. d   4. a   5. b   6. a   7. d   8. d   9. c   10. d
11. d   12. b

Chapter 40
1. c   2. b   3. d   4. c   5. d   6. b   7. a   8. d   9. c   10. d
11. d   12. d   13. d   14. a   15. d   16. d   17. a   18. d   19. d   20. a
21. d

Chapter 41
1. c   2. b   3. d   4. d   5. b

Chapter 42
1. d   2. d   3. a   4. b   5. d   6. b   7. b   8. c   9. b   10. a
11. d   12. a   13. d   14. d   15. d   16. d

Chapter 43
1. a   2. d   3. d   4. d   5. c   6. d   7. b   8. c   9. d   10. d
11. c   12. d   13. b   14. a   15. d   16. b   17. d   18. d   19. d   20. c
21. d   22. b   23. a   24. b   25. c   26. d   27. b   28. d   29. a   30. d
31. d   32. d   33. a   34. d   35. a   36. d   37. c   38. d   39. b

Chapter 44
1. d   2. a   3. c   4. a   5. b   6. a   7. a   8. d   9. d   10. d
11. d   12. d   13. b   14. d   15. b

Chapter 45
1. b   2. d   3. d   4. d   5. b   6. d   7. d   8. d   9. d   10. d
11. d   12. d   13. a   14. c   15. c

Chapter 46
1. c   2. d   3. d   4. b   5. c   6. d   7. d   8. b   9. b   10. a
11. a   12. c   13. b   14. b   15. d   16. a   17. b   18. d   19. b   20. d
21. b   22. b   23. d   24. d   25. b   26. a

Chapter 47
1. b   2. d   3. d   4. d   5. d   6. b   7. d   8. d   9. d   10. a
11. a   12. d   13. b   14. b   15. a   16. d   17. b   18. d   19. d   20. c
21. b   22. d   23. c   24. d   25. b

Chapter 48
1. c   2. d   3. d   4. b   5. b   6. d   7. d   8. d   9. c   10. b
11. a   12. d   13. d   14. d   15. d   16. d

Chapter 49
1. b   2. a   3. b   4. a   5. c   6. d   7. d   8. c   9. b   10. d
11. a   12. c   13. c   14. a   15. a   16. d   17. d   18. b   19. d   20. d
21. d   22. d

ANSWER KEY

Chapter 50
1. d 2. b 3. d 4. a 5. d 6. d 7. b 8. c 9. d

Chapter 51
1. b 2. c 3. d 4. b 5. a

Chapter 52
1. a 2. d 3. d 4. d 5. a 6. d 7. b 8. d 9. a 10. d

Chapter 53
1. d 2. d 3. d 4. c 5. d 6. a 7. d 8. d 9. a 10. c

Chapter 54
1. d 2. a 3. d 4. b 5. d 6. d 7. c 8. a 9. a 10. b
11. a 12. b 13. d 14. b 15. d 16. d 17. d 18. a 19. a 20. d
21. b

Chapter 55
1. c 2. b 3. d 4. d 5. c 6. a 7. d 8. c 9. a 10. d
11. b

Chapter 56
1. d 2. a 3. c 4. a 5. c 6. d 7. c 8. d 9. d 10. a
11. d 12. d 13. d 14. d 15. d 16. a 17. d 18. d 19. d 20. b
21. d 22. d 23. d 24. d 25. d 26. a 27. b 28. c 29. d 30. a

www.ingramcontent.com/pod-product-compliance
Lightning Source LLC
Chambersburg PA
CBHW080729230426
43665CB00020B/2679